G103

CP

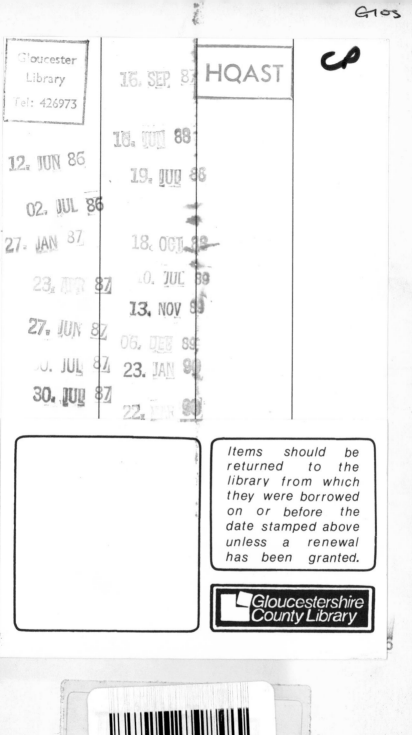

AGAINST OURSELVES

Disorders from Improvements Under
the Organic Limitedness of Man

Against Ourselves

Disorders from Improvements Under the Organic Limitedness of Man

by

D. G. GARAN, Ph.D., J.U.D., LL.D.

Author of *The Paradox of Pleasure and Relativity,*
Relativity for Psychology, and
The Key to the Sciences of Man

PHILOSOPHICAL LIBRARY
New York

Copyright, 1979, by PHILOSOPHICAL LIBRARY, INC.
15 East 40 Street, New York, New York 10016

Library of Congress Catalog Card No. 79-83603
SBN 8022-2243-9

Manufactured in the United States of America

TABLE OF CONTENTS

FOREWORD

Many readers will find the central idea of this book unacceptable. But the main value of the book—whatever its faults—is that it tries to explain a causal fact about ourselves which seems impossible yet is objectively true and important.

The simple most universal fact about man is that he exists as an inexorably limited organism which conserves its sameness to the tiniest detail. Because of this organic limitedness of man he can have satisfactions, inner values or pleasures only upon equal needs as nonsatisfactions, inner disvalues or restrictions. In a limited system you can have an advance, a movement upward or energy expenditure only upon equal receding, movement downward or energy accumulation by restriction. Also, if the normal energy reserves in the limited organism are exhausted, by excessive enjoyment, the organism restores them by equal, restrictive, opposite processes.

Thus the causation of value reactions through their opposites inevitably results from the organic limitedness. Organic values are possible only through equal organic disvalues. Satisfaction or pleasure release requires equal need or restriction. Since all human values derive from the organic values, and since values determine everything man feels, does or even thinks, the opposite causality governs practically everything about man.

But this opposite or relative causality is as unacceptable to man as is his own limitedness extending to all his values. Men cannot live with the belief that their striving for inner values is futile, inevitably limited to the requirement of equal value opposites.

That is why true human sciences, which would have to proceed by this opposite causal logic, have not evolved. The physical, exact sciences, now imitated in all fields, have advanced enormously, be-

vii

cause they require only the humanly acceptable like-from-like causal logic. Otherwise, human sciences would have been the first. For men can feel or know directly all the value reactions inside themselves.

The point is that in all fields dealing with man, the proper causal logic—which this book explains—is exactly contrary to the usual human and the presently dominant scientific causal logic.

In present human and behavioral sciences it is always assumed that positive, satisfactory causal backgrounds or experiences create positive motivations or value reactions. If this were so we all would be supermen. For we constantly start with and pursue only the most positive feelings and experiences. This then would create more of the positive value reactions, satisfactions, or pleasures, which constitute our positive motivations and capacities.

In reality, every satisfaction or pleasure release has to be "earned" through equal accumulation of conditioned needs as nonsatisfactions or restrictions, its value opposites.

Still the "scientific," like-from-like causal logic is presently the only way of thinking in everything said or written about human behavior or inner value experiences. Consequently, this book has to oppose the very logic of present thinking in the fields dealing with man. We know that our repeated assertion of our "impossible" logic, against the views of the best authorities, in this book, can only make it appear more graceless—in addition to its distasteful, relative view of values.

But we have no choice. The opposite or relative causality is scientifically true and important. To test our new logic we have to check it against the present truths. We have to confront the best authorities—in a seemingly disrespectful, percursory way because of lack of space.

We have to use the hard facts established by the authorities. There is no lack of such facts and we do not have to make new investigations. Then we have to compare these facts with other equally hard discoveries and conclusions. Our findings, shown in the book, reveal vast, increasing confusion and total lack of causal explanations in all fields dealing with man. At the same time, the concept of the opposite causality offers explanations that are almost self-evidently true for all facts.

To give an example—that also may show the importance of the problem—we may look at our modern functional diseases which now kill three fourths of the men best cared for. All the facts, by any authority, show that modern man enjoys prodigious improvements in the conditions that can give him greatest immediate increase in his functional enrichment. But the result is equal worsening or impoverishment, causing the diseases, in the enjoyed functions. This is recognized by the best authorities, who also admit that the causes of these diseases are not yet understood.

Actually, the causal explanation is simple. Within the inexorable limitedness of the organism the excessive improvement or acceleration of a function has to result in equal exhaustion or impoverishment. If this is overcome by more improvement the impoverishment deepens, as a stress, which is generally recognized as the immediate cause of all functional diseases. The simplest example is the use of drugs. They give perfect, wondrous improvement of reactions but lead to their equal worsening. The insidious, vicious-circle way in which functional overenjoyment deepens the impoverishment is explained in detail in the book.

The same is true of all human reactions, feelings and behavior. They are certainly overenjoyed by the modern man with his prodigious skills, affluence, and a liberal, logically "scientific" attitude. As certainly he has brought on himself unprecedented impoverishment in the form of opposite, negative reactions. These are, automatically, as prodigious or "ingenious" as are the overenjoyments. No assumption of the Unconscious is necessary.

But the modern human scientists, proceeding by the nonopposite, like-from-like causal logic, have no explanations. There are as many controversial theories as there are noted behavioral and human scientists. The functional diseases, like heart attack, cancer, or diabetes, are admitted mysteries causally. For each functional disease doctors frankly admit that the cause is still unknown. In fact, doctors die of heart attack three times more often than ordinary people. For mental disorders the picture is the same; and psychiatrists commit suicide at a rate five times higher than the average.

Insight into the opposite causality offers a causal, that is, scientific explanation for the functional diseases, as well as for the behavioral or social disorders that modern men bring on themselves. Science of man will become possible when its own causal logic, of the opposite causation which determines everything about man, is established. Such science will become as tremendously effective as the physical or technologic sciences are. Man then will be able to do virtual miracles with himself, beyond the present imagination and prejudices.

The idea of the relativity or limitedness of our inner values, that the opposite causality implies, is as distasteful to us as to everybody else. It can easily justify relativistic and defeatist attitudes. But we have to overcome distastes when we can explain fundamental causal, that is, scientific principles. The book shows that not defeat but unimaginably miraculous future awaits man at the end of his scientific, causally understood progress.

The relativity may also be too commonplace, but not recognized because it is unacceptable. Thus its idea may seem simplistic as well as be repugnant. But it is—no less because of its commonplace universality—true and practically decisive for everything man feels, does or even knows. It is the key to a causal, scientific understanding of the world of man—and of the scourge of self-inflicted ills of the modern men.

The very logic of the relative or opposite causation is "impossible," seemingly paradoxical. It is therefore repeatedly explained, in the book, to make understandable our statements of the relative causation wherever they may otherwise appear illogical. Clarity may be more important than the risk of being repetitious, in our effort to explain a strangely new but practically important view of causal facts.

D. GARAN

I

THE MODERN MEN DESTROYING THEMSELVES

The modern men best cared for die of diseases caused by the way they live, in epidemic proportions. They also suffer from similarly caused mental disorders at an appallingly increasing rate. The causes of these diseases and disorders are not yet understood, as is empathically admitted in medicine and psychiatry. Stress and anxieties of modern life are blamed for these diseases—and for the other increasing, behavioral or social self-inflicted ills.

But the modern men have attained prodigious resourcefulness and skills *to have or do anything they want.* The progress here has been as unprecedented as is the epidemic increase in the mysterious self-inflicted diseases. The arguments about inevitable stress, anxiety or other negative feelings of the modern life are incongruous. They imply the absurdity that the resourceful modern men do not know when they are hurting themselves. Even a dumb animal knows to avoid what is unpleasant.

And *there is nothing more unpleasant than stress or anxiety.* That is why drugs that relieve stress or anxiety are sought above everything else. Modern man knows these feelings perfectly. In fact, he uses all his staggering resources and skills first and most of all for eliminating and avoiding these tormenting feelings in everything he experiences, does, pursues or enjoys.

Logically, if there ever was, in history, a chance to overcome these dreaded feelings, it would be now that we, with our power and improvements, should be living free of any stress or anxiety and the disorders it brings.

That just the reverse is the case proves how totally wrong are

1

the "logical" usual arguments and ideas about stress, anxiety or other negative reactions. The key to understanding the paradox involved here is *the organic limitedness of man.* The organism conserves and restores its inexorably limited sameness to the tiniest details, statically and dynamically. If any function in it is "improved," accelerated, strengthened or increased, the result is an opposite reaction, worsening, deceleration, weakening or decrease in the same function, as the organism restores its normalcy or sameness, by opposite processes.

The greater the functional "improvements" overenjoyed by modern man through his unprecedented skills and power, the deeper the opposite reactions—functional worsening or stress. Moreover, as such worsening is overcome by still more improvements, it only deepens, in a vicious-circle way.

Negative reactions after overenjoyment, through narcotics, or through emotional imbalance, are not so strange, to anybody. We are only establishing the cause of such opposite reactions, which is as universal as is the organic limitedness of man. Certainly, the rich and skillful modern man is inventing means and ways of "improvements" more effective and subtler than narcotics or other gross enjoyment means.

Unparalleled, Modern Epidemic of Self-Inflicted Ills

The ills that the modern men bring on themselves are increasing at an epidemic rate, and range from functional diseases and disorders to crime, violence and social turmoil. They are all due to the impoverishment of human capacities and motivations, that deepens in the way just indicated. The exact causation of the self-inflicted organic impoverishment through overenjoyed improvements will become clear as our discussion proceeds.

We may look first at our grave functional, as we shall see, self-inflicted diseases, caused by the overimprovements of modern life. The latest statistics of deaths in this country[1] show that since 1970, in the average, only fifteen percent of the deaths have been due to infectious diseases, congenital and organic defects, and "all other causes," while *over eighty percent have been due to the functionally caused diseases* (discussed in detail later). Thus over fifty-five percent have been due to major cardiovascular diseases, twenty percent to malignancies, and ten percent to other functionally caused disorders like diabetes, cirrhosis, emphysema or kidney diseases.[1]

It can be said, without hesitation, that *three fourths of modern men die of functional diseases, caused by the way men live*—by the Stress and not by organic defects or external, pathogenic causes. Moreover, the other causes of deaths, like infections and organic ills, become fatal, mainly, due to functional impairment or impoverishment.

Often it is argued that the modern men best cared for die more of functional diseases, like heart disease or cancer, because they live longer. But the natural ways of deaths show that the argument is not true. Older animals, in nature, die of infectious diseases, accidents, adversities, or general, undefinable, gradual weakness. The *dramatic, abrupt, deaths of heart disease or cancer,* with the organism still continuing otherwise strong, are completely different.

Incidentally, only the average longevity has been extended in the more developed countries, because the early-age and infant mortality, from infectious diseases, has progressively declined. Real old age is attained more often by individuals in the less developed countries—as the *U.N. Demographic Yearbook* shows—and such old persons do not suffer or die from functional disorders.

The main truth about functional diseases, heart disease or cancer, is that they are *extraordinary, unnatural abnormalities,* mostly incurred continuously, long before the old age. This is clear for cancer, of which animals under natural conditions do not die at old age, and which is incurred by man during any, sometimes a prolonged, period of his life. It is a clear abnormality.

The same is true for the modern *heart disease.* It is clearly an abnormality, created by the modern man, by his way of life. It has increased by 400 percent[4]—some experts say by 500 percent[3] —in the last fifty years, while the average longevity has increased by less than 25 percent, in this country.[1,3]

Statistics show that we are contracting heart disease *beginning with early years* and are dying of it at increasingly earlier age. Now the young people "just barely out of their teens, have definite signs of beginning atherosclerosis".[5] Autopsies on a number of young Americans could be performed during the World War II and the Korean War. It was discovered that the young men, in their early twenties, had already the typical changes of cardiovascular disease.[5,6] The Korean-War autopsies showed that the hardening of arteries had already occurred in eight of every ten cases. In ten percent of the men the atherosclerotic process had already narrowed the arteries by 70 percent or more.[5]

Recent observations have shown that now men at the age of thirty have more coronary artery disease than forty-year-old men had twenty five years ago.[5] *The increase of heart attacks for younger people* is the unfortunate trend.[5,6] The "most foreboding statistics" show that "since 1950 the heart attack death rate for men between the ages of twenty-five and forty-four has gone up almost fourteen percent."[7]

Typically, strokes occur in "the most productive years," forty-five percent before the age of 59.[6] The peak period of deaths from heart attack, for males, is at the age of 55 to 59, and that peak starts building up at the age of 30 to 40.[8] By the age 40 to 44 heart disease is already the leading cause of deaths.[8] It is "an epidemic like no other."[5] There is "convincing evidence that heart attacks are not matters of advancing age but of advancing disease."[5]

The disturbing central fact about coronary disease—as about all other functional diseases—is that *its cause is not known*.[3,5,8] Here we have an unparalleled epidemic of wihch most of modern men die, but the modern medicine does not even know what it is causally. This is constantly, empathically admitted.[3,5,6,7] It is equally recognized that the disease cannot be treated as long as its cause is unknown.[5,8]

At the same time, we have here a remarkably uniform, natural phenomenon, repeating itself endlessly and uniformly to the minutest details. As such it can only have one simple natural causal principle; nature does not know complex principles. Scientists are demonstrating their superior insight when they see the Stress as

the general causal principle here.[2,9] Only, because they are proceeding by the usual, "scientific" logic, which is totally wrong here, the unsolvable confusion is compounded.
Stress is generally viewed as the cause of all functional diseases.
[2,5,9] Actually, stress is the reaction to the improverishment of the affected organic function. We can visualize such reaction as a restriction, functional decrease, energy limitation, and so on. This agrees with most of the concepts about stress, including that of Hans Selye, the foremost authority on stress.[2,9] What leads to confusion is the disregard of the ever-present limitedness of the organism.

Because of this limitedness, restriction or functional restraint is necessary before or after any increased functional release or acceleration. The limited organism can expand or accelerate only upon previous retraction or slowing down. If it uses up reserves, which are potentials of expansion or acceleration accumulated by restriction, it has to restore the reserves by subsequent restriction. *The restriction is felt as the unpleasant stress.*

Necessity to impose extra stress indicates abnormal condition, but stress itself, as the restriction, is the beneficial reaction that restores normalcy. Nature in its miraculous purposiveness imposes the stress because it is the remedy.

As the stress follows the overenjoyment, the modern man, in his unlimited resourcefulness, overcomes it by more improvement, thus making more stress, as restriction, necessary. The result is a *vicious circle,* that can deepen the exhaustion or impoverishment of the enjoyed function to any degree. Moreover, the continuous, vicious-circle effort to overcome the restrictions or the limitation may finally efface or damage the restrictive mechanisms. Unrestrained exhaustion of the function, as well as malignant growth, is the result.

Doctors do recognize the normal function of stress. Dr. Selye is emphasizing repeatedly the *necessity of stress in life.*[2] So are other scientists.[3,9,10,11] What is not recognized is the generality of the opposite causation within the organic limitedness. All stress, patiently lived through, is beneficial. The overenjoyment or functional "improvement," which causes the stress, is damaging or exhaustive. But this *opposite causal logic*—of clear, experimentally registrable improvement causing the worsening—is contrary to the "scientific" tenets of modern medicine.

Doctors, realizing that the wondrous nature itself imposes the stresses, talk of good stresses and bad stresses.[3,9,10,12] Dr. Selye sees as beneficial the stresses of altruistic effort, "neighbor's love," creative involvement, or satisfactory career.[2] Drs. Meyer Friedman and Ray H. Rosenman suggest striving for "things worth being" instead of having, "finding yourself," or enjoying the events that give "real" pleasure.[3] Dr. Lennart Levi advises finding stresses that are not injurious but relaxing and productive.[9]

It is, certainly, advisable to concentrate on the traditional, morally approvable, idealistic and productive or altruistic pleasures. They are already restrictive. One can hardly overenjoy them. But the organism or *nature does not know a distinction* between moral or cultural, and immoral or uncultural enjoyments. Any enjoyment as functional overimprovement exhausts the function.

The point is that, under the usual "scientific" logic, doctors see the restrictive, unpleasant, hard stress as injurious, though it restores normalcy. They view the positively felt increased stress-free enjoyment or improvement in well-being as beneficial, though it turns, under modern conditions, into overenjoyment as cause of functional exhaustion and abnormalcy.

The paradox of functional improvement turning into worsening —because of the organic limitedness—is the decisive fact. Modern doctors, as "scientists," can never accept this paradox. But it is clearly proved by the very recognition of stress as the cause of our ills. As we saw, modern man attains, to a degree never reached in history, every functional improvement in his feeling of well-being—everything that is furthest away from stress. But the result is the overwhelmingly increasing stress as the syndrome of the deepening functional impoverishment.

The stress and anxiety as psychological causes prove that *the ills of the modern man are self-inflicted.* However erroneous their causal logic, the doctors recognize that men themselves choose their stressful reactions—that it all depends on the way the person reacts.[2,8,9,11] The authoritative work here is, apparently, the book by Meyer Friedman and Ray H. Rosenman, *Type A Behavior and Your Heart*.[3] It proves conclusively that the way person responds or behaves, and not any other, outside factors, is decisive.[3]

In fact, the Type A behavior equals overenjoyment behavior in its widest practical sense. The person here has found the inexhaustible source of enjoyment—the competitive success in what he is doing. By concentrating on special, limited goals he can always have the success or win. That is why he hates to be interrupted from his routine work, is always competitive, hurrying, impatient, aggressive or ambitious.[3] He tries to attain "maximum number of achievements in a minimal amount of time" or to "increase and satiate the appetitive" for the success.[3]

It may be argued that he does not pay attention to the quality or enjoyment of his work, only concentrates on numbers and deadlines.[3] But the concretely real, practical value of success is always to be measured in numbers, or dollars, and time periods. The efficiency "expert" that the type A person is knows this perfectly.

Nobody could ever become so unrestrainedly involved in the "hurry sickness" if he did not enjoy it all as an ever-present source of pleasures of success. If somebody does not like what he is doing—if he feels it as stressful—he finds hundreds of ways how to do less of it, and to ignore numbers or time limits. The supposed type B person easily forgets his work, is less ambitious and finds enjoyment in other, wider, "really satisfying," cultural and esthetic pleasures, hobbies or interests[3]—as substitutes for the rougher enjoyments.

The "logical" interpretation of behavior A and B is erroneous. The type A person does not seek to be hurried, rushed or enslaved by stressful work. Nobody would. He merely enjoys the competitive success, in his limited area. That is why he is *not worried, anxiety-ridden, disturbed, or showing signs of stress* in any form, as Friedman and Rosenman,[3] or other authors, have to admit.[9,10,12] Of course, a deeper, hidden anxiety is assumed.[9,10,11]

Men who are particularly concerned with numbers and deadlines, which are the real measures of accomplishment, are not type A persons. In various studies, notably by Lawrence Hinkle,

Henry I. Russek, or Stewart G. Wolff,[5,8] it has been found that the people like higher executives, who accomplish most, are not excessively suffering from coronary disorders.[5,6,8] They are capable to force themselves to do such really stressful work—and do not suffer from it.

The "logical" explanations are dangerously misleading, here as elsewhere. People are urged to avoid stressful—supposedly type A—behavior or work, which is actually never overdone and can lead only to a peaceful, healthy rest. All kinds of "real" enjoyments—supposedly the type B behavior—are recommended, instead.[2,3] In reality, the kind of enjoyment does not matter, since the organism does not make cultural or esthetic distinctions. All enjoyment involves acceleration or intensified use of organic functions. Therefore it leads to the vicious-circle impoverishment, within the limited organism.

The organic impoverishment through overenjoyment, through the *prodigiously effective, logical improvements by modern men,* explains all modern functional diseases. These are, as we saw, the self-inflicted causes of three fourths of our deaths. The enormity of this self-destruction is comparable only with the enormous power and the unique, liberal determination of the modern men to pursue greater satisfactions everywhere. We shall explain in detail later the overenjoyments as causes of the various functional diseases.

Hypertension is the main syndrome of heart disease. According to official statistics 23 million Americans suffer from it,[12] but the actual number is thought to be around 40 million.[8,12] It is starting at increasingly earlier age, even in the twenties.[5,8] Again, the personality, the psychological cause, or "the game people play," is found to be the determining factor.[8] Hypertension appears to be the main contributing cause of the deaths from heart disease and stroke.[8]

Other disorders contributing to heart disease are arteriosclerosis, with atherosclerosis as its critical part, and various other forms of deterioration of the circulatory system.[5,6] They, together with renal malfunction, are recognized as the underlying causes of hypertension.[8,12] Evidently, *as many people must be suffering from these disorders as from hypertension.* In fact, the autopsies during the Korean War disclosed, as we saw, signs of arterial abnormalities in eight of every ten of the killed men, in their early twenties.[6] Other studies have shown similar findings,[5,6] as well as the fact that these disorders are caused by the modern way men choose to live[5,8,10]—including the Type A behavior.[3]

Second to heart disease is *cancer* in its dreadfully increasing fatalities. Deaths from cancer have quadrupled since the beginning of this century.[4] Whatever its mysteries, cancer is a disease brought by man on himself, by the way he lives. Animals in their natural state do not die of cancer. We shall explain later that overenjoyments or overimprovements more than mere pollution of environment, are the causes of cancer, Mere poisons, once adjusted to, rather extend lives, as has been found since the famous, surprising experiments by Alexis Carrel.

A less dreadful, but more widely suffered functional disease is *arthritis.* Reportedly, more than fifty million people in this country are afflicted by it, often without knowing it.[15] Seventeen million are patients seeking help, most of them women. Arthritis has always been found to be a disease caused by the way the people live. Its overenjoyment or "improvement" causes are evident from its syndrome of stress, or stress-hormone imbalance.[15] These causes are as insidiously persistent and paradoxical[15] as can only be man's pursuit of functional improvements, and their effects.

Diabetes, supposedly, afflicts ten to twenty million Americans.[16] Some four million are seeking help or being registered. Diabetes is an "improvement" disease, since it is as rare in poorer countries as it is prevalent among people enjoying the modern improvements.[16] The paradoxical effect, on diabetes, of poor and rich foods as well as of stress,[16] confirms here the overenjoyment as cause.

Peptic ulcer is a typical affliction of the modern men suffering from excessive stress. Such stress can reach its inordinate levels only through the vicious-circle overenjoyment. People living under conditions of grave stress do not suffer from peptic ulcers, as we shall see later. In any case, this disease, suffered by four million Americans exposed to "pressures" of life, is a self-inflicted disorder, since it depends on the psychological reactions of the person.

Other diseases and disorders suffered by modern men are similarly dependent on the way we live, on the stress or psychological reactions by which we respond.[2,3,5] It is well known in medicine that even infectious diseases become virulent only if the body is functionally impoverished[2,10,11]—mostly through the paradoxical effects of "improvements," showing in stress and anxiety.

Thus, whether it is the functional diseases, of which three fourths of modern men die, or other diseases and disorders, the fatal, or contributing cause is the functional exhaustion that modern men bring on themselves. Presently Stress is seen as such cause. But within the organic limitedness of man, only the vicious-circle overenjoyment, through the prodigious modern added improvements, can deepen the stress to the critical, disruptive levels.

Mental disease and disorders of modern men reveal an equally epidemic self-inflicted scourge, of unprecedented proportions. These diseases have increased to the extent that one in every ten persons in this country will spend some time in an institution.[17] According to the Institute of Mental Health, six percent of the persons born in 1960s will suffer from schizophrenia, the gravest of mental diseases.[1,17]

The number of mental patients has *increased fourfold,* to seven million· since 1955[1] when the greatest "improvements," by use of the revolutionary modern mental drugs, started. Most of this increase consists of outpatient cases,[1] because most disorders are now purely functional, not organic; and the big new trend is, finally, to keep patients out of mental institutions.[17] But even the rate of inpatient cases has increased, by 38 percent.[1] And the increase, in all mental patient cases, has been rising progressively.[1,17]

Evidently· at such increase in mental disorders, the epidemic can reach appalling levels in a few more decades. And there can be no doubt that it is caused by what we are doing to ourselves, how we are reacting to the best life men have ever had in history.

Our social self-inflicted ills are more difficult to measure. But if our more permanent, organic functions are so deeply disrupted by our "improvements" one can estimate what happens to our more delicate, carefully evolved cultural and social behavior. One measurement of our social or cultural "disease" is the *increasing crime* in our society. As we shall explain in detail later, crime is ultimately due to lack of positive motivations and capacities. These can be attained only through restrictions. Instead, overenjoyment is the dominant tendency in our society.

Particularly our juvenile, lower and minority groups are living by this tendency, as the freedoms and satisfactions have increased for them at an unprecedented rate. This increase has been enormous in *relative terms, which are the only ones that really matter.* And during the decade of the greatest such improvements, before the last recession, the *crime in this country increased at a yearly rate of fifteen percent.*[1] At such progressive increase, if it resumes, with return of normal conditions, we shall in a few more decades be committing crimes or struggling against them, each one of us, every day. No society in history could have survived for long with a similar progressive increase in crime rate.

Another measurement of our cultural self-destruction is the *disintegration of our family life.* Family has always been recognized as the foundation of our culture· that it is. The rate of divorce has increased in this country more than five times since 1910.[1] It has more than doubled since 1960.[1] The number of persons of opposite sex living together unmarried has tripled since 1970 and is already 1.9 million. The rate of illegitimate births has increased 390% since 1950, and for teen-age mothers this increase is already a dismaying 1020%. Now one in ten of our, unmarried teen-age girls becomes pregnant.

The essential disintegration of our family and culture is particularly evident from the rapidly deteriorating relationship between children and parents. The *"generation gap"* is the fact of our life, confirming that most of our young have nothing but hate and despite for their elders, who have lost all control over them. Is it not revealing that the juvenile delinquency increased sixteen-fold—yes, 1600 percent—during the twenty prerecession years?

The modern moral revolution, against almost everything in the traditional culture, is unique. It has brought more cultural "progress," actually rejection of cultural restraints, in few decades *than has any culture experienced during thousands of years.* One has only to think of the changes in our moral habits, like the pre-marital intercourse, the "toplessness," or nudity. They may not mean much in themselves, or may be rather amusing under a relative cultural view. But they would have been a complete outrage even thirty years ago.

This merely shows how the modern man has rejected the total past culture in a few decades. The grave, ominous part of it is the *rejection of the past tradition of general restrictions,* which are painfully evolved through millenia and are the only ways of preserving our physical, mental and social normalcy.

The results of the rejection of restrictions should be the same for our social "disease" as they are for our mental and physical functional diseases. In both, the cause is the same—as is explained next. If statistics for the social "disease" are not available, we can infer its extent and progress from the statistics of functional diseases. Those statistics, as we saw, show that *our self-inflicted ills are increasing by one hundred percent every decade and are fatally afflicting three fourths of us.*

Social or cultural ills have the same source as the functional diseases—the impoverishment of our reactions and capacities, somatic as well as mental, through the general modern overenjoyments and freedoms. This is equally well understandable under the accepted concepts of stress and anxiety as the general causes of all our diseases and disorders—with the right, opposite causal logic. The modern social disease is accumulating as an undercurrent, since the cultural tradition externally continues by inertia.

The nature of this "disease" is evident from *the degenerate syndrome of our social license and turmoil* even more than from the above progressive increase in crime and family disintegration. Our modern lawlessness, violence or terrorism are committed for the sake of mere destruction, spite or willfulness, not because of dire need or inhuman oppression, as in previous times. In objective terms we should have no social violence at all, since everybody is ensured of subsistence. The present destructive, willful violence and terrorism are the signs of social degeneration—of which we may soon suffer at the same epidemic rate to which functional diseases have increased.

Unique Modern Improvements

With his staggering scientific and technical progress modern man has at his disposal every resource and skill. He can enjoy, do or understand virtually anything. In his modern, unrestrained pursuit of satisfactions, he understands, chooses and enjoys to perfection—and to excess—the most pleasant experiences. He never miscalculates here, however involved the trade-offs or efforts needed. Nothing is simpler or clearer than pleasures and displeasures.

And *stress* is man's most unwanted, unbearably tormenting feeling—as the use of drugs against it indicates. The resourceful, liberated modern man invents and enjoys prodigiously ingenious ways and means for *avoiding the stress perfectly, and excessively,* in everything he does. That is how he is destroying himself.

The reason is the organic limitedness, under which added enjoyments as intensified "improvements" of a function lead to its equal exhaustion. The organic response to such exhaustion is a seemingly diseased restriction or worsening, as the organism restores its sameness or normalcy by opposite processes. This is felt as stress. Intensified efforts of the modern man to overcome this opposite feeling or stress, by still more improvements, evidently, lead to increased exhaustion or worsening, at every turn. This vicious circle can deepen the exhaustion, and stress, to any conceivable, malignant degree.

The continuous *perfected addition of improvements is essential,* in the overenjoyments by which the functional disorders are incurred. For instance, heart disease is suffered more, even four times as much, by workers who are sitting, instead of standing or moving.[5,9] In particular, the studies on the London bus employees and Israel kibbutz workers have brought this out.[9] The sitting may seem a minor accomodation. But it is what makes the perfect enjoyment during the work possible. You cannot enjoy relaxation, or anything, if you cannot sit down. Enjoyment through constantly added intensification of the function at deepest levels keeps the malignant vicious circle running.

It is always the enjoyment element that induces man to over-drive his innermost living mechanisms and thus to incur the disease. In absence of enjoyment nobody would deepen the ill so persist-ently. Overimprovement is the key. That is why the person feels excellent and is markedly vigorous before the functional disease appears, as if from nowhere, or suddenly. This is generally noted, particularly in regard to heart disease, as an insidious peculiarity of such diseases.[2,4,5,6]

The awesome inventive perfection of the modern improvements is the decisive factor. Modern men have spent most of their time on inventing new ways of adding to their enjoyed improvements. To mention only our food, think of the hundreds of thick cook-books offering every conceivable exquisite combination of improve-ments. If there is any possible way of increasing the feeling of well-being, in any function, the modern men have brought it to perfection. "Enough is never enough" for the modern man,[10] as he improves and invents new comforts around him. His goal be-comes "surfeit in every direction."[14] New "whipped up longings"[10] are created by our ingenious industry, bursting with new capacities.

Of course, the work or profession is the most important part of our lives. We spend most of our time and energy on it. Expectedly, the modern man, in his endless ingenuity, has brought *every pos-sible improvement to his work.*

The efforts here have been so persistent and thoroughly inven-tive that finally most of professions or work has been turned into a *genuine interest* of our lives. The right, most enjoyable work or profession is sought for everybody, in endless ways, including early development of our interests or enjoyment tendencies.

That is why the Type A behavior is indulged mostly in the person's work, and is as we saw equivalent to a continuous over-enjoyment of one's professional successes. The person here has all his interests and ambitions invested in his work and enjoys them in every possible way. He finds *so much pleasure in what he is doing,* and does it so resourcefully, that even Friedman and Rosenman could not find any signs of "external" stress or anxiety in such, type A behavior.[3] Other doctors reject the Type A idea because no worry, tension or stress can be observed in the behavior leading to heart disease.[6,12]

Hardships and monotony of work are often blamed as causes of stress.[2,9] But the hardest, traditional, physical work has been observed to be the best protection against functional diseases. In a *reversal of previous medical beliefs,* physical exertion is now recognized as healthy and indulgence of relaxation as harmful.[5,8,13] Exercises, like the jogging, are becoming fashionable—and probably are overenjoyed, with deleterious effects, raising controversies.[3,6,7]

Hard, unpleasnt work is best for inducing the Type B behavior, as the person forgets the work when it is finished and turns to other interests. Cranky, fretful reactions from work arise when its hardships are covered up or compensated for by unwarranted overenjoyments which then, irritably, lead to opposite pressures, as the normalcy or reality is reestablishing itself.

Research and studies show as *crucial not any working conditions in themselves but the way the person reacts to them.*[2,3,5] Of course, too deep involvement in work is possible only when it is overenjoyed in some, direct, or conditioned and compensatory way.

The decisive fact is that under the modern, "scientific" attitudes our interests in work are *conditioned through emphasis on enjoyments* rather than on restrictions or hardships: we are to *seek and find increased enjoyment* through our work, directly or as expected success and improvements of life.

Even the much deplored routine and assembly-line work is an outcome of people's enjoyment tendencies. Most men view work as a necessary evil. They want to invest in it as little of preparation, study or worry as possible. The nonroutine work, of greater interest, "self-expression," initiative, pride, or responsibility, requires investment of exactly equal tensions, needs as nonsatisfactions, worry, hard learning and effort. This vexatious side of the interesting or responsible work is avoided by most people. Employers or industry adapt themselves by offering the routine and assembly-line work. In short, such work as well comes together with the modern indulgence of easier life.

Next to work, our *living conditions* are the most important factor to be considered. Needless to say that exactly those modern men who suffer most from the functional diseases live in conditions superior to any in history.

Ben Wattenberg, in his book *The Real America,* is demonstrating, by use of statistics, that we are enjoying historically unprecedented improvements in every form of living conditions, from use of effort-saving devices, particularly cars and appliances, to every comfort of home, or enjoyment of travel, sports, entertainment and relaxation. Also, the improvements enjoyed by our minority groups have risen at a uniquely high rate in relative terms which are the only ones that count in behavior.

It is truly amazing that the modern experts, in their confusion, *claim the conditions we live in to be harder than those of more primitive people,* who suffer less from functional diseases. In every way, including food, the more primitive peoples live under incomparably worse physical and psychologic conditions. This is clear from most studies;[3,5,6] we may refer here to Daniel Brunner, or Jeremiah Stamler.[5] The general, deepest sources of stress and anxiety, the threats to survival, are enormous in more primitive societies in comparison with ours.

It would be a hair-raising experience for us to live with the imminent dread of death, disease, or helplessness that primitive people face every day amidst hunger, infection, lack of protection and threats from nature or other men. Even the conditions of our early frontier days would be scary for the modern man insured and assured for everything, from birth to grave. Nor do primitive people enjoy more peace of mind. As Margaret Mead points out, the idea that primitive people enjoy lives free of stress "is cooked up out of our heads."

Primitive men have demons, ghosts, deadly curses and witchcraft all around them. It is remarkable how every aspect of primitive life is permeated by constant fear of such ever-present dread, as M. J. Field shows in his study on rural Ghana. If modern men had one tenth of such fears, doctors would really have a logical proof why our lives are full of stress.

Revealing is the fact that functional diseases of which modern

men die did not afflict the *inmates of the Nazi concentration camps,*
not even those who had suffered them before. Among such inmates were very many doctors. After the War they compared, in
Israel, their observations and found that they did not see "a single
case of heart attack or angina" among the inmates, including
those who had been previously sick with heart disease.[5] Harold
G. Wolff has written about similar observations in regard to other
functional diseases, peptic ulcer, colitis, asthma, or psychoneuroses.

Leonard Tushnet, studying the reports of Jewish doctors in the
Warsaw Ghetto under the Nazi terror, points out the absence in
it of almost every functional disease—heart attack, diabetes, arthritis, peptic ulcer, asthma, allergies, pellagra, neuroses and psychoses.[18] Rather, surprising recoveries, from diseases like diabetes,
are noted. Even epidemics of infection were less severe, though
infectious diseases, like tuberculosis were, naturally, acute and
fatal for the starving young.[18]

It is always the perfected avoidance of stress, under *conditions
of skillfully enjoyed improvements,* that deepens the stress to its
malignant degree. Experts have often referred to the remarkable
study of Italian immigrants in Roseto, Pennsylvania.[5,9,11] As John
Bruhn reports, these people had, at first, only one fourth of the
rate of heart attacks suffered by their neighbors.[11] The Italians
ate "heroic" amounts of pasta, oil, lard, or other foods rich in
cholesterol and fats. They were also overweight. But they lived
to ripe old age.[11]

Ten years later, they had become Americanized, had executive
positions, watched television, had highly paid jobs, were freely
buying and showing off. Their heart attack rate leaped to three
times the national average.[11] Dr. Bruhn concludes, "these people
have given up something to get something, and it's killing them."[11]

Evidently the old Italians of Roseto were clumsy amateurs in
their enjoyments, hindered in hundreds of ways by the restrictive
traditions of their homeland. What they acquired in the ten years
were the perfected ways—from more intense, genuine enjoyments
to the "scientific," liberal attitudes—that people in this country
have ingeniously "improved" under their unique affluence. Nobody

would learn so much of anything that was really stressful and therefore most unpleasant.

We may repeat, for emphasis, that *men never miscalcualte in choosing only what is more pleasant.* Pleasure and displeasure are the clearest, simplest things for man—even for an animal. And anything is most unpleasant to the extent it is *stressful.* Experts asserting that primitive conditions are different, freer of stress, are implying that the modern man, able to have anything, somehow chooses the more unpleasant, stressful conditions, because of some miscalculation.

Crowded urban conditions and social or cultural restrictions have been blamed as causes of stress.[2,10] But people live in crowded cities exactly because they like it. Studies on dislocated people show that they prefer to relocate as crowded groups.[2] Isolation is clearly recognized as conducive to stress.[2,9] In the city the person gets the best of both the opportunity for social intercourse or variety and the anonymous freedom within the crowd when he does not want to be restricted by his group. Social and moral restriction by a close community can be one of the most stressful conditions, as anthropologists have repeatedly observed.

The effect of loosening of social or cultural restrictions is particularly clear from the modern *liberation of women.* It is too obvious to miss that women were kept in clearly more restricted or stressful conditions. Now these conditions of stress, limitation, boredom and denial of "self-expression" have been progressively removed. The women's lib movement has been gathering force for decades.

The result has been the increasing rate of functional diseases, particularly of heart attacks, for women.[3,5] The same phenomenon has been observed in Japan after the War, when the role of restriction and subordination for women there was changed.[3] Even the crime rate for women has increased, fivefold, in this country, during the last twenty years, of the highest progress for women.

Variety and social intercourse together with freedom from restrictions by close community is attained best through the extreme *mobility of people in this country.* The use of mobile homes is typical, and their number has increased sixfold in the last fifteen years. In his book *A Nation of Strangers,* Vance Packard demonstrates, by well documented statistics, that we are virtually becoming a nation of wanderers. Everybody is moving around at increasing rate. Whatever the interpretations, it is clear that without the underlying pleasure of enjoying it all the mobility would not have increased as it has. Four million Americans have mobile homes for enjoyment.

The combination of social intercourse together with opportunity for anonymous freedom is offered also by our rapidly *expanding suburbs.* A suburb, certainly, is "the most luxurious locale for middle-class living known to history."[10] Expansion of suburbs and the epidemic of functional diseases have come together.

Our *inner cities* are generating such diseases at a not much lower rate because the overenjoyment tendencies there are often even stronger. The *relative unique* increase of improvements for the people there is to be kept in mind. Experts sometimes correlate incidence of the modern diseases with "stressful" areas of cities. Actually, the stressful conditions, of crime, drug addiction or moral license, are products of the same—here relatively unique—improvements, in satisfactions and freedoms, that bring all the self-inflicted ills.

The general *amount of improvement we enjoy is as extraordinary* as is the rate of incidence of our functional diseases. Americans constitute only five percent of the world's population but consume thirty percent of world's resources and energy. Considering the ingenious, all-inclusive drive by man to improve his feelings of well-being or happiness, we must have increased our functional enjoyments by an equally disproportionate amount. Which has been the scourge of our self-inflicted ills.

We are suffering from functional diseases at *inordinately high rates in comparison* with peoples who have least of resources or skills—and thus of the opportunities for improvement of their enjoyments. This is confirmed by numerous studies, of Eskimos, Navajo Indians, Bantus, Masai, Somali, Negev Bedouins or Yemenis, as well as peoples living under clearly greater difficulties of life, in China, Korea, Japan, or Yugoslavia.[3;5;6]

Even experts have to admit that opportunities for enjoyments of life are greater in this century.[3,10] But they blame various frustrations—which inevitably come with higher expectations. It is revealing that during the years of recession and inflation, since 1973, the rate of deaths from heart disease has declined, from its high level, by three percent yearly, in the average, for the first time in decades. A similar decline has been recorded for the crime rate during the years of the recession and inflation.

The total, *massive quality of the enjoyed improvement is decisive*. The enjoyments have to reach a higher level in their totality and perfection, as they do in this country, before they become the sources of the malignant, vicious-circle exhaustion. The studies of the various peoples have shown that no one causal factor is decisive.[3;5;12] The overall emotion is, and its causation is not understood. As the American Heart Association states, "wrapped up somehow in the whole business is the subject of emotion."[8] Doctors find that a "meaningful definition for harmful stress" is missing.[7] Nothing in our richest and freest life correlates *logically* with the stress we suffer from.

The traditional definition of sins, "wrath, sloth and gluttony,"[14] seems to fit better than scientific explanations. Doctors as "scientists" have to aim at removal of the clearly negative stress, by improvement of emotions—logically, through improved, more pleasant conditions of life. The great authority on stress Dr. Selye has *urged the increase in pleasant emotions, in every form*.[2] So have other experts.[5;9;11] Is not the stress removed perfectly by the use of drugs, which then deepen it to malignant levels?

The critical overenjoyment is reached by perfected improvements. Doctors, of course, have every means and skill of attaining such improvements. No wonder that *doctors suffer from functional heart disease three times more often* than ordinary people.[19] Overenjoyment effect of the improvements that doctors attain is evident. A statistical study of British physicians revealed their "special disposition to drug addiction, suicide and mental disease."[2]

Dr. Daniel DeSole has made a similar study in this country. He concludes that "to a degree unknown in other professions, the physician is unable to reduce psychological tensions stretched to the breaking point."[11] The suicide rate for the physicians was found to be four times higher than average.[11]

Without the totality of improvements—with a vexatious absence of some enjoyment factor—the stress can not start on its vicious circle of intensified added improvements of the feeling of well-being. It was found, in one study, that Benedictine monks ate as much of the rich foods as general practitioners but suffered only one fifth of coronary diseases.[5]

Is Disorder from Overenjoyed Improvement So Strange?

Everybody can observe how an aftermath or opposite after-effects are suffered after an overenjoyment, induced by alcohol, narcotics, or psychological stimulation. The organism, strictly limited in its system and dynamics, has to *return by opposite processes to its normal state* after any excess. If a function was accelerated or expanded, then slowing down or recession has to follow. We mentioned the use of drugs as the simplest example.

A drug provides a perfectly improved feeling in the organic well-being in every respect. If the drug effect did not reverse we would all be using scores of strongest drugs, to make ourselves virtual supermen in every way. As the reversal inevitably follows, more of the drug has to be used. Naturally, this creates a deeper aftereffect, to be overcome by increased use of the drug. The result is addiction, a typical cause of disorder from improvement.

Addiction is as general as is the present inability of science to explain it causally. It ranges from drinking of coffee and smoking to use of drugs and alcohol. We live continuously with "habits" we have in eating, working, relaxing or enjoying ourselves. We cannot stop them even if we know they are endangering our health. We have become compulsively "used" to them, because we feel the worsening unless the improvement we have been enjoying is continued or increased.

Modern science cannot understand addiction causally because experimentally or "scientifically" the addictive means has always a direct positive effect. *The negative, opposite aftereffect cannot be logically connected with the direct effect which experimentally shows to be positive at every stage.* Only practical insight tells us that overenjoyment brings equal opposite aftermath. Experts are classifying most of the addictive means, even alcohol and cocaine, as nonaddictive.[17] In the present controversy about marijuana, it is still not decided whether it is addictive or not, good or bad, though a half dozen thick official volumes have been filled with reports and studies.

Typically, *alcohol* is repeatedly found, by modern doctors, to have beneficial effects. It, supposedly, relieves stress, reduces fats in blood, and acts as an enjoyable tranquilizer or sedative.[14] If stress is the cause of heart disease, alcohol is a logical means of lessening it.[6] Alcohol helps relaxation, blunts anxieties and acts as vasodilator that reduces hypertension.[6,14] Since the immediate effect of alcohol is the lowering of lipids and of cholesterol in the blood, as well as vasodilation,[5,8] it is viewed to be more beneficial than harmful, by many doctors.

Of course, the longer-range aftereffects of alcohol are just the reverse of its immediate, experimentally registrable, positive effects. Those aftereffects are well known in practice. Drinking leads to stress, anxiety, as well as constriction of blood vessels and increase of fats in blood or body.

Doctors, expectedly, are adding that alcohol should be used "in moderation."[5,6] It is not understood that, as the opposite effects start, the person has to take more than the "moderate" amount of alcohol to get the relief. Otherwise all the negative effects, that alcohol relieved, start appearing at once as the aftereffects. The usual result is a progressing addiction, under deepening negative reactions.

Similarly, *smoking, coffee or other means* of stimulation and relaxation can be viewed as beneficial or at least not harmful. A cigarette, certainly, is "the perfect type of a perfect pleasure."[3] Nicotine is known to act in the way "ganglionic blockers" do.[13] They are used to relieve hypertension. The immediate effect of nicotine is the relief of tension or of stress, anxiety and other negative feelings. That is why people smoke. It is well known, though, that the aftereffects of smoking are the exact opposites.

The vicious-circle efforts to overcome these aftereffects become the addiction. Volumes have been written about smoking addiction. Everything, from the need to keep hands busy to unconscious oral complexes, has been "discovered" as cause. The simple, opposite causation has not been recognized.

Coffee, like many other stimulating means we use, counteracts stressful reactions, and as a vasodilator relieves blood pressure. The gradually deepening aftereffects of a mild stimulant like coffee may not be seen as connected with it. Doctors may only notice that statistics, from hospital admissions, show coffee drinkers to be suffering more often from heart disease.[14]

Stronger stimulants, like amphetamines, lead to aftereffects of stress and anxiety so strong that they cannot be distinguished from syndromes of psychoses. All kinds of stimulants, foods, drinks or other means we usually enjoy are more subtle, evolved through centuries. Their aftereffects are less noticeable directly, therefore rather more insidious.

Here we may emphasize the ingeniousness and intensity by which man seeks the improvements of his feelings of physical and mental well-being. Naturally, *the opposite aftereffects follow with the same intensity and "ingenuity."* It can be said that to the extent a person attains every most positive feeling he wants, he ends by suffering every aftereffect he wants least—because of the organic limitedness.

To take a typical example, Howard Hughes could afford in every physical and psychological way anything he wanted. His life became a nightmare, as James Phelan describes in his book. Hughes suffered from as many functional and mental negative reactions and disorders as were the perfect improvements he could enjoy. The total, effortless leisure ended as a monotonous boredom unrelieved by change, which would have required effort. To conserve his glamorous image, without further effort or risk, he had to hide from the world. All kinds of behavioral obsessions and phobias became inevitable. (Any overimprovement in an indulgence or in avoidance brings opposite reactions, deepening in the vicious-circle way.) Fixations intensified, since new sources of enjoyment can be developed only by equal new needs as non-satisfactions. Drugs became the easy relief.

Even animals can be induced to destroy themselves through perfect overenjoyments. The NIMH built a Paradise for Mice, in 1974, providing in overabundance everything mice could want. After initial spurt of increased reproduction, the mice became indifferent to the environment, suffered from stress, turned autistic, spiritless, and lost normal interests. The colony, started from four pairs, sharply declined to zero, after reaching only half of the 4000 that were planned for.

Nonsatisfactions or restrictions are the sources of normal satisfactions or pleasure releases as our capacities. But nonsatisfactions and restrictions are felt as stress. Evidently, *by bearing normal stress one can avoid the malignant, deepening stress* from exhaustion or impoverishment of his functional capacities.

That is why the experts on stress, while blaming it for our various ills, constantly emphasize that "good" or normal stress is necessary.[2,5,9] However, the paradox of the requirement of opposite reactions, within the organic limitedness, is not understood. Dr. Selye has classified stresses into healthy and unhealthy. He has also blamed too much and too little stress.[2] The confusion is fundamental. The very logic of "scientific" thinking is contrary to the seemingly paradoxical opposite causality that governs our capacities, normalcy and health.

The theories on stress of Dr. Selye are generally accepted.[5,6,9,11] Because of their direct, one-sided causal logic, they are misleading. It is claimed that our energy of adaptation or of general vitality is limited and can be exhausted by stress.[2,11] Nature is never so rigid or resourceless. Dealing with stress is the normal business of the organism, and it adapts limitlessly. It can become insensitive to prolonged stressful conditions, even stop functioning, as in simple fainting. But it recovers, day after day, and restores its normalcy—if the normal stress, as restrictions, is not avoided.

The wrong causal logic shows in the conclusions on the adaptation experiments by Dr. Selye and others. Rats, "prepared" for stress syndrome by administration of corticoids,[2,5] showed under stress at first an increased resistance but then total exhaustion.[9,11]

Rats not receiving corticoids did not show this syndrome under similar stress.[2,5] The opposite effects, as increased resistance and then exhaustion, are to be expected under the corticoid stimulation.

But the experimenters as "scientists" could not accept the logic that a factor which induces a positive reaction at first leads to a negative one subsequently as a matter of course. They had to postulate a grave reversal in the organism itself, its exhaustion, or poisoning of itself by its own products as Dr. Selye claimed. This contradicts the miraculous capacity of the organism to cope with its usual conditions, of which stress is the main one.

The theory that stress exhausts our life energy itself[2,11] is untrue and regrettable. Stress, as we saw, is the natural organic way of restoring normalcy and capacities. Nor does it become destructive. Even in the experiments by Dr. Selye, the "prepared" rats, if conditioned for a few days to the stresses to be expected, survived the most violent conditions, of being thrown abruptly around, electroshocked, and so on; if not so conditioned they eventually died. But man is never thrown around or shocked, in any sense, without knowing what is happening to him or without being able to react to it. Animals are as limited by their instinctive reactions as man is not.

The seemingly paradoxical effects of stress and enjoyment are perhaps best evident from *suicide*—caused by what must be the ultimate despair. More suicides are committed by the lucky, rich, beautiful, stardom people than by the miserable wretches whose every hour of life would be a torture to us. Economic conditions do not correlate with suicide, except that "downward mobility" increases its rate and that professional people commit suicides more often.[20]

We saw that psychiatrists and physicians commit suicide at a disproportionately high rate—and that overimprovements must be the cause. Suicides by very successful people, like movie stars, are frequent. One can think here of Marilyn Monroe and Freddie Prinze. Or of Bridgitte Bardot, who tried to commit suicide. During wars and disasters—the most often invoked instances of stress—suicides are committed less.[20] Suicides as well as other, mental disorders are frequent in springtime, the most enjoyable season.[11,20]

It is surprising how *little is understood about the cause of suicide*. Authors point out constantly the total confusion as well the endless multiplicity of unproved theories about it.[20] At the same time, detailed statistics for suicides have been accumulated for a century. All that experts have to do is to put the statistics and the historically known conditions together. But thousands of studies have failed to provide a causal explanation. Evidently the very logic of thinking is wrong.

Practically, anybody can see that a person who has held a prominent or very enjoyable position suffers deeply if he has to accept ordinary conditions. *The relative change, not any objective condition, is what matters.* Improvement creates equal worsening if return to previous condition is required. This is always the case with improvements within the limited organism. A person's life is not so limited, but the relative causal logic applies to all our experiences.

If a person sees his way ahead to be only downward, he may feel that it is better to quit. The mysterious theories by great experts, from Durkheim to Freud, cannot explain much if this relative or opposite causality is not recognized.

It should be added that the precipitating factor in a suicide is always some bigger and sudden trouble, causing a factual, or merely emotional, downward descent. If the trouble is smaller or gradual it brings relief before the great decision of suicide is made final or carried out: as the gradual troubles lower the position the descent ahead seems less steep.

The effect of *descent from a higher position* to a lower one is the same in other experiences. The descent can sometimes be only emotional, without immediately corresponding factual causes. Retirement neuroses are an example. During his work, for years, the person may compensate for its hardships with enjoyments by anticipation of his pleasures of retirement. There is an emotional accumulation of great expectations against which the reality of retirement is a letdown. Men accumulate enjoyments by expectations in various conditions and subsequently live through equal disappointments. Prisoners of War may suffer disorders or stress after they are liberated.[2,11]

Problems of change in the lives of modern men have been claimed as sources of stress, by many experts.[10,12,14] In his book, *Future Shock,* Alvin Toffler blames most of our disorders and diseases on the clearly tremendous changes of the modern life. Changes in one's life, work, home or family are clearly stressful. Doctors have even established lists with stress values for each change.[12,14] Actually, the stresses the person feels here are the organism's restoration, or building up, of release "reserves" expended, or needed for the efforts that changes require. This is a normal organic reaction. It can cause no disorder, if lived through without emotional compensations.

But changes do bring disorders, for a very different reason. Most of the modern changes become emotionally excessive because people want and enjoy them eagerly—as can be seen also from Toffler's book. The *overenjoyments* then bring the *opposite aftereffects,* functional impoverishment and stress. But a change, even a radical one, that is not emotionally enjoyed or compensated for requires only difficult, complex, technical work, at which nobody gets emotionally too involved. Modern changes cause deep disorders and diseases primarily because they are means of strong overenjoyments.

In addition, any change in a person's life easily leads to over-enjoyments—and therefore to stress—because the traditional restrictions are more easily discarded when environments change. Everybody tends to get rid of the restrictions imposed on him and sustained by the environment of his cultural conditioning. *Changes offer him an opportuniy to discard the restrictions.*

For instance, a person put in a concentration or prison camp and then liberated, lives through so much change that he loses all normal standards of restriction. He therefore easily yields to overenjoyments, both by anticipatory compensation during the imprisonment and by direct enjoyments after the liberation. The result is a cumulative overenjoyment, followed by stress disorder, only partially counterbalanced by restrictive difficulties lived through.

Before we conclude, we may mention one more important modern ill that we bring on ourselves: *the economic recessions.*

Economic booms and slumps follow each other, as causal opposites. They are little understood causally—because of the opposite causation involved. The confusion is recognized by economists themselves. John Kenneth Galbraith has described the efforts to predict the booms and recessions as "a modest profession in which reason, divination, incantation and elements of witchcraft had been combined in a manner not elsewhere seen, save in the primitive religion."

We bring on ourselves economic recessions, much like other disorders, by exhaustion through overenjoyment, in economic terms. The foremost authority, Paul Samuelson, says that one explanation of business cycles would be people becoming "alternately optimistic and pessimistic, each stage leading as inevitably to the next as the manic stage of disturbed people leads to the depressive stage."[21] This is exactly *what happens in all exhaustion through overenjoyment.* In recessions such exhaustion is both economic and psychological.

In economy the primary stimulus or motivation is consumption. During a boom the consumption stimulation increases to excess, as everybody enjoys it and welcomes the expansion it brings. But as the consumption intensifies, and capital accumulation correspondingly decreases, everything becomes more inflationary, costly or difficult.

This in itself would not create the recession. It should be emphasized that a recession is much like a psychotic paralysis, under which people are unable to work and produce though they desperately want to and would be perfectly capable to do so. Evidently, the contributing cause is psychological.

As the above difficulties start, apprehension becomes general, because recession in one sector or business intensifies it in another. The decisive fact is the *reversal of the excessive, unwarranted optimism into equal, unwarranted pessimism,* by "the opposite error of optimism" in the words of Keynes.[21] Psychologic overenjoyment always leads to an equal opposite reaction. As the pessimism spreads under the above interdependence, and people start fearing the fears of others, everybody seeks to limit his business before it is too late. Thus the people stampede each other into a panic.

Economic exhaustion through increased consumption enjoyment combines here with psychologic overenjoyment reversal to create a general self-generating paralysis, under the economic interdependence of all business. But under a direct or "scientific" logic both the promotion of consumption and the stimulation of the optimism are the primary goals to be pursued unlimitedly all the time. We shall explain later the seemingly paradoxical effects of consumption and of capital accumulation.

In conclusion, we may note that people well know in many intuitive ways the truth of worsening from overenjoyed improvements. They know that they would be free of their functional ills if they could resist overeating, overweight, smoking, coffee, beer, or their lazy indulgences.

But "logically," even experimentally, each one of the enjoyed improvements is immediately beneficial. The person knows better than anybody what oppresses or ails him. *His overindulgences are perfectly selected immediate ways to lessen these ills.* Such means stimulate, or relax him by accelerating the inner living processes, or by decreasing ordinary organic demands. Naturally, opposite processes, the worsening, has to follow as the organism has to restore its normalcy.

It also should be noted that the means of such immediate improvements used by man are extremely subtle. He avoids using means, like drugs, that bring the aftereffects too clearly. With his awesome ingeniousness he invents improvements that are far more effective but lead to the inevitable equal aftereffects in ways which he logically or scientifically sees as unconnected with the "beneficial" improvements.

In the end, all the prodigious efforts of modern man are directed at increasing such "scientifically" beneficial, pleasant improvements of his feelings of well-being and freedom from stress everywhere—in his work, home, foods, relaxation, enjoyments or entertainments.

That is why the most resourceful, modern men suffer and die epidemically from diseases that animals, not knowing how to invent improvements, are free of. Peoples in least developed countries, unable to afford such improvements, suffer from the functional diseases at surprisingly low rates.

Of course, experts demonstrate, expansively, that our stress is different from that of primitive men. It is, exactly as different as are our overenjoyments in *avoiding stress, the general most unwanted feeling.* Our stress is fraught with haste, materialism and mechanistic complexity, because we constantly rush to enjoy the material wealth and technologic inventions as the concretest means of enjoyment which begins with the freedom from stress in everything we do. Our stress is vast because we expand our enjoyments through extensive additions in our physical and cultural improvements. It hurts us at every step, because we overenjoy our experiences everywhere.

Let us face it. We can have practically everything, and we want most and first of all the freedom from stress. We are far too smart ever to miscalculate in gaining this simple foremost enjoyment, however complex our increasing, self-defeating efforts and means. We overenjoy the freedom from stress vastly and prodigiously, almost as strongly as by use of drugs. The inevitable result is an equally vast and strong malignant stress.

II

WHY AND HOW WE ACT
AGAINST OURSELVES

Man as organism is limited to its sameness. No function in the organism can be increased without equal subsequent decrease. But man as a conscious planning being, striving for more pleasure or increased feeling of well-being, tries to expand, accelerate or "improve" his organic functions or reactions. Inevitably, the organism has to return to its normalcy by *equal opposite* processes, by restrictions or slowing down of the functions.

Thus opposite feelings follow every overenjoyment or "improvement" and appear as unpleasant, restrictive or "diseased" reactions. To overcome them, the modern prodigiously resourceful man uses still stronger means of "improvement." This leads to still stronger negatively-felt reactions, to be overcome by still more improvement. The result is *a vicious circle* of functional impoverishment deepening through progressively increased improvements.

But this opposite causality, as well as the very limitedness of man, is contrary to human beliefs. Men cannot live with the conviction that there can never be any pleasure gain, that under the organic limitedness every pleasure or satisfaction requires equal displeasure or need as nonsatisfaction.

Moreover, the modern scientism—from physical sciences—proceeds by a logic contrary to the above opposite causality. For *experimentally the "improvements" as added satisfactions or pleasure releases show to improve* the enjoyed function or performance. The opposite reactions that follow after the experimental observation are not seen as connected with the improvement, because they are totally different from it. The requirement of equal opposite,

31

restrictive, negatively-felt or seemingly diseased reactions is never recognized, in common thinking or in science.

All modern, experimentally "logical" science proceeds by the causal logic that satisfactions or pleasure releases, as organic capacities, come from causal sources of same nature. Also the humanistic thought is based on the belief that our positive values, which are our positively felt satisfactions, derive from sources of alike —never opposite—nature.

Of course, if the satisfactions or pleasure releases, which constitute our values and capacities, derived from satisfactory causal backgrounds, the world would be an alchemic utopia. For we always begin with and strive for the greatest possible satisfactions, and these would create more satisfactions. Or, if no equal hard nonsatisfactions or restrictions were required, why not find the right formula or technique for enjoying only the satisfactions?

The modern sciences about man have, indeed, turned into *virtual alchemies*. They are trying to obtain the satisfactions or releases —our capacities—by removing restrictions, making satisfactory improvements, and discovering easier ways or the right methods and ideas for having more of the positively-felt, pleasurable experiences. Thus our greatest treasure, our capacities, are to be created with the ease of added satisfactions or of techniques and ideas, which cost psychologically or organically as little as reasoning.

The Inexorable Limitedness of Man as Organism

The limitedness of man as organism to its sameness is the key factor that determines why and how every excessive improvement turns into equal worsening or disorder. Man as organism lives by and for the conservation of its sameness, to the tiniest detail, statically and dynamically. To understand this better we have to go down to the very fundamentals of the existence of living forms. First of all, only that exists which is capable to persist. This is the ultimate principle of everything existing. But a species can continue existing only if it conserves the sameness, to infinitesimal detail, in its every form or function—eye, heart, proteins, blood, breathing or rate of metabolism.

The conservation by the organism of its sameness is *so general or commonplace* that nobody even notices it as anything significant. But its very commonness or universality reveals that we have here a universal causal law.

In a word, the conservation of organic sameness is the only possible "purpose" or principle of "design" of the organism. And any *higher, more detailed form or function in the organism derives from its lower* ones which exist by that "purpose." Human feelings and reactions, however complex or advanced, can derive only in the same way and follow the same "design." The conservation of its sameness by the organism is the source of all its values—let us call them value reactions—of everything and the only thing that has meaning for it. Thus all human values derive under the same causal law.

But could not the organism be changed, or some of its functions increased so that its capacities are expanded? Modern science can do miraculous things. It is, however, preposterous to imagine that any genius could reorganize a living process. Living mechanisms work with myriads of elements at every point and instant. Nobody can create the tiniest living tissue or produce the simplest living process. Scientific means, like drugs, are ridiculously crude in comparison with living molecules consisting of millions of atoms and purposively organized in cells containing billions of molecules.

By use of artificial means we change living processes either by destroying or disturbing something in them. The organism then only can restore its normalcy, by opposite reactions. What is more, even if we managed to change the organism, the new organism would, again, exist by the conservation of its new sameness or normalcy. Men can live only as organisms, which can exist only by conservation of their limited sameness.

Practically, the organism conserves its sameness by finding *satisfactions,* for restoration of its normalcy, after experiencing *needs* or disturbances. And all human values are, ultimately, satisfactions or experiences of return to normalcy after change. Evidently, there can be only as much satisfaction or restoration as there was need or disturbance. *Changes,* as the sources of value experiences, can work only within the principle of equal *opposite changes,* since the organism has to remain the same.

Another important fact has to be added. The organism, naturally, has to have *reserves* of motivational capacities, that satisfactions are. Since the satisfactions can be increased only by increasing the needs or nonsatisfactions, the "reserves" are created by extensive, biological and cultural, restrictions as conditioned nonsatisfactions. Thus a rich source of satisfactions or releases is created by increasing their opposites the nonsatisfactions as needs or restrictions.

Schematically, we can think here of the potential of the living energy or the *life flow itself being kept back,* as if "dammed" up, so as to be used or released when necessary. Since the life flow or energy is identical with pleasure—we shall explain the details later—organic capacities can be best understood as pleasure releases. Naturally, if the releases are overspent, by overenjoyed or accelerated living, they have to be restored by opposite processes, by equal restrictions, felt as stress, anxiety, slowed down living, "slow death," or seemingly diseased reactions.

Thus the concepts of *release* or pleasure release, and *restriction* are useful for explaining the dynamics and economy of organic capacities and reactions. We shall use these concepts constantly. They can be as easily understood as is the concept of stress, used generally. Stress means the exhaustion of living energy; this agrees with Selye's theory on stress.[1] The exhaustion is accompanied by the constraining, seemingly diseased restrictions, felt as anxiety and mental impoverishment. The restrictions always have to equal the exhausting releases, since the normal reserves have to be restored sooner or later.

If an amount has to remain the same you can have additions in it—corresponding to enjoyed satisfactions or values—only upon previous subtractions from it. And if you have a reserve that always has to be, at least, kept the same, equal saving up is necessary upon each spending. This "reserve" here, of course, is that of painfully accumulated restrictions or conditioned nonsatisfactions, as sources of releases or satisfactions. The valuable positive motivations and capacities, that satisfactions and releases are, do not come without equal effort.

The basal, physiologic *mechanisms of restrictions* or reserves are innate. They are evolved, through the long history of selective evolution of organisms, because reserves of capacities are big advantages. One can feel the innately maintained restrictions as little as he could feel a "pain" caused by some inborn abnormality that would be tormenting if inflicted on him otherwise. The higher a species is, the more of restrictions as reserves it embodies. Under the restrictions the organism becomes more elaborate and longer-living.

The *brain* is larger in higher animals. It is essentially a system of restrictions. That is why numbing or incapacitating of the brain, by alcohol or narcotics, brings pleasure. The same happens in cases of illness of the brain, like syphilitic paresis, or upon debilitating brain operations—as doctors have commented.[7]

Of course, man's unconditioned *natural needs, as desires* and "lusts" are mostly destructive or useless. Also, to the extent they are fully satisfied, immobility results and the person resorts to overenjoyment. Such needs have to be conditioned, by nonsatisfactions or restrictions, into culturally or practically usable needs as sources of desirable satisfactions or interests.

But the *cultural and educational conditioning* is little noticed because it is so general. Men do not notice universal conditions, like the atmospheric pressure, they live in. We are conditioned every minute of our lives. We want to grow up like other men; to be as good or human as others; to be loved, particularly by our parents, which ensures our survival; or to be superior and fulfill ourselves, in the fixationally valued ways we see around us, which is again part of our growth and survival needs.

This continuous, omnipresent conditioning is strongest exactly where it is so universal as to remain unnoticed. Equally our fundamental ever-present needs, of survival, growth or superiority, are not noticed because of their universality.

Thus the universal conditioning and the general needs that are conditioned have *remained practically little noticed* in modern science. Psychologists, imitating the scientism from physical sciences, cannot accept feelings or inner value experiences, which constitute these needs and their conditioning. Pleasure is the core here, and it does not exist for psychologists as scientists.[3,6,8] Psychologists deal with the conditioning that can be "scientifically" demonstrated, in experiments conceived on models of physical sciences.[7,8] The Pavlovian conditioning is generally accepted as the classic example because it corresponds to such scientism.

Most psychologists know that our natural, animal drives can be transformed into the completely different, civilized behavior only by conditioning. They speak of conditioning through handling of infants, their feeding, toilet training, teaching to avoid fire, or to say "please" when hungry.[3,7] Such experimentally or "scientifically" structurable forms of conditioning are the infrequent, rather unusual therefore well noticed, exceptions from the *minute-by-minute inner conditioning.* No wonder that humanists and educators can dismiss the whole idea of psychological conditioning as baseless— or as insult to one's education.[12]

We have to stress the *value atmosphere* as the conditioning medium. One's sense of values depends on the standards and length of experience of the values around him. If he works only two days a week he will feel lazy among people working daily. But he would feel virtuous among people not working at all. Everybody's sense of what he should do thus depends on others; and theirs, on still others, further on. The atmosphere in the whole community or culture becomes decisive.

The most important universal therefore little noticed factor in human behavior is the *pleasure.* As we saw, it is the force behind all satisfactions, especially those derived from the "reserve" as satisfaction potential accumulated by restrictions or nonsatisfactions. Pleasure becomes a particularly important factor because of the efforts and skill of man, as a conscious being, to obtain pleasure beyond its natural, evolutionary function. Animal, unable to plan or increase its pleasures is free of functional diseases or self-inflicted, overenjoyment disorders, which have become the scourge of modern man in every field.

When pleasure centers in a rat's brain are wired so that they can be activated by the animal, it goes into a frenzy of bar pressing that gives the pleasure, forgetting all other needs, until total exhaustion.[9] Men are far more inventive in obtaining their pleasures, even beyond the point of mere exhaustion.

The *universality of pleasure* in our lives cannot be overemphasized. We clearly act in pursuit of pleasure in ninety percent of cases, if we consider that for man a future pleasure also becomes a present pleasure, determining the choice of action. By pursuing the pleasure we choose what we do in our eating, drinking, sleeping, reading, work, entertainment, play, hobbies, interests, planning of life, marriage, career, or striving for anything we want.

In perhaps ten percent of cases we may do what is seemingly unpleasant. But we do this because we are conditioned to gain pleasure from doing so. We know that fulfilling one's duty or following the "voice of conscience" gives satisfaction. These conditioned pleasures can derive only from the natural pleasures or satisfactions, like those of survival or superiority.

The identity of pleasure with the life force itself has to be stressed next. Seeing pleasure as merely a feeling is missing an important insight. Animals, or organic mechanisms, do not feel pleasure, but they strive to do only that which we know is pleasant. And by doing so they are finding, out of millions of possible choices, only what is best for their normal existence. Evidently, what we know as pleasure is the ultimate, self-explanatory principle of existence by virtue of survival, realizing itself in living nature.

Pleasure is, thus, identical with the life force itself that creates and controls everything in the organism. In man as a conscious living being, governed by conscious reactions, it had to become consciously felt, as the pleasure, to serve as such determining causal principle. Pleasure is a conscious representation of the very force of life realizing itself through endless, otherwise ungraspable living processes.

It is truly unbelievable that the pleasure, as the clear and simple mechanism that makes man tick, is *disregarded in psychology and behavioral sciences.*[3;6,8] The reason for this is that pleasure has no meaning under the present scientism, from physical sciences. Pleasure seems to be mental, not physical. Moreover, it decreases upon addition, derives from its opposites and works contrary to the "scientific" logic in every way. It would not matter if sciences used some other name for what pleasure is; but there is no concept in modern sciences that could stand for that of pleasure, as our continuous central drive.[6,7,8]

Pleasure is also *miraculously precise and mechanistic* in providing us with causal "information" about the organic processes we live through. As the pleasure guides the organism to its tiniest details or reactions, it has to take into account all the mechanisms and their causal meanings, evolved through mililons of years. For if the organism does not choose the right food or the right response —determined by the evolutionary past—it perishes. Our feeling of pleasure gives us the answer on such myriad questions by simple yes or no, of pleasure or displeasure.

When you taste a piece of food you "understand," in few seconds, how the food will meet your complex past and evolutionary needs, after passing through equally involved digestive, metabolic and circulatory processes. Scientists working for years would not gain such understanding. Other pleasure experiences, like those of self-protection, beauty, or sex are even more "insightful"; one look at a beautiful woman reveals to you how well she could conceive, bear, nourish and endow your progenies.

All living forms, individual animals as well as mechanisms inside them, are equally "insightful." One can think here of salmon finding their spawning grounds, birds flying South, bees communicating with other bees, or dolphins, whales and apes "talking." In all such behavior, the performances are ungraspably complex but purposefully miraculous. The animals here respond, under the pleasure guidance, with uncountable mechanisms, evolved through ages, in causally precise, scientifically hardly understandable ways—just as in the above tasting of food.

Nature all around us is unfathomably miraculous, in its infinite multiplicity and purposiveness. This is true not only of the above kind of "insights" but of every performance by living forms, particularly the myriad mechanisms inside the organisms.

This does not mean that nature is metaphysically superior to human mind. The two, simply, work by different methods. The mind has to reduce phenomena to generalized "ones," to deal with them, because man thinks or feels as a unified, one organism. He responds in the same way to outside world. That is why man is able to think only of one thing at a time. In contrast, nature works with myriad factors at every point and instant.

Pleasure "explains" as well as governs, in purposive integrated ways, every mechanism and function in the organism. By managing the pleasure—with understanding of its paradoxical causality— you can manage simply and directly the organic processes so complex that no scientist or doctor can fully understand them.

Our modern diseases and disorders, that we discussed, come from our simple excessive drive for pleasure, however complex the means used. They could also be overcome by simple restriction of the pleasure. But doctors and scientists trying to find explanations and remedies by studying the detailed organic processes and causal factors have admitted their inability to understand these diseases and disorders causally. Generally, the simple commonsense rule shows that hard effort, actually restrictions of pleasure, are required to attain any lasting capacity. This indicates how men can use the simple pleasure management as guide in solving the practical problems that are bothering the modern man most.

The organic limitedness of man does not preclude him from increasing his capacities. Satisfactions or releases are the motivations and forces behind the capacities. They can be enriched by increasing their causal sources, the needs as nonsatisfactions, or restrictions. This can be done unlimitedly. Human knowledge and understanding, of abstract facts, can be equally unlimited. They grow as the systems of endless traces left by the past experiences of the equal satisfactions and needs, or releases and restrictions.

It should be noted that *all knowledge and thought derive from value processes,* from conscious varied experiences of the satisfactions or pleasures. These are the organic values or value processes, things that have significance for the organism. To the extent that this value significance is absent, no thought or knowledge results. You can watch TV scenes or read sentences, but if you do not follow it with conscious evaluation you will not remember that you saw or read anything.

This evaluation consists of experiencing the organically significant values, however involved or minute. They may be mere peripheral "disturbances" and restoration of normalcy, as in the vision, of extreme multiplicity. But the law of the organic sameness, and of equal opposite value processes thus applies to them. Inner values and disvalues, like satisfactions and needs, derive from each other as opposites. Restoration of normalcy, or satisfaction can arise only upon disturbance; but also, disturbance is possible only if there was the corresponding normalcy.

This is important for understanding how all knowledge and thought work—by *differentiation* or finding of opposites. For anything is "different," ultimately, to the extent it contains opposite elements. Thus everything known is always relative, derived from something else that is opposite.

Understanding of this relativity of cognition would be revealing, particularly for the problems of knowledge and value. Why, for instance, has philosophy become "something that cannot be done?" Or, why do theories about mind and values become so helplessly confused—and more complex with every effort to explain them? We shall see in detail later that philosophy is impossible and the humanistic value logic totally misleading because cognition and values are relative.

The unlimited, ever changing *world of thought* may seem to deny the limitedness of organism to its sameness. Actually thoughts are only endless, *minute* elaborations and combinations of the *tiniest* phenomena of the opposite value processes and of the traces they leave. That is why thought is so powerless, in spite of all appearances and general belief. If thoughts had power there would not be one problem in the world. For we all know what would be perfect behavior, like having satisfaction, interest or love in everything we do. That would make us supermen, limitlessly successful in everything we start and enjoying harmony with everybody.

But the force that can move us in such behavior, of interests or love, is that of satisfactions or releases—to be gained through the painfully hard nonsatisfactions as needs, or restrictions. Men always explain their behavior as being guided by reason, because the very function of reason is not to leave anything unexplained.

One can see, though, that those who claim most to be reasonable are least so. Thought can be so expansive or grandiose exactly because it does not involve the organically weighty reactions. Thoughts are mere rehearsals for trying out countless possibilities.

The organism is limited in its *dynamics,* as well as in its forms. It is often argued that we can grow without stopping, particularly in our spiritual vigor, to reach new powers and experiences. But human growth is predetermined, by evolution, to its tiniest details. And this organic growth is the basis for all higher elaborations of growth experiences.

If growth is increased or accelerated during one period, the organism slows it down at the next, so that the normal state of growth or aging is reestablished. It is rather amazing how strict, and predictable, the order of the cycles of growth is in the organic life, which is the only one that matters, in the end. We certainly can grow in our capacities. But not by direct increase or acceleration of the growth. Rather, we have to restrict the growth or life flow—to "dam" it up—so that its reserve, or potential of releases as capacities is accumulated.

An interesting proof that man is the most restricted of animals is his *unique capacity to laugh.* He bears within himself surplus restrictions, which can be released by laughter. It is clear, even from the way laughter goes off, like bursts of steam from a boiler, that it is a release. But release is possible only if there was tension or restriction. It is also clear that laughter is caused by realization of unseriousness. Laughter is a relief from the tensions of seriousness—from the *restrictions* on full life flow, that underlie all our normal or *serious* adjustment.

The very universality of these restrictions and of the inherent seriousness of all adjustment makes them unnoticed. Hence the curious inability of theorists to discover the general natural, therefore, necessarily, simple cause of laughter. They realize that it bears on unseriousness and is a release—from something they have not discovered. Theories on laughter are many, but the nature of laughter has remained unexplained.[10] The best known theorists, Bergson, Schopenhauer or Freud, have emphasized contrast or conflict, in various forms. But contrast is the method of all experience.

We may add that the unseriousness causing the laughter has to be of a specially original, previously unsuspected kind. Moreover, we have to be led, by a trick, into logically accepting it. We cannot laugh all the time. Therefore all the usual and not logically inevitable realization of unseriousness has long been counteracted by one's continuous concern to uphold the seriousness or the restrictions. If this concern is weakened, as by inebriation, the release through more laughter is readily enjoyed.

Finally, we may mention the concept of *homeostasis* which is synonymous with that of the preservation of sameness by the organism. As René Dubos has explained, the "dynamic stability" that conserves the "morphological identity" of the organism is a *universal property of life.*[11] It is interesting to note that "homeostatic tendencies are now found to be more prevalent than was previously believed," according to the more recent, humanistic theories in psychology.[12] Psychologists recognize, in a general way, the universality of homeostasis as the principle under which the organism keeps its conditions within its normal limits.[3;6;7,8] But this general view of homeostasis becomes misleading because it leaves out its most significant, opposite effects.

The organism restores its normalcy after overenjoyments or "improvements" by *equally excessive opposite,* negative reactions—which are deepened by efforts to overcome them by further "improvements." This is what causes the mysterious modern diseases and disorders. They have become as extensive as is the modern man's resourcefulness in adding new improvements of his feelings of well-being, in his experiences, or in organic functions. The homeostatic theories, explaining that organism always conserves its normal state, rather lead away from such causal insights, in these most important modern problems.

The Opposite or Relative Causation and a Vicious Circle

If the preservation by the organism of its limited sameness is recognized, the opposite or relative causation becomes self-evident.

Value experiences—which determine everything we feel, do or even know—can arise only upon some change in the organism. But the organism has to remain the same, statically and dynamically. Consequently, equal opposite change becomes necessary for every value experience. Generally, the organic change is some disturbance or need, to be met by equal satisfaction or restoration of normalcy.

But the converse restoration of organic normalcy, actually of its normal reserves, upon overexpenditure of releases, is the most important in practice. The restoration here requires imposition of restrictions. These appear as negative or diseased reactions and are overcome by more pleasure release, which leads to still more restrictions. Drug use is the simplest, more evident example.

Clearly felt, even experimentally provable, *improvements,* successfully attained by the modern man, become causes of equal *worsening* or disorders under the opposite causation. In natural conditions, animal strives for intricately limited pleasures or satisfactions because they lead to conservation or restoration of normality. But man as a conscious being, governing his feelings of pleasure, starts to pursue pleasures beyond the natural limitations.

Such pleasures, however derived, are always felt as improvements in the organic well-being, whatever the function enjoyed. Man always feels that he is improving when pain or stress is stopped, though removal of pain by, say, cutting off the nerve, would amount to organic destruction. Of course, such clearly destructive means are not used by man. Modern science has invented the subtlest means for obtaining the feeling of well-being or freedom from pain and stress.

The point is that the improvements men seek are *pleasures or feelings of well-being* which exhaust the organic resources but still are felt as beneficial. Moreover, the modern experimental scientism can never accept the opposite causal logic. Experiments always show that upon increase of releases or satisfactions performance improves. It has never yet been mentioned that, because of organic limitedness, the added release or satisfaction has to be paid for by equal opposite reactions.

The staggering inventiveness and richness of modern science and life are important. After men are able to produce and use the subtlest, intricate, most deeply effective "improvements," they are bound to deplete the limited organic normalcy, by nothing more than constantly added experimentally clear improvements.

What we shall call the *vicious circle* becomes decisive here. The "improvements" that modern men enjoy are subtle, almost imperceptible depletions, not gross exploitation which would be readily seen as harmful. Such slight depletions can accumulate to any, incredible degree through the vicious circle. As the opposite, restrictive reactions follow a direct "improvement," modern man overcomes them by using more of the same means of improvement or changing to a more powerful means. This then leads to still stronger restrictions, which are met by still more improvements, and so on. The deepening of the exhaustion thus can reach any imaginable extent.

Such effects are almost inevitable as long as the modern man can enjoy the rich modern means and is encouraged, by our "scientific" and hedonistic attitudes, to improve unrestrictedly his feelings of well-being. Of course, the means used are as varied as the life itself: foods, drinks, conditions of work, relaxation, entertainments, or psychological improvements, from "positive thinking" to drug therapy. They all are to provide the added satisfaction or pleasure release—but lead to the deepening exhaustion or impoverishment.

The opposite causation is never noticed. The pleasant past improvement is always so different in everything from the resulting exhaustion that no causal connection is seen. The two, as opposites, seem least related causally. That is why in a functional disease, like heart attack, or in a psychic disorder, like depression, the real cause is never perceived. The person seems to have been completely well, and the attack to have come suddenly without serious cause. The negative effect is usually attributed to the closest precipitating factor.

In all overenjoyments, the added stimulation keeps the opposite reactions at bay, until the breaking point. Then some negative, *even tiny factor* can precipitate the beginning of the negative reactions. Doctors and psychiatrists have often attributed disorders to such weightless, directly precipitating causes—under various, confusing, specious theories, so typical of the modern psychiatry and psychosomatics.

The deeper reason why the opposite causation is not recognized is the natural *aversion of man to ideas of value relativity.* The opposite causation is a form of relative causality. Both rest on the principle that values derive from their opposites or are dependent on equal disvalues. The relative causality is of course humanly unacceptable.

Men cannot live under the conviction that their strivings, always for some value, are futile because values have to come from, or bring, equal opposites. Relativistic attitudes are degenerative, therefore repulsive, like offensively smelling foods that are bad for survival.

But the relative causality has been, rationally, recognized wherever practical considerations are not involved. *In abstract philosophy* it has been noted in most of the leading systems.[2,4] The polarity of values was, supposedly, accepted by Pythagoras, Socrates, Plato or Aristotle.[12] Plato noted that a pleasant state follows an unpleasant one, and vice versa. Stoicism grew from the insight that pleasures bring equal pain. Sophists and cynics wanted to extend the value relativity to practical views—and were, deservedly, branded as ridiculous degenerates. Necessity of evil for discernment of good was recognized by St. Augustine. Comparison as method of cognition was noted by St. Thomas.[4] Some great later philosophers, Leibniz, Hobbes, Spinoza, Spencer, Hamilton or Whitehead, were relativists, in many ways.[2,4] And the modern positivists, pragmatists or analytic philosophers are practically relativistic on their main subject, the cognition. They find that knowledge or answers are possible only upon relevant, pragmatic questions[4]—as the satisfaction and need correspondence requires.

In psychology the relativity concept is frequently recognized, or implied, particularly in the Gestalt psychology, the Weber-Fechner law, or the phenomena of perception, where the modern, experimental psychologists cannot miss noticing it.[7,8] Everybody can see that a gray figure appears darker on a lighter background. And recognition of the relativity of perception does not, directly, involve practical problems. But in general, psychologists want to be practical and scientific, therefore cannot afford to recognize the value relativity.

In psychology, and in all science, the logic that values increase upon addition, or decrease upon subtraction, is axiomatic. This logic is used in everything scientists do, observe, or experiment with. But in value causation, addition of value decreases it. The highest total of satisfactions amounts to satiation and zero potential of value. Subtraction from value, or addition of opposite value like nonsatisfaction or need, creates or increases the value potential, of satisfaction.

Even in the clearest cases *psychologists are misled by the "scientific" logic*. For instance, everybody knows that a hard period in one's life, like a difficult school term or a heavy work week, makes the vacation or weekend so much more pleasant. Yet all psychologists, as scientists, have blamed the difficulties or frustrations in a person's past for his later negative reactions. It should be noted that a frustration may lead to negative effects, but only if it was compensated for by unwarranted inner satisfactions, which then as overadjustments lead to opposite reactions.

Actually, the relative or *opposite causation should be clear to psychologists from everything else they accept as true*. They recognize the homeostasis as conservation of organic sameness.[3,8] Add to this the fact that all experience derives from organic change, as all psychologists know, and you have the opposite causation. If the organism has to return to its sameness after change, the opposite process is the result. Psychologists would, further, admit that such basal organic phenomena determine all other "higher" experiences. Also the interpretation of behavior in terms of needs and satisfactions is fairly general in psychology.[6,7]

But psychologists have turned for explanations of effects of the opposite causation to the *concepts of the Unconscious*. Man certainly brings on himself all the disorders and diseases, with intense ingenuity. He does so, as we saw, by his uncessant pursuit of added feelings of pleasure or well-being. As he uses the most ingenious and intense means, in such pursuit, the opposite reactions, necessarily, follow with the same "ingenuity" and intensity.

The only logical explanation for the psychologist then is that an ingenious and intensely persistent Unconscious inside the person acts against him, without his knowledge.

A very general *proof of the opposite causation is the addiction.* We saw how general and causally inevitable addictions are as consequences of overenjoyments. We may add that under the vicious circle the negative reactions deepen into unbearable torment to be held at bay by continued use of the same or stronger means of "improvement." Hence the compulsion even if in the end the person gains no enjoyment, and only avoids the torment.

The thousands of addicts around us are a living proof, as real as life, of the opposite causation. But psychologists, ever averse to the logic of the opposite causality, are virtually mystified by the phenomena of addiction. They have only controversial and inconclusive endless theories, even on the simplest everyday addiction problems, as we shall see in discussing drug addiction.

Perhaps the most general evidence of the opposite or relative causation is the inability of man to attain the only goal he lives for—pure *happiness.* In final analysis, the happiness, pleasure or positive feelings are everything and the only thing man strives for. To the extent that he reaches happiness or satisfaction he wants nothing else. But happiness belongs in fairy tales. And the purest happiness which is, necessarily, the unrestricted natural pleasure, has to be branded as sin.

Happiness can be enjoyed to higher degrees through many means, like narcotics. But everybody knows that the results are disastrous. Happy people are those who live restrained lives of toil—who do not even strive for happiness.[5] Unhappiest are the overenjoyers, narcotics, or emotionally unrestrained psychopaths. It may seem *as if a curse has been imposed on the search for happiness,* the only goal of man.

There is more to happiness than mere feeling. Satisfactions are found to be the sources of interests, love, health, success or any positive reaction. This discovery is expounded in hundreds of ways[5] by "experts," sophisticated, and simple, urging us, excitedly, to profit from this bonanza. One can easily see that he could attain everything if only he could have satisfactions or pleasure in what he is to do or in how he wants to behave. Happiness or satisfactions are the most precious capital in the world. But it has to be paid for by equal nonsatisfactions or displeasures.

Psychologists and behavioral scientists hold that our irrationality and mistakes prevent us from attaining satisfactions. They argue that our faulty learning or conditioning is to be blamed; or that we are ruled by irrational instincts; or that our misconceptions, wrong ideas and lack of understanding become the causes of our negative reactions; or that we have substituted the materialistic and technologic rat race for true, inner satisfactions.[5,11] But our intelligence and rationality are supreme. We can understand and build stupendously intricate systems of adjustments, while the acceptance of positively felt saitsfactions is the easiest thing to learn, understand, find, choose, enjoy, get conditioned to, or be ruled by.

Men are far too clever to miss what they really want or what is most *satisfactory*. We pursue the materialistic comforts or enjoyments because they are our truest, deepest satisfactions, as we simply know it. Who else could know or feel it for us? We make no mistakes when we evaluate satisfactions. Nobody can be so limited that he would not know what is pleasant.

Surely, the material enjoyments, actually our truest overenjoyments, bring impoverishment—as do all overenjoyments. Then the "true" inner satisfactions are, indeed, missing. But this is so *not because of the materialism*. The material and technologic progress could be used as the necessary, effective means for building a constructive future, with vast systems of enriching education, actually of restrictive conditioning, which would create men with rich reserves of the inner satisfactions.

The source of all his satisfactions for man is his existence as ensurance of survival. But the most perfect, fullest existence, without variations or disturbances in it, is the boredom itself. Only when existence is threatened its value becomes apparent. Then everyone can see that no other satisfaction or value has meaning apart from the existence. The *paradox is true of any value,* or of satisfaction as the source of values.

Satisfaction or pleasure is what we live for and want to enjoy but full satisfaction is immobility, that gives no feeling. In fact, full satisfaction is a condition leading to disorders. Its immobility is unbearable, and the fully satisfied person seeks further satisfactions, above the organic normalcy. The overenjoyment then leads to the opposite reactions, and the vicious-circle impoverishment.

But man as conscious planner always pursues his satisfactions or feelings of well-being to their fullest. If he succeeds—as the modern man does—the opposite reactions, deepened by the vicious circle, then follow, step by step, his each overenjoyment. It may seem *as if his every successful "positive" effort is mimicked* by an equal negatively felt or disordered opposite aftereffect.

Finally, we may look at two very general phenomena of the opposite or relative causality: *contrast* and *fixation*. No value can be experienced without a previous or subsequent disvalue, and vice versa. Everything is known or evaluated through differentiation, which ultimately means through contrasting of opposites. If the world around an object had become a hundred times larger, the object would be seen as hundred times smaller and nothing else would seem to have changed. Every value can be changed, or reversed, in the same way, by changing what it is compared with.

If we could distort everything in one way, say, make it curved to one side, then normal shapes, or straight lines, would appear distorted in the opposite way. In experiments, subjects saw straight forms as curved after they had worn glasses that curved everything in the opposite way.[7] The same was observed with tactile distortions.[7]

There are *no values or qualities in themselves*. An object can be made to appear light or dark, yellow or green, depending on the opposite value of the background. The only limitations to the rule of total contrast are due to the incapacity of our organism to experience physically very much. If we could experience temperatures to the extent of a thousand degrees, we could make a hundred degrees appear either warm or cold depending from a previous opposite experience. The same would be true for colors, tastes or smells. And *psychologic* or mental values are not limited to any degree.

Since differences as contrast are necessary in order to experience, differentiate or know something, *the most universal—therefore causally most important—conditions or factors are not felt or "known."* The atmospheric pressure, as well as our most general needs, of survival or growth, are not "known" as anything particular. We shall see that even the most universal causal reality, in physics, is not known, because of its absolute universality— much as water is not known to fish.

Psychologically, one may live in his inner world of security or superiority without noticing it, then experience anxiety or inferiority when forced to face normal reality. Thus the disorder may seem to have no cause—to emerge under normal conditions. Since men are turning into a general atmosphere their most wanted feelings, they are bound to suffer "without cause" the opposite feelings they want least. Hence the mystifying theories about unconscious, existential or other arcane causes of disorders.

The requirement of contrast for any experience confirms that you get less value by addition, and more by subtraction or addition of opposite value. If you try to intensify the red color in your room, by making everything red in it, you will get only the experience of shades of gray, and no red at all. The same applies to the feelings of satisfaction, pleasure, security, goodness, or of any other value.

Fixation is, probably, the second practically most important phenomenon of the relative causation. The strength of values or satisfactions derives from the possibility of relating them with past backgrounds or pre-established channels of needs-satisfactions. Something may be, objectively, highly valuable, but if there is no background for evaluating it, no value experience arises. Particularly our cultural and social values gain their strength or meaning from the way they can be related to our own-created past backgrounds. You would not care to become the President of a country you know little about.

Fixations *deepen themselves automatically.* As a value object is enjoyed, first even accidentally, the background for its evaluation increases, the object becomes more valuable and is sought still more for enjoyment. The result is a vicious circle, that can deepen the value to any, irrational, degree.

Even when the enjoyment of a fixational value starts fading, the compensatory overenjoyment is sought still through the same, readily available, strong value background. The result is that men are *going in circles on their own tracks,* with increasing intensity, in their social and cultural value enjoyments. Fixations may become similar to neuroses, in which a previous means of overenjoyment is resorted to for further avoidance of the rising opposite, negative reactions.

Fixations can be observed everywhere—from the way you enjoy your breakfast sitting in the same chair to the seemingly unique value of the job or affair you have been engaged in. Particularly the cultural and social customs become increasingly elaborate or rich as well as indisputably valuable or "true," through the vicious circle of fixations. Every reason and justification is found for such fixations, for *it is the increasing value feeling that makes the reasons true.*

The result can be a virtual self-enslavement by a people to their own-created ghosts. Fixations are bound to deepen, irrationally, as long as we live with the humanistic beliefs that our rich and deep values are sacred treasures. The fixational values are always the richest, deepest and most convincing. Fixations become important in many fields of behavior, as we shall see repeatedly.

Under the fixations our values, as expressions of our ways of life, are *not causally different from taboos and totems* of more primitive peoples. Of course, fixations grow only where the value object or performance yields some satisfaction, however self-defeating, even pathologic this becomes if overenjoyed. But fears and anxieties equally become objects of fixation, because their avoidance is a great satisfaction. Then as the avoidance of threat is overenjoyed, the anxiety arises as aftereffect, which is overcome by more enjoyment of the avoidance, and so on. Taboos or avoidance customs thus can deepen into incomprehensibly terrifying obsessions.

Before we conclude, we may have to answer the question whether under the law of equal opposite feelings *everybody gets as much of pleasures or satisfactions as of displeasures or nonsatisfactions.* Yes, it cannot be different, because all such feelings derive from organic value reactions and the organism is limited in every way in its performance. If there is some continuous added growth during early age, it is taken away by later decline and death. Organically, it all comes out to zero, with which man starts and ends. However intricate the ascents and descents of a plane that lands at the same level it started from, they inevitably equal out.

A second question would be whether under the relativity of reactions *every feeling extinguishes itself as it is being continued.* Under the relativity of perceptions, a continuous noise, smell, light, temperature, or pressure does cease to be felt particularly. But no major organic value reaction extinguishes itself completely. Feeling of hunger or cold may decrease, but never ceases, until death.

The reason is that all such feelings are rooted within deeper and deeper organic mechanisms. As a feeling ceases on one level, a deeper reaction takes over. The cessation of the feeling finally does result, but only after the whole organism, with its every mechanism and reaction, of growth and decline, has been totally involved. This is fully attained only at death—when also all feelings become equalized by their opposites.

In conclusion we may emphasize that the opposite or relative causation is almost self-evident but is "impossible" because the relativistic world view and the reversal of logic it implies are unacceptable. The dependence of satisfaction or release on equal need as nonsatisfaction or restriction is, though, clearly necessary within the organic limitedness.

Even in the more elaborate, higher experiences, of perception, the relativity is clear, as is already recognized in psychology.[7,8] Such recognition has arrived there because it does not involve practical values. Generally, a relativistic view of values would be degenerative in practice; and we are not trying to convert anybody to a relativistic world outlook.

We are explaining the relative value causation—without much pride—only because causal understanding is the first requirement for having a science; and value feelings determine everything man feels, does or thinks. The science of man requires its own, relative causal logic—true for value causality—exactly contrary, as we saw, to the logic of the presently authoritative, physical sciences.

Of course, if the opposite causation is true, then it is clearly understandable how man brings on himself the disorders and organic impoverishment through his very success in attaining increased enjoyments, by added feelings of well-being or by improvements in his organic functions.

A Virtual Modern Alchemy

If the opposite causation is not recognized, the human capacities must appear, in every way, as easily attainable. These capacities are the most precious human capital. But they are also satisfactions or pleasure releases. We saw that pleasure is the motive for everything we do and equals, ultimately, the life flow itself. It is clear to everybody, including scientists and "experts," that we can attain every success if we only have satisfaction or pleasure for what we intend to do. We never lack perfectly good wondrously useful intentions.

Practically, in managing our behavior, we could easily perform any act, follow any method, or expand any stimulation, if it all did not require, or entail the displeasure: the hard restrictions and nonsatisfactions as needs; or negative aftereffects of enjoyments. Easy, "costless" and pleasant means, drugs, techniques, formulas, ideas or perfect reasons could be used. Moreover, under the logic that excludes the opposite causation the satisfactions, our capacities, would be increased by addition—by us enjoying more and more satisfactions. Thus an *alchemy of gaining our most precious capital with perfect ease,* even with added satisfactions, would be at our disposal.

Indeed, every modern scientist or theorist proceeds by the direct *"scientific" logic* under which increase in any value is attained by addition. This like-from-like logic underlies all modern, experimental scientism—from physical sciences. Also, all our humanistic thought is governed by the logic that positive values derive from like, positive value sources. Everything written or said, in behavioral sciences, or psychology, perpetuates the logic that our positive behavior comes from positive causal backgrounds.

It can be said that in the sciences about man the modern scientism is a *virtual alchemy*. The like-from-like logic, of the physical or exact sciences, is absurd for the sciences of man, who is governed by value reactions in everything he feels or does. These reactions follow the opposite causation, of the pleasant satisfactions and releases requiring equal hard needs as nonsatisfactions, and restrictions. No values come easy or without equal difficult effort. The most perfect ideas and reasons, which are always easy, cannot help us.

The virtual modern alchemy is vast. The most general, "scientifically" logical approaches expound *direct increase in positive feelings,* satisfactions, interests, love, joys of life, "peak experiences," satisfactory attitudes, optimism, faith, happiness, or pleasure in doing things. The experts here range from Norman Vincent Peale to Erich Fromm, Abraham Maslow, Karl Menninger or Norman Cousins. The theories and explanations may be intricately sophisticated or straighforwardly simple. But the purpose and logic are the same: to increase the clearly beneficial, positively felt reactions in the seemingly only possible way—by addition of the positive and avoidance of the negative value feelings.

Other approaches may stress *reasons and ideas* as the ways to increase the positive feelings or to avoid the negative, "irrational" reactions. The various kinds of analyses, in psychology, aim at discovering the ideas and reasons, in the minds of the persons, and at providing them with the right insights. Particularly in social sciences ideas, reasons, perceptions or ideational attitudes are considered as decisive. In fact, everywhere "attitudes" are seen as being determined by perceptions and ideas.[6,7,8]

But all such ideational reactions and experiences are *easy and weightless.* The greatest idea, that would be most satisfactory, can be formulated in minutes—if only it could be carried out. We saw that merely having more satisfaction in our experiences, of interests or love, would bring us superb benefits. But even the best understanding or perception of this simple truth cannot help.

Here we have to mention *learning,* which is, perhaps, most

generally accepted as the decisive factor in behavior. This can be seen from works of our leading, classic psychologists, such as Hobart Mowrer, John Dollard, or Neal Miller.[3] But learning is, equally, an ideational, perceptual, or cognitive experience, therefore has no causal weight. You could learn in one hour the insights and truths about all the positive reactions, including the love and interests, that could make you a total success.

Actually, to the extent one really learned to enjoy more effectively his positive feelings—as the theorists and experts urge us to do—he would fall victim to overenjoyments. There is only one, nonalchemic way to accumulate the satisfaction potential, and learning is not it. Of course, psychologists see that mere learning does not help. But under their "scientific," analytic approach, a thoroughly understood, faultless addition of satisfactory or avoidance of unsatisfactory experiences seems the only possible way.

Consequently, the theory becomes as complex as it is inherently unfounded. Psychologists tend to use more involved formulistic, secondary concepts of learning, like generalizations, cues, signs, verbalizations, and their assumed displacements.[3,12] These supposedly increase or exacerbate negative reactions.[3,7,12] But man, striving for pleasure, will use any generalization, sign or cue to improve his positive, pleasant reactions—which then does lead to the opposite effects.

Conditioning theories are equally important in behavioral sciences. Behavior of a person is certainly a result of the conditioning of his fundamental values, of survival or growth. But modern behavioral scientists view conditioning in terms of the Pavlovian kind of conditioning by which animals *learn,* to expect awards or dangers. Learning is here the decisive element.

The best known expert on conditioning and experimental neurosis in this country, H. S. Liddell, recognized that the "neurotic" or anxiety reactions induced in animals were due to learned expectancy of danger.[7,12] For modern scientists conditioning is mostly such *learning.*[6,8,12] Consequently, what we said about learning applies here. We may add that the cultural "learning" of behavior is actually a very different, hard conditioning, of our emotional values or pleasures. It imposes conditioned nonsatisfactions as needs, or restrictions—therefore is not alchemistic.

The theories of learning and conditioning are intended to explain why man acts against himself, why he adopts negative behavior disorders, which are unproductive as well as unpleasant. But who would ever want to learn something that is *unpleasant and useless?* The very force behind learning is pleasure, or at least usefulness. Nobody can miss noticing what is painful or disturbing, as one's disorders are. The same can be said of conditioning. Who would want to condition anybody, or himself, to have the clearly useless, unpleasant behavior disorders?

True, the animals can be conditioned to have "neurotic" reactions or anxiety—as expectancy of danger. This is so because they can proceed, by instinct, only in one way and if they learn there is danger on that way they feel the anxiety. But man has freedom to choose, from unlimited number, the most pleasant ways, in his life. That is what he does excessively, and suffers the compulsive, negative aftereffects. It is million times more probable that one will learn or be conditioned to obtain what is pleasant and positive than what is both unpleasant and useless, as anxiety or disorders are.

In all present theories of behavior the inevitably *strict "economy" of value experiences is disregarded*—as it is in the learning theories. Behaviorism, the strongest movement in behavioral sciences, rejects value experiences completely, as "mentalistic." Instead, conditioning techniques and external behavioral effects are relied on.[12]

Even where feelings are actually dealt with, the explanations never show any concern about the economy of value experiences. One can think here of the behavioral therapies and practical behaviorist conditioning methods, notably those suggested by H. J. Eysenck or B. F. Skinner.[7] Typically, Skinner stresses the use of only satisfactory reinforcements. The alchemy of mere techniques, and of added satisfactions is thus implicitly accepted.

The theories on *unconscious behavior,* which are probably next in importance, perpetuate a pure alchemy. By very definition the unconscious experiences are not felt. For to feel is to be conscious.

Such experiences are assumed to be inner hidden reasonings, perceptions, fantasies, reasoned conflicts or ideas. If they had been experienced, as past suffering they could make the later experiences easy or satisfactory, by comparison. The alchemy of never-experienced feelings, expectedly, engenders methods and treatments that rely on analyses, discovery of ideas and insights, endless symbolism, role playing, and dozens of purely formulistic mechanisms like identification, substitution, or projection.[7,8,12]

Various other theories explain that men unwittingly act against themselves by way of *mistakes,* because of their unwillingness to learn, past failures, fears, faulty learning, or constricting habits.[6,7] But the positive, pleasant reactions are the easiest things to learn or enjoy—when they are available. They are so simply and immediately pleasant, as well as beneficial, that we are always ready to have them, whatever our past failures or fears.

Habits do become constrictive. But the reason is our overenjoyment tendencies. Habits become traps, as pursuit of easier, nearer enjoyments and values brings opposite aftereffects which are compensated for and deepened by further fixational recourse to the same easier enjoyments or values.

Conflicts are often blamed as causes of disorders. They are recognized as mainly cognitive difficulties of decision. A generally noted explanation, by Neal E. Miller, dealing with concepts of "approach" and "avoidance," is typical.[7] The conflict here is a difficulty of cognitive evaluation, preceding actual value experiences. The involvement, therefore, can be only a cognitive effort (followed by rest) not a self-deepening emotional impoverishment. Surely, disorders embody a conflict. But it is not a difficulty of choosing or deciding.

The person knows perfectly that he wants the simple pleasant, positive and normal behavior. Exactly when he acts free of any "conflict" and enjoys the feelings of the pleasant behavior without restraints, the resulting overenjoyment deepens into a disorder. This is the real and continuous, self-deepening conflict.

Finally we have to mention the practically most dangerous alchemy, of trying to increase our capacities by *artificial means, like drugs.* The initial improvements in capacities that drugs bring are spectacular. Stimulants like amphetamines enable a person to work with amazing outburst of energy. Even a highly disorganizing drug, the LSD appeared to offer wondrous enrichment, at the beginning, when its effects were first widely discussed. The later aftereffects showed it to be equally disastrous. Still the use of artificial means is viewed as one of the main promises in behavioral engineering.

Stimulation, or tranquilization, by drugs, electricity or hormones, can be so effective, initially, because organic *restrictive mechanisms can be easily interrupted*. Living forms can be easily disturbed or destroyed, though no genius can construct them. The artificial influences are, of course, counteracted by the organism, through opposite processes—and the vicious-circle disorders follow. So many drugs and other means have been reported as providing wondrous initial effects that, it would seem, all our problems should have been solved by now.

The above alchemistic theories and efforts can have decisive effect on all fields of modern science about man. For it is our management of the strict economy of organic releases or satisfactions that determines whether we are well or ill, rich in our capacities or impoverished and disordered, organically and mentally.

The virtual modern alchemy results from emphasis on the scientism that has been so successful in physical sciences. The practical life shows *how blatantly wrong this scientism is for human sciences*. If the logic of increase of values by addition was right here, we would be living, as we saw, in a paradise of unlimited satisfactions or positive capacities.

Yet the modern alchemy is as entrenched as was the Medieval alchemy, for the same reasons. The old alchemists—in search of the philosophers' stone—based their elaborate theories on philosophy which then was the system of scientific certainties. The modern "alchemists" have the authority of physical sciences behind them. The everyday realities bother our "alchemists" as little as they did the old alchemists. What is more certain, in day by day life, than the fact that for every value, capacity or enjoyment you have to pay with equal effort or hardship?

But the very immaturity or irrelevance of our human sciences permits easy and free, "alchemistic" approaches. We shall not repeat how our human scientists expect to increase our capacities through more satisfactions or mere techniques. However, the simple truth in all real sciences is that you never get something for nothing or without equal countereffort or counterforce. Because of this, real sciences are constricted to one or few, exact, difficult possibilities—as in the release-restriction equality.

To the extent that a "science" is not so constricted and deals *with irrelevant factors or logic, everything is easy,* attainable through specious means or inventive formulas. It becomes an alchemy. In modern psychology, or behavioral and other human sciences, this is evident from the incredible multiplicity of theories, formulas, concepts or techniques offered as solutions without inherent difficulties or equal effort.

Everything is easy because it is all causally irrelevant. Any theory is as good as any other. The theories and techniques become so endlessly varied, actually conflicting, that nobody even cares to contest opposing views. The old alchemy was equally rich in elaborations and unconcerned about controversies, or about the requirement of equal "payment."

Some human scientists, particularly doctors and psychiatrists, have tried to find some unified causal explanation, particularly for functional diseases, which are uniform enough to imply existence of one natural, therefore simple, causal principle. But they are frankly admitting their failure to find any causal explanation. Here we have to note that *the modern alchemy is more than a harmless futility.*

It becomes the most dangerous fallacy ever foisted on man in the name of scientism. Through its gigantic elaborations it imposes the logic and methods of physical sciences on the fields of sciences of man with enormous inertial impact. And that logic is as dangerous as it is diametrically wrong for the human sciences. We saw how the modern, epidemically increasing diseases and disorders grow through the "scientifically" logical addition of experimentally clear direct improvements.

In the *physical world,* added movement or change keeps a system moving or changing; but it creates countermovement or counterchange in the *organic world*. Added heat to a physical object warms it up, but addition of heat to organism creates the reaction of cooling. And it is this reaction, not its antecedent, opposite physical influence, that determines what the organism does. Even if the physical influence is beneficial, still the organic reaction, the satisfaction derives from a need caused by preceding opposite, adverse influence. Thus all organic reactions arise by a logic contrary to that followed by phenomena of physical sciences.

But the scientists know only the usual "scientific" logic. *The opposite causality has not yet been thought of in any way.* Actually, its recognition would require a total change or abandonment of the previous "scientism"—of the whole gigantic present system. No scientist could think of that. The more erudite or experienced he is, the less he could do so. It would mean rejecting everything he has done, learned or aspired to be respected for. Moreover, the *simplicity or commonplace* nature of the opposite causation would make the scientist accepting it appear simplistic.

As we saw, the opposite causality, though humanly "impossible," is evident from the simplest, universal or commonplace facts: the preservation by the organism of its sameness; the need-satisfaction equivalence; the dependence of a feeling, like pleasure, on its opposite, like preceding pain; or the requirement of extra restriction as effort for extra release as organic energy or capacity. The very simplicity or universality of these facts is why they are proofs of universal causal laws. But for the modern scientist, steeped in the logic and methods of physical sciences, these facts are simply not scientific—neither "scientifically" remarkable nor logically fitting.

Here we may think about the first universal law of chemistry and about alchemy. That law is the permanence or equivalence of matter—which could be compared with the equivalence of releases and restrictions. The alchemists would have found that law a meaningless commonplace of no scientific interest. For it neither permitted any "scientific," profitable inventiveness, nor had ever been mentioned in the "scientific," highly sophisticated disciplines of philosophy, as the authoritative science of their time.

In sum, the causal logic of exact or physical sciences is presently applied to sciences of man. Increase in positive human, organic values, satisfactions or releases, is sought through their direct addition or improvement. *What can be easier than adding satisfactions or pleasure releases?* This is a perfect alchemy. It has led to an endless multitude of easy theories, about mere techniques, formulas, methods or reasons and ideas as sources of enrichment. Perhaps the simple wisdom that man has to "pay" for everything he gets would have helped here to see the causal truth: the requirement of equal opposites in the value reactions.

To conclude, we may point out the universality of the opposite causation, as an inevitable consequence of the inexorable limitedness of the organism. If we add the incessant pursuit of the fullest feeling of pleasure or well-being by the modern man, we can see how he is destroying himself. As he overenjoys or intensifies his capacities or functions, the organism responds with equal opposite, restrictive or "diseased" reactions—which the modern man overcomes by further prodigious "improvements." The result is a vicious circle that can deepen the exhaustion or disorder to any, incredible degree.

It may seem as if every intense and ingenious effort of improvement is mimicked here by an equally intense and "ingenious" worsening. That is how we act against ourselves—without help from any ingenious unconscious.

III

MODERN DISEASES AND THE BLUNDER
OF OUR AGE

The modern diseases of which eighty percent of people in this country now die are caused, as we indicated, by the way we live. Stress in our organic functions is a typical, generally accepted concept for explaining the immediate cause of these diseases.[1,2] But stress or anxiety is more tormenting than any other feeling. Modern men, having unprecedented resources and skills, are ingeniously and *excessively avoiding and suppressing every reaction of stress.*

This is done in the most effective ways, by adding constant, prodigious improvements in everything we feel, enjoy and do. We far exceed here the method of attaining improvements in our feelings by the use of drugs. The inevitable result is the deepening of the organic impoverishment and stress, in the vicious-circle way, to an equally prodigious extent.

Perhaps the most important fact here is the feeling and belief by man that he is improving or regaining his health when his reactions of organic well-being are improved, whatever the means used. His doctors are helping him in such improvements. They would, of course, avoid eliminating pain reactions by cutting a nerve or paralyzing an organic mechanism. But it is never recognized that, because of the strict limitedness of the organism, every functional improvement added from outside amounts to an *intensification or "enrichment" of the functions that is inevitably reversed* at the next phase. And as these opposite reactions are further overcome, by more intense improvements, the functional exhaustion or impoverishment can reach, through the vicious circle, any intensity.

Thus the modern medicine, by its inventions and approval of perfected modern functional improvements, is contributing to our self-inflicted scourge of functional diseases. Its emphatically admitted inability to understand the cause of these diseases,[2,3,4] in spite of its gigantic efforts, is a confirmation of its fallacy in its very logic or way of thinking, about the functional diseases.

The progress of the modern medicine in its technical or professional achievements and erudition is awe-inspiring. One only can feel humble before it, and we shall use or refer to the findings of medical experts, with deepest respect. But, as definitely, we are opposing *the causal logic* or way of thinking of the modern medicine. We are explaining the "impossible" but self-evidently simple and universal limitedness of the organism. By recognizing the "paradoxical" causal logic following from this limitedness the modern medicine could use its phenomenal skills for helping the modern man, instead of contributing to his self-destruction.

Functional Diseases from Overenjoyment of Improvements

Functional diseases, like heart disease, cancer or diabetes, are caused not by any organic defect but by what we are doing to ourselves. Stress, anxiety or other negative reactions, accepted as causes, show that we are exhausting or impoverishing our functional capacities by emotionally excessive behavior.[1,2,3] There is only one way man can bring this about so intensely and generally. That way is his unrelenting pursuit of improvements in his feelings of functional well-being as the ultimate source of all his pleasures or happiness.

The paradox and the vicious circle of the effects of functional improvements have to be emphasized. The paradoxical reversal of an intense and ingenious improvement or enrichment into an equal worsening or impoverishment is, as we saw, due to the limitedness of the organism. The self-evident way of how a functional worsening can reach a degree of extreme exhaustion or malignancy is the vicious circle.

Man uses all his ingeniousness to increase the improvements as the worsening starts appearing. This, of course, only deepens the worsening. The effort here becomes so persistent and inventive that finally the very mechanisms of restrictions may be effaced. The result is a disordered exhaustion of the normal, inherently limited function, or malignant growth.

Without the vicious-circle improvements a functional disorder does not develop. If restrictions, as the stress, are not prevented, they restore the normalcy. That is why *animals, not knowing how to improve their reactions, do not suffer from functional diseases.*[3,4] But as soon as men attain means rich and powerful enough to overcome their negatively felt, restrictive reactions, the vicious-circle impoverishment becomes inevitable.

The restrictive reactions, naturally, seem diseased. They are opposites of the intensified, expanded or "improved" functional performance. Of course, an improvement in one function may evoke the worsening through a quite different other function, just as nutrition can affect circulation, or smoking, the nerves.

It should be noted that functional improvements can be attained by a *general* intensification or acceleration of the function and may not require specific means. In fact, *one stimulating or stress-relieving drug or hormone like the cortisone can "cure" temporarily a series of functional diseases.*

Donald Cooley, writing on wonder drugs, finds that the "variety of human diseases that are eased by cortisone is astounding,"[6] though this hormone is so simple that it can be produced synthetically. He says, "what confounded and baffled doctors was that these afflictions have no cause common to all of them, yet cortisone affected them all as if it attacked some unknown common cause."[6] J. Harold Burn states in his book on drugs that "the astonishing ability of cortisone apparently to turn disease off and on at will marks the opening of a new era in medicine."

The cortisone action is only a more typical example. All main hormones can act in the same way, "as if they affected something that is fundamental to almost all disease," according to Burn. Drugs have similar effects. For instance, MAO inhibitors, chlorpromazine, meprobamate, or even the simple aspirin can "cure," temporarily, series of both psychological and physical disorders.

The best logical conclusion is that such cures are attained by "protection against stress," as Burn points out.[4] Of course, whenever an ill seems to be due to the stress, one can be sure, as we saw, of general functional overimprovements as causes, under the opposite causation.

The above *essential simplicity of the etiology of functional diseases* points to one simple, universal but extremely persistent cause. Man's excessive striving for functional improvements, as the sources of all his pleasures and happiness, is such cause. It is not recognized only because of its seemingly paradoxical, opposite-reaction logic.

Of course, the ways the modern overimprovements are enjoyed can be as complex as life itself. To attain some of the unique improvements offered by modern affluence, the person may accept difficulties or work harder, sometimes by resorting to compensatory functional overenjoyments. But *however the opportunities are manipulated,* greater satisfactions are the final, clear attainment, enjoyed by anticipation or directly. And the core of every greater satisfaction or enjoyment is more freedom from stress. Overavoidance of stress becomes a unique achievement and an equal calamity of the modern man.

Psychosomatic etiology of functional diseases has been very popular,[18] because the causes here are ultimately psychologic or behavioral. Everybody can see that these diseases are causally connected with emotional difficulties or stress—that they come and go together with emotions. Also, the psychosomatic explanations offer ways of getting around the paradox that the modern life creates the stress while providing the unprecedented improvements against it.

Psychosomatic explanations permit you to invoke anything as cause: a personified unconscious agency, symbolism, hidden complex, or self-punishment. The classic work on psychosomatics, *Mind and Body,* by Dr. Flanders Dunbar,[18] shows that such mystifying causes have been accepted by doctors as explanations for almost every functional disease. Supposedly a mere idea "he makes me sick" brings a disease or "a load on my chest" becomes a physical symptom. Or, a person may "consciously want to be cured, but his needs are often better served by illness." The sophistry is endless.[18]

Psychosomatic approaches are now followed everywhere, by doctors and non-doctors, who can easily observe the psychological or behavioral causes in functional diseases. But psychosomatics builds on the direct logic that restrictions as the stress, that they are, cause disease. The Freudian theories are accepted because they view restrictions or repressions as sources of disorders, and because they permit the endless mystifications.

The decisive fact is the ever-present *limitedness of the organism.* If any organic function is improved above its narrowly limited normalcy, the worsening, its opposite, has to follow inevitably. And almost *every organic function can be improved or overenjoyed* beyond its usual, normal limits. The modern man enjoys such improvements to excess, and suffers equal worsening, deepened into disease by the vicious-circle, in all his main bodily functions.

Equally important is *the role of stress as restrictions.* The organism is a humanly unfathomable miracle of purposiveness. It imposes the stress, with such persistence and inevitability, because stress is the remedy against our persistent, consciously planned excessive enjoyment of releases or improvements. The recognized fact that excessive, malignant stress is prevented by acceptance of normal stress[1,3] points to the overenjoyment etiology.

Even abnormally high demands on a function can be met without incurring exhaustion. Satisfactions or pleasure releases constitute all our capacities, and their potential can be increased unlimitedly by accumulation of conditioned needs as nonsatisfactions, or of restrictions. That is why the organism imposes pain, stress, restraint or "incapacities" when it suffers from harm or danger.

Overimprovement Etiology of Heart Disease and Cancer

We shall discuss, briefly, major functional diseases merely to illustrate he seemingly paradoxical causality of these gravest of ills that the modern men bring on themselves. We have nothing to say or add in regard to the awe-inspiring professional and technical knowledge of the modern medicine. But we shall explain that in the field of functional diseases the modern medicine is a danger rather than help. There it *is not even a science:* it cannot explain the causation of these diseases,[1,2,3] because its very logic of thinking here is exactly contrary to causal truths, that follow from the limitedness of the organism. It sees our constantly added "improvements" as beneficial while they actually cause the functional diseases.

HEART DISEASE. As we saw, fifty-five percent of people in this country die of functional heart disease.[2,5] In general terms, the *heart function is the center of our enjoyment experiences,* as even languages invariably indicate. Consequently, the heart bears the brunt of the aftereffects. The modern man, of course, uses here the endless, subtle means, that we discussed, and thus deepens the vicious circle of the overenjoyments. Think, in illustration, of a person taking stimulants to exclude fatigue and increasing their dosage to overcome the deepening need for rest, until final collapse.

The modern "improvement" means have become so perfected that nature has no protection against such direct, planned attacks on the heart. The unprotected mechanisms, ungraspably complex and delicate, are necessarily very vulnerable, when directly reached by the modern phenomenally efficient and incomparably grosser means of "improvements." Consider how a tiny clot formed by a chemically hardly noticeable imbalance can kill the person, while a drug can change that balance enormously either way.

The efficiency and determination of modern man in overcoming the naturally sickly feelings of strained or aging heart are decisive.

Nature uses exactly such "sickly" reactions to protect the heart. In natural state animal or man becomes unable and painfully unwilling to exert or enjoy himself upon organic exhaustion. Life continues as an unexciting slowed down or aged living. This may be sufficient for monotonous work and even advantageous for intellectual life, freed from natural drives. In any event, left to a natural adjustment man would never die of sudden functional heart failure and stroke that now kill most of the modern men. Animals do not die of such attacks.[2,8]

The overenjoyment etiology of heart disease is confirmed by the fact that the things which people enjoy most, like smoking or overeating, are also clearest causes of heart disease. This has been proven by countless studies, particularly in the Framingham project, so often referred to.[3,5,7] Similarly, indulgence of continuous relaxation is now found damaging to heart, though in its direct effects it clearly relieves heart. In a reversal of medical beliefs, it is now discovered that hard work or physical effort is beneficial.[3,5,8] A 22-year study on 3,600 San Francisco longshoremen showed that even irregular strenuous physical exertion is good for heart.

The greatest risks lie in the use of various drugs, because of their strong and gross "improvement" effects, and aftereffects on the delicate inner mechanisms of the heart function. Some doctors are very enthusiastic about drugs. We are advised to take nitroglycerin tablets for everything, even if a hundred tablets have to be taken daily.[9] But other doctors see all use of drugs for heart disease as fatally dangerous.[4,6] Even the use of digitalis has been condemned as a definite "blunder."[4]

Of course, *the general, continuous behavior* of the person, particularly in the work or profession of his life, is the most important factor. This has now been brought out by the study of the Behavior A and B, by Friedman and Rosenman, to which we have repeatedly referred.[2] We saw that the Behavior A, which leads to heart disease, practically amounts to an overenjoyment behavior, in the continuous, main pursuits of the person's life.

As to the Stress, the generally recognized cause of heart disease,[1,2,8] we can only repeat that the prodigiously resourceful modern man is excessively eliminating and overriding stress as his most tormenting feeling, in everything he does, therefore suffers to an equal extent from opposite reactions or excessive, malignant stress.

HYPERTENSION is viewed as the main underlying cause of heart disease and is its accompanying syndrome.[3,5,7] As in heart disease, the overenjoyed-improvement and stress etiology here is clear, for the same reasons. That is why the extensive directly logical or "scientific" efforts to explain hypertension causally have failed.[5,7]

In simplest terms, hypertension is a result of increased vaso-dilating stimulation and circulatory tranquilization. The overstimulated circulation becomes restrictive or exhausted, but has to meet increased work load because tranquilization has left the various circulation needs unattended. As the increased circulation requirements have to be carried out by a restricted or exhausted system the tension results. Any added stimulation or tranquilization can, naturally, lessen the tension—to make it worse in the end.

The most remarkable thing here is the excited *effort by experts to explain that drugs exist for easy relief of hypertension* and that by using them we can prevent or cure it.[5;7;9] One can only wonder why has not everybody been cured of this main contributing cause to heart disease. Doctors have known for decades, particularly since the development of the modern tranquilizers, in the late 1950s, that they can lower blood pressure anytime they want. As Donald Cooley wrote, "scarcely a month passes without appearance of a new drug for lowering of hypertension."[6]

If the drugs did not have the opposite aftereffects, hypertension would have disappeared years ago. Still, various campaigns are mounted to bring the benefits of drugs to the hypertension sufferers. Even the leading, practical expert, in the noted such campaign at the New York Cornell Medical Center, Dr. John H. Laragh, sees drugs as the main means of combatting this "quiet killer."[5]

Of course, drugs cannot change the organism in its myriad complexity. They only induce "improvement" effects, which are followed by equal opposite aftereffects. We saw that alcohol, coffee or other relaxants and stimulants equally relieve high blood pressure, but in the end make it worse.

Hypertension is the organism's reaction to the exhaustion through the stimulation and tranquilization, of the circulatory and renal functions. If not overridden, the blood pressure makes the person cut down, painfully, in his enjoyed foods, drinks or smoking and to live moderately. Even the heart takes more effort and increases its muscle.[3,5]

The danger lies in improving the feeling of well-being so that the person pursues further his enjoyments, or a "normal" life. Without added, stronger improvements hypertension cannot become malignant. It was discovered in one comparative study that Japanese had the "highest frequency of hypertensive disease [but] only one fourth to one twentieth the rate of heart attacks in the United States."[9] Apparently the Japanese had not yet learned or acquired the superior "improvements" we have perfected in this country. To the extent that hypertension is "cured," general heart disorders result.

ARTERIOSCLEROSIS is the most clearly evident syndrome of heart disease, and atherosclerosis is its main, fatal form. As all other functional diseases, it has remained a mystery causally. The experts are constantly confirming that its cause is unknown.[2,3,9] Dr. Irvine Page thinks that "it will be a long time before its inner nature will be known so that it can be prevented and cured."[18] It is also found that the arterial degeneration disease is "rarely if ever reached in the normal wild state of animals."[9]

Overenjoyment of "improvements" is evident as the cause of arteriosclerosis. People living under all kinds of stressful conditions suffer from it least. This has been shown by studies on people under war conditions, in concentration camps, under the apartheid conditions in South Africa, or generally in the underdeveloped countries unable to afford improvements.[2,3,4] Persons having emotional difficulties suffer also from excess fats, lipids, fatty deposits and cholesterol that accompany arteriosclerosis.[2,9] Of course, malignant emotional difficulties can be caused only by overenjoyments.

It should be noted that functional diseases are better understood if one thinks *in terms of generally integrated enjoyments of a function, and their opposite aftereffects.* Because the suppleness and unimpeded action of arteries is overenjoyed, their hardening and clogging, as opposites follow. On a more detailed level, the increased protoplasmic vigor and efficiency of tissues reverse into exhaustion and saturation with metaplasmic, inert material, as in all exhaustion or aging. On a still deeper level, numerous mechanisms, hormones or biochemicals reverse in their infinite effects.

But, in the end, it is equally informative yet less confusing to stay on the most general level of reactions, miraculously integrated by the feelings of pleasure. Going into depths leads to confusion amidst the unfathomable complexities of the living organism. There are, supposedly, 20,000 kinds of proteins in it, each performing its complex functions.

It is practically more reliable to find out which overenjoyment, say, of a food, induces the "improved" suppleness of the arteries, therefore leads to their hardening—with every minutest mechanism integrated in the process. Thus by dealing with the more general reactions, of enjoyment or "improvement," the disease can be controlled in a less confusing, simply understood, practical way.

CHOLESTEROL has been endlessly studied as a cause of heart disease.[2,3,9] But this has led only to equally endless controversies and confusion. The increase of cholesterol may be—much like any negative reaction or pain, or rising temperature—rather a protective measure. As Friedman and Rosenman write, on cholesterol, "the question is the old familiar one: how do we distinguish a symptom or sign from a cause."[2]

Various experiments, particularly by Dr. Stewart Wolf, and at the NIH, have shown that exposure of subjects to stressful conditions dramatically increased cholesterol, fats and coagulants in their blood.[18]

Evidently cholesterol, as all functional "disease," restriction or stress, serves to prepare the organism for emergency, or to restrain releases in order to restore their reserves. Cholesterol is known to restrict nerve stimulation.[2] Surely, a functional restriction creates a "diseased" condition, a feeling contrary to enjoyment of well-being, and it may turn the person into a weakling or partial invalid. But so do healthy reactions to danger, that actually prepare and finally strengthen the organism. All the person has to do is to live through such "diseased" reactions patiently and avoid the overenjoyments that cause them.

The organism regulates its cholesterol precisely, and produces more of it if less is supplied by food.[2,3] The great authority on nutrition Ancel Keys says "the cholesterol we ingest has little or no effect on cholesterol concentration in the blood."[18] Animals that eat foods containing cholesterol, like rats or dogs, showed *no abnormal increase of it in their blood even when fed enormous amounts of it.*[2] Various drugs can reduce cholesterol, but the organism counteracts them so strongly that they have had to be discontinued.[2,3,5]

Cholesterol is a tasteless fatty substance most richly contained in brains, egg yolk, kidneys or sweetbreads.[2,3] Nobody would consume it excessively. People in this country eat the protein rich foods freest of cholesterol, while foods of poorer people contain much of the tasteless cholesterol. Somali camel drivers and Masai tribesmen were found to consume excessive amounts of cholesterol, in milk, but to be free of heart disease, as are all peoples consuming the poorer foods.[3,5,7]

Surely cholesterol can be proven, experimentally, to come together with heart disease. So does stress, and we saw its paradoxical, protective role of restriction. The danger is increased by efforts to overcome such reactions through further "improvements," which the organism has to meet with still stronger opposite, restrictive processes. The ensuing vicious circle can drive the production of cholesterol to excessive levels while the whole disorder is deepened to the limits of organic collapse.

In heart disease, as in any functional disorder, its cause is *our excessive, unrelenting pursuit of added improvements, that inevitably lead to the opposite worsening,* deepened to extremes by the vicious circle. The strong overimprovement means, particularly drugs, can induce prodigious effects, and equal countereffects. Against such inventiveness of man using his awesome intellect the heart has little natural protection, and can fail "if only for a few seconds or minutes" its function is disrupted.[2]

The efforts to understand heart disease have been gigantic, involving 100,000 people in one project and 40,000 in another.[2,3] But the result is always the same: more mystery and confusion. This is inevitable as long as the direct, "scientific" logic is used. For, experimentally, overimprovement always shows as a direct benefit and the restrictive protection as a "diseased" stress, in their various forms. It is significant here that doctors die of heart disease at an abnormally high rate.

CANCER. Almost every characteristic of *functional overimprovement* is apparent in cancer. We find in it the unrestrained increase or acceleration of the most fundamental function, of growth, concurrently with the exhaustion of the normal, restrictive potential of growth. The paradox of worsening through improvement is confirmed by the fact that the same carcinogenic agents which cause malignant growth also provide temporary relief from it. Also, cancer advances while the person feels perfectly well, enjoying his habit, like smoking.

Overenjoyment as cause is evident from the causal connection of cancer with overactivity of the hormones that control the functions serving emotional enjoyments.[18] The most usual cancers can be easily related with overindulgence habits. Equally significant is the often demonstrated correlation of cancer with negative emotions and emotional difficulties—which can become malignantly excessive only through the vicious circle of overenjoyments. Cancer has increased progressively, fourfold in the last seventy years,[18] together with equal increase in the modern enjoyments of life.

On the opposite effects of carcinogens J. Harold Burn writes: "many of the agents which are used in the treatment of cancer are themselves liable to produce cancer under certain conditions."[4] Similar observations have been reported by Charles Huggins, winner of the Nobel prize.[18] Among the ambivalent causal agents are steroids, sex hormones, enzymes, various carbon compounds, mineral-enriched preparations, X-rays, ultraviolet rays, the folic acid and growth hormones.[4,18]

The most typical modern overindulgences, smoking and overeating have been clearly, statistically related with cancer. Restriction of food, in experiments with animals, reduced the incidence of cancer remarkably. The most pleasant, affluent diet, of beef correlates statistically with the main cancer of the alimentary tract, the cancer of the bowel. Drinking causes cancers of the mouth, throat and liver. Pills taken for alleviation of menopause can increase the risk of uterine cancer five times, according to a study at the University of Washington.

It may be significant that *chemicals which affect organic pleasure mechanisms induce chromosomal changes,* that can cause cancer.

Drugs like LSD, the use of amphetamines, or of saccharin, even the glue sniffing, have been found to induce chromosomal changes. Typically, exposure to anesthetic gases can double the risk of cancer, according to the American Society of Anesthesiologists. Pleasure as the mechanism that controls, in a perfectly integrated way, everything in the organism, is a determinant of all changes in it. Further, *the chromosomal changes can be inherited* as the chromosomes reproduce themselves.

Research should center on such changes induced by pleasure-controlling *drugs and hormones.*

For instance, the "marvelous" aspirin, now used for generations, controls the prostaglandins that act through almost every cell and affect most of organic reactions. The accumulating effect of aspirin can therefore be decisive inheritable changes in the cells. Steroid hormones, controlling the most important, pleasure mechanisms, of growth and sexual life, can have similar effects. Modern man has evolved various means of how to control these hormones which "cure"—and then deepen—a series of disorders, from arthritis to cancer. Drug effects causing cancer in children of users of a drug have been particularly noted in the cases of DES, used for relief by pregnant mothers and causing cancer in daughters later.

Unfortunately, the modern medicine does not expect damaging effects from drugs and hormones providing pleasant "improvements." It promotes and supports the use of such drugs or the hormone stimulation. Rather, it blames the mysterious cell abnormalities on environmental pollution, as the hedonistic fashion requires.

Poisoning of environment is blamed for malignant disorders. Poisons certainly have clear direct injurious effects. But the organism wondrously counteracts and adapts to straight injuries. It rather becomes stronger through them—by growing a thicker healed bone, or by evolving a healthier heart upon its "aggravation" by hard effort.[3,5]

Malignant disorders are completely different from straight injuries or poisoning. They are insidiously unnoticeable while they grow, because they are directly pleasant rather than injurious. A couple of decades can pass before the cancer appears as an injurious disease. Its accumulating persistence, during the years, is possible only because of some continuous (therefore little felt) vicious-circle enjoyment, since nothing else could be pursued so persistently. Pollution is quite different from such influences.

Environmental pollution shows as cause of cancer in *statistics* because it is a necessary contributory factor in many cases. The overenjoyment that causes malignancy can often be purely physiologic, rather than psychological like smoking or overeating. Every cell or tissue in the organism also strives for release of living energy (which would psychologically be felt as pleasure). Normally the balance in the cell is maintained by equal restrictions. But these can be overcome if some unnatural, even merely distorting influence "helps." Any persisting chemical or even physical influence can do it. Then the overenjoyment starts, on the purely physiological level, and deepens through the vicious circle into the disorder.

Probably any active material if injected persistently or in gross amounts can become an influence having the above effect. That is why so many materials can start tumors in selected experimental animals.

But in addition to such influence the *enjoyment effects are decisive*. In one of the clearest examples, asbestos workers have a higher lung cancer rate, but only if they smoke. Typically, mice exposed to tobacco smoke did not develop cancer; but dogs did, evidently because they acquired taste for smoking and became addicted to it, as the experiments of W. G. Cahan and O. Amerbach showed.

The purely physiologic "overenjoyment" tendencies could, conceivably, be stopped by some strong alarm influence. In the presently most promising research, on immunotherapy, notably promoted by Robert A. Good, the best results are obtained by injections of strong bacteria, viruses, or extracts from tumors similar to those of the patient. The BCG, a vaccine from live TB bacteria, has been used by the National Cancer Institute and by scientists in a dozen of countries.

Similar effects of the TB bacteria and of strong infections have been long observed, particularly since the remarkable pioneer work by William B. Coley.[18] Apparently, strong *alarm reaction is at work in the immunotherapy*. It may be significant that bacterial toxins evoke "a very strong shocklike reaction in human beings which is often alarming," according to Dr. J. Harold Burn.[4] Interferon, a protein appearing upon destruction of cells by viruses, serves as an alarm agent in protection of other cells against malignancy, as was particularly shown in the research by M. R. Hilleman and his associates. Vast research on the interferon now has been started at the National Institutes of Health and the National Cancer Institute.

The immunotherapy, using the agents having alarm effect, could be viewed as supplement to the prevention of our conscious overenjoyments, like smoking or overeating. It thus can make the protection against overenjoyments complete. Of course, the "paradoxical" causal logic about improvements and worsening is required to deal with any kind of overenjoymnet. This would be *contrary to the usual, "scientific" logic of the present medical thinking.*

We can rather expect continuation of direct improvement treatments. It may be claimed that, because the state of patients becomes clearly better, they live longer, though nobody knows how much longer they would have lived without the improvements. In functional disorders the improvement amounts to intensification of the function and rather exhausts it. Cancer has increased with the intensified, accelerated modern living but is also the disorder of the exhausted, slow, old age.

The overenjoyment etiology is not contradicted by correlation of cancer with trauma. In all overenjoyment disorders the precipitating factor is some negative, often insignificant event. Also, overenjoyments are possible under hard conditions. In the simplest case, people may compensate for lack of stimulation in their food —good in itself—by using strong, spicy additives. All kinds of compensatory enjoyments are possible while logically the hard conditions may be blamed.

Nor is the overenjoyment etiology contradicted by the theories about *viruses* or by evidence of *inherited predisposition* as cause.

Viruses are always present in the body, often as the "orphan viruses."[18] But here as in all diseases, even infections, the functional impoverishment or exhaustion is what makes the virus, or any agent, virulent. As to the inherited predisposition, all overenjoyment tendencies are inherited, but it depends on the person, or his conditioning, whether overenjoyments become his way of life.

Perhaps the clearest evidence of the overenjoyment etiology of cancer would be its *dependence on psychological causes*. Such dependence is, indeed, being repeatedly demonstrated. At the Conference on the Psychophysiological Aspects of Cancer, psychological factors, particularly the negative feelings and reactions, were convincingly shown to be causes of cancer.[10] Among the participants were experts who have done extensive work on the subject: Lawrence LeShan, David M. Kissen, William A. Greene, Fred Brown, Gotthard Booth, Roy R. Grinker, and others.[10] The various proofs and arguments are too many to discuss. But the emphasis on the negativity of feelings, on stress and emotional complexes as causes has been general.[10,11]

Here again, the negative feelings and stress can reach their excessive intensity only through the vicious circle of overenjoyments. All emotional complexes or disorders result from excessive enjoyments, of satisfactions as well as of avoidances. Typically, the negativity of feelings is not overtly observed in the "cancer personality" and is only inferred as a hidden, unconscious tendency.[10,11]

But intense dominance by emotions of people who become cancer patients is, apparently, too evident.[10,11] It all supports beliefs and theories about a cancer personality and negative emotions as causes—which practically can mean only overenjoyment etiology.

In spite of colossal efforts, *the cause of cancer remains a mystery*. As cancer attacks different functions, the effects are naturally different. But it acts in a remarkably uniform way, by unrestrained, primitive growth, upon exhaustion of the function. As a uniform natural phenomenon cancer can only be governed by a simple causal principle. Also, such principle should be evident at any level, of detailed processes as well as of integrated reactions, feelings or pleasure.

The functional overenjoyment or overimprovement is such principle. It is as uniform as is cancer and as varied, in its effects on the various functions overenjoyed. It is manifest, as we saw, throughout the causation of cancer, particularly if the paradox of disorder from improvement and the vicious-circle exhaustion are understood.

But functional overimprovement as cause of malignancy can never be understood in modern medicine. This etiology is exactly contrary to the "scientific" logic and everything believed, thought or done in modern medicine. We can only agree with scientists that understanding of the cause of cancer would be a breakthrough in dealing with it. But to reach that, *medicine would have to move in a direction it presently cannot even think of.*

Overimprovement Etiology of Other Functional Diseases

We may look, briefly, at other functional diseases to point out their overimprovement etiology. They all originate in functions that can be strongly enjoyed by man. Emotional involvement or stress is clearly evident in these diseases. Their syndromes correlate with negative experiences and feelings—which can become excessive only through the vicious circle of overenjoyments. Ilogical, seemingly paradoxical or capricious appearance and disappearance of these diseases point to the disorder-from-improvement causality. So does their development during long periods of excellent well-being.

Above all, causes of these diseases have remained mysteries, in spite of enormous efforts to understand them. Apparently the very logic of thinking in such efforts leads away from finding the necessarily simple causal principles of these fundamentally uniform natural phenomena.

ARTHRITIS reveals all the above characteristics. Its experts are invariably repeating that its cause is not yet understood.[12,13] The function involved here is certainly one that can be strongly enjoyed, and arthritis, as certainly, constitutes the opposite of such enjoyment.

What is enjoyed here is the ease, suppleness and vigor of the bodily movement, which can be constant sources of pleasure. The various reactions of arthritis and rheumatism are concrete malignant opposites—logically unrelatable, as opposites always are—of such overenjoyed ease, vigor or any other quality of the movement. That is why arthritis, in its various forms, affects the movement in so many ways.[13] We explained that the reactions on the most general level of integration reveal best the concrete causation of functional disorders.

The paradoxical overimprovement etiology is confirmed here by the *curious effects of cortisone on arthritis*.[12,13] The initial effects of administration of cortisone to arthritics can be virtually miraculous. But the aftereffects are equally extraordinary in their devastation and crippling.[12,13] A most revealing explanation of the cortisone effects has been offered by Dr. Philip S. Hench, winner of the Nobel prize and foremost authority on the cortisone treatment.[12]

In his later research he found that it is not the simple deficit of adrenal hormones that causes arthritic reactions, but a change in the circulating hydrocortisone from abnormally high to low levels. He observed that the disease flares up when the cortisone tide ebbs, and that the letdown in long-term cortisone treatment is due to the same phenomenon; understandably, continuous increase in the cortisone level is impossible.

Dr. Hench found that his observations required a theory so new that he did not expect other doctors to accept it. In truth, the relative descent, not any actual level, in any improvement factor, causes the negative reactions in all functional disorders. Reaching higher levels of improvement leads to opposite effects because descent becomes inevitable—as the use of narcotics shows.

Dependence of arthritis on emotions is repeatedly confirmed.[12,13] Stressful conditions aggravate and enjoyable experiences relieve it, dramatically. It is significant that aspirin, the general improvement drug is the best medicine for arthritis.[12] Psychosomatic explanations abound,[18] because the psychological causation here is often too evident.[18] Stress, in its various forms, is viewed as the main contributory cause in arthritis.[12,13] Opposite fluctuations of arthritic symptoms are constantly noted. Doctors are puzzled by "curious remissions and exacerbations" of arthritis, as it "waxes and wanes in severity for reasons as yet unknown."[4,12]

All this confirms the paradoxical, confusing, emotional over-improvement causation of arthritis. Unrelenting overenjoyment of a function leads to the malignantly deepening opposite reactions. Typically, immunosuppressive agents, like cytotoxic drugs, can relieve arthritis.[12,13] They suppress the complex restrictive reactions of the organism—and only can lead to a deepening of the disorder—as cortisone does.

We have to add that functional *overenjoyments may not be noticed* by the person, or his doctor. They bring a complete, actually a superior sense of normality, and after a while may not be felt as anything special, particularly after the opposite reactions start emerging and are only kept at bay by the "improvements."

Furthermore, *overenjoyments can be incurred even while the person lives through unpleasant hardships,* but attains "normal" reactions under the abnormal conditions. This explains why people who work hard or are exposed to climatic hardships suffer more from arthritis.[12] But a hardship met in full, with all the natural restrictive, painful reactions, causes no ill. Understandably, the modern medicine never finds a logical relationship between arthritis and any factor, like climate, physical exertion or diet.[12,13]

This may help to see how mysterious the functional disorders can become. A typical mystery is the *backache,* which seems to be attacking everybody in strange ways. It may appear suddenly, from nowhere, and for no reason—actually after the most "normal" long enjoyed condition. Functional overenjoyment here is to be expected, since the back must be taking prominent part in the function of movement and in its enjoyed improvements.

The role of medicine would be to discover and control the means the person is using to "improve" his functions of movement, even if he is only attaining more "normal" reactions under abnormal external or internal conditions. The modern medicine, with its enormous skills, would be more than capable to do this.

The help would be practical, and clear, under the right logic. Of course, stopping the enjoyments is the hardest thing to do for the people, who often already know, intuitively, that some over-indulgence is causing their troubles.

DIABETES is a typical functional disease. First of all, its cause is still a mystery in modern medicine,[14,15] though it afflicts, supposedly, from ten to twenty million known and unknown diabetics[14] and is a major contributory cause of our main fatal diseases.[14,15] Doctors admit that in spite of enormous effort we are as far from understanding diabetes causally as ever.[9,14] In fact, the newest observations have led to increasing controversy, and a *reversal of previous certainties.*

Thus the central medical truth about diabetes, that it is due to *insulin deficiency,* is contradicted by more detailed findings. The newest research, particularly by Gerald Reaven, Lester Salans or Lawrence Power, has shown that insulin and insulin-like activity is actually higher in the blood of diabetics—who, apparently, have a specific capacity for functional overenjoyment here. Also, it is now recognized that increasing the dosage of insulin leads to the worst diabetic reactions.[14]

Concurrently, the *drugs* universally used for relieving diabetes now have been found to do more harm than good.[14,15] Sulfonylureas, traded under the names of Orinase, Tolinase, Dymelor and Diabinese, prescribed for most of the diabetes patients, have shown, in several studies, to double the risk of deaths from heart attack.[14,15] The FDA, AMA and ADA have warned doctors of the risk. Similar effects have now been found for the other widely used drug, phenformin, traded as DBI and Meltrol. The ensuing controversy is intense, and doctors continue prescribing the clearly effective drugs.[14,15]

The other central *belief, that diets rich in carbohydrates cause diabetes is also being contradicted.* Now the American Diabetes Association has advised doctors to "encourage diabetes patients to eat the same proportion of carbohydrates" that other people are eating.[14] Studies in this country and in England have shown that, actually, higher-carbohydrate diets are better because they induce a more strenuous use and thus the strengthening of the "metabolic machinery" that is weak in diabetics.[14]

Americans eat the enjoyable protein-rich foods, that contain only half as many carbohydrates as those of poor peoples[15] and that stimulate directly the body metabolism. This is why such foods are so much more pleasant and invigorating. But diabetes is surprisingly low among people eating the poor foods,[15] which consist predominantly of carbohydrates. Various studies on diets, during the War, and of primitive peoples have shown this.[3,18]

The rich, enjoyable foods are more stimulating and their initial effect is a lowering of blood sugars. But the *opposite reactions follow, in the form of diabetes,* which is very high in this country. The opposite causation, though, is not understood, and it is, logically, argued that "the low blood sugar syndrome may be a form of diabetes."[14] Of course, the invigorating enjoyment may continue for years before the diabetes breaks out.[14,15]

It all proves that stimulation here, as functional improvement, of the metabolism, leads to metabolic exhaustion or impoverishment, in ways contrary to "logical" views. Experimentally or "scientifically," increased insulin, stimulating drugs and enjoyable, invigorating foods clearly counteract diabetic reactions. But the end result is the opposite.

The overenjoyment factor in diabetes is also confirmed by *its dependence on emotions.* Various psychological disorders and negative reactions have been correlated with diabetes.[14,15] Stressful or unpleasant emotions aggravate diabetes and enjoyable, stimulating experiences relieve it dramatically.[14,18] Sharp changes in the blood chemistry of the diabetic are observed upon variations in his mood.[14,15] Again, it is the vicious-circle overenjoyment that can deepen the emotional impoverishment to its excessive, malignant levels.

As in all functional diseases, the causal factors in diabetes can be *best dealt with on the most generally integrated level,* of the overenjoyments and their opposite aftereffects. Going into the myriad complexities, on the deeper levels of the reactions, is endlessly confusing—and misleading if the "scientific" logic is used—as the above controversies confirm. In simple, practical terms, doctors have merely to find out and restrict the means and ways the diabetic is using to attain his functional overimprovements. Even now it is recognized that restriction in diets, and in other indulgences can relieve diabetes, while the insulin may be required only for ten percent of diabetics.[14,18]

The metabolic functions that diabetes eventually afflicts can certainly be *deep sources of enjoyments*. Therefore their overimprovement becomes almost inevitable as the modern life and medicine progress. That is why diabetes incidence rate is so high in this country and is rising in all advancing countries.[15]

The most insidious fact here, as in other functional diseases, is that the "improvements," which ultimately lead to the disorder, *are felt by the person as beneficial*. Nor do doctors doubt the effects of direct improvements. Typically, the general improvement drugs —aspirin, antihistamines, sulfa compounds or vasodilating drugs— can relieve diabetes.[14,15] Even smoking and alcohol can be shown to be immediately beneficial,[18] though they clearly lead to opposite aftereffects.

PEPTIC ULCER reveals its functional improvement etiology by its clear dependence on emotions and by its increase with the modern improvements.[16,17] Also, the way the peptic ulcer is caused has remained a mystery.[17] Stress and negative emotions correlate directly with peptic ulcer though the way they cause it is, admittedly, not understood.[16]

The people who enjoy the best conditions and have all the means of improvements, particularly executives and doctors, have more ulcers.[18] In experiments, the "executive" monkey who could avoid shocks developed peptic ulcer while the one who could not did not get the ulcer. In this country, where people have the best means and ways for avoiding stress, four million are suffering from peptic ulcer.

In peptic ulcer the *determining factor is a conflict* between the person's "improvement" drive and the incapacity or resistance of the organism to meet it. In the simplest physiologic terms, ulcer is caused by excessive gastric-acid and pepsin activity eroding the stomach wall that remains inert and does not secrete enough of necessary, protective mucous substances.[17]

Higher peptic and stomach-acid activity is, of course, a quality of vigor and youth. It is resorted to in case of stress, to create additional energy or performance. But if the person suffers from a general functional restriction—which may be a response to over-enjoyment—the stomach wall does not follow through adequately with the "improvement" sought through the stomach-acid increase.

Partial necrosis, or vascular anoxia of the stomach wall is inferred in stomach ulcers.[16] In experiments, inactivation of stomach, by cooling, tranquilizers, or clamping, leads to ulceration if, concurrently, increased acidity is induced, by cortisone or by requirement of exertion.[17] Etiology of peptic ulcer thus appears to be simple. But "logically" nothing agrees in it, because the functional responses, as well as the negative emotions or stress, work here in seemingly paradoxical ways.

The conflict, and the *decisive role of emotions,* in the ulcer causation has been always recognized, particularly in the psycho-somatic explanations.[18] The ulcer patient is found to be a generally submissive, passive, retiring person forced to play an aggressive, active or assertive role.[16,18] Such conflicting emotions could well find expression in the above physiologic conflict.

In any case, stress or emotional difficulties, demanding extra releases of functional energy, can be recognized, by anybody, as the cause of ulcer. But stress, as we saw, can reach disturbing intensity only through overenjoyment. Peace of mind is, recognizedly, the best protection. *Logically therefore relaxation is seen as a goal,* and direct means for enjoying it, like drugs, alcohol or smoking, are often approved.[18] Also, since the organic reactions against overenjoyments are restrictive, emotional restrictions may be blamed as causes, here as in all functional disorders.[18]

The *conflict aspect* of peptic ulcer explains some peculiarities about it. For instance, the ulcer fluctuates in its intensity with seasons, and with day-and-night periods. It may disappear during the summer and winter, while being worse in the spring and fall.[16] The reason is that no conflict persists in the summer, when the whole organism yields to overenjoyment; nor in the winter, when all overenjoyment tendencies have subsided. Further, it is noticed that while ulcer continues there is no danger of cancer—because there is no general, unopposed overenjoyment. Conversely, the cancer-prone, easygoing, obese people do not have ulcers, because with general overenjoyment there is no conflict. Also the cardiac Type A people have ulcers rarely, for the same reason.

OVERWEIGHT is the most prevalent physical health problem of affluent people, and the main contributing cause to all functional diseases. It is a glaring embodiment of the overenjoyment from food or from the nutritional function. Because it is a product of overenjoyment, it becomes a puzzling, paradoxical problem.

Hundreds of means for reducing weight have been proven effective, often spectacularly so, but have failed or made the problem worse in the end. The reason is that any means which provides stimulation or accelerated rate of living, and is weight reducing at first, leads to understimulation, slowed down metabolism and overweight.

People in this country enjoy the tastiest foods, which are pleasant because they invigorate, accelerate the body reactions and therefore *reduce weight, in their first effects. But the end result is the "overweight society."* Of course, fats in diet are logically blamed, because clear fats are a dull unstimulating food. Experts, offering such explanations, talk as if they had never seen an affluent modern diet.

The kind of fats that could be associated with the fats in the body are totally excluded from our affluent diet, because they are unbearably tasteless. Only the poor people, Eskimos, Indians, blacks, or similar groups studied eat such fats, and suffer from overweight least. The equally unstimulating or tasteless, polyunsaturated fats are also weight-reducing.

Yet the great diet experts, like Dr. Ancel Keys, the author of *Eat Well and Stay Well,* still see solutions in stimulating and experimentally weight-reducing, tasty diets, even in direct stimulation from food or drink.[18] Typically, alcohol is the best means for burning off fats in the body and thus for initial reducing, but also for incurring the overweight. Experts then blame the clearly insignificant calorie amounts in the drinks.

Equally confused are the *arguments about people choosing the wrong foods by mistakes.* Dr. Jean Mayer, as the Chairman of the White House Conference on Foods, blamed advertising and promotion for the wrong choices. Actually nothing in the world can deceive man about what is pleasant, as are the stimulating, initially invigorating foods. We eat "junk" foods because they are artificially concentrated in their stimulation to the point of resembling artificial means or drugs. Of course the stimulation effects reverse. The general confusion is reflected in the psychosomatic "explanations"—about overweight's symbolic meaning of impregnation, or about various oral symbolic associations and unconscious complexes.

The central cause of overweight is metabolic sluggishness, from functional overenjoyment. Overstimulation is particularly dangerous for individuals suffering from innate metabolic weakness or incapacity to derive enough stimulation from foods. Such individuals are bound to *suffer additionally strong sluggishness upon overstimulation,* leading to requirement of more stimulation, more food. The result can be a particularly insidious vicious circle.

But exactly for such individuals the expert is suggesting more stimulation through diets and drugs, to make them act more "normal." Doctors are often surprised to find that a person eats little and still accumulates fat. The reason is that the stimulation he receives from food is not sufficient to make him exert, move or work enough to expend the calories consumed. In brief, the problem is one of the economy of stimulation; and that is governed by the paradoxical logic of the opposite causation.

In all functional disorders, a direct increase in a function, "scientifically" showing as clear improvement, and felt as such, decreases or exhausts the function. Restriction or opposition is the way evolutionary and cultural selection has produced the higher forms and capacities. Medicine should proceed by the same method— *even by infliction of difficulties, in the way it does in inoculation, which is the greatest medical success of all time.*

But the modern medicine is doing the reverse and promoting progressive increase in the direct improvements. The result is an equal increase in functional diseases, of which three fourths of modern men die and which have remained admitted mysteries causally.

The Medical Blunder of Our Age

In all ages and cultures people have lived with peculiar medical blunders, crudely primitive as well as sophisticated. When Charles II of England was dying, 43 elaborate cures were used that rather hastened his death. The people who eagerly sought such cures were as intelligent as we are and as anxious to follow the science of their time.

The only protection against such blunders is a true scientism, which cannot begin without causal understanding. And, as we saw, *there is no such understanding in the field of our main, functional diseases.*

The direct improvement logic is the central fallacy of modern medicine, and it is best illustrated in the treatment of pain or any negatively-felt reaction. If we did not feel pain, upon being hurt or infected, we would not last for long. But man avoids the feeling of pain more than anything else. He identifies it with disease, as does his doctor. The goal of "logical" treatments becomes removal of the pain-causing reactions, which are ultimately organic restrictions. The enormous medical effort is directed at increasing the positively felt improvements, which man already overenjoys through most ingenious means.

Medicine thus combats that side in adjustment which needs most support and helps the side which has to be counteracted above everything else. This is an inevitable result of the failure of the modern medicine to recognize the logic of the organic limitedness.

The total *difference between artificial and natural removal of pain* should be noted. Under natural adjustment pain has to be removed. This is the very purpose of pain as the guide in avoidance and counteraction of an ill, through complex readjustments. But when pain is removed artificially or nonorganically, by the medical means or drugs, it is like blinding a man or getting him drunk when he has to face a complex, dangerous situation.

Two misconceptions have to be emphasized here. First, it is universally assumed that the doctor treating a functional disease removes or counteracts its cause. In truth, even when the doctor makes detailed analyses or tests of body products and processes, *he only gets reactions* of organs, cells and tissues. All these act as limited integrated wholes reacting to stimulation and disturbances, by releases and restrictions. They show improvement upon increased stimulation, that may lead to exhaustion; and they show worsening or restriction upon meeting disturbances, that actually serves to sustain normalcy.

Thus the doctor deals only with organic reactions, *which actually follow the paradoxical logic* of opposite causation. The doctor could properly use the direct scientific logic and treat the *causes* of the functional diseases if he could deal with the biochemical factors, in their myriad multiplicity, at every point and instant— and if he understood the principle of life in the first place. Of course no genius in the world, and no human mind can deal with such multiplicity.

Second, it is as *generally assumed that organic processes can be improved,* changed or added to by the advanced medical means. In truth, all the doctors in the world using every skill could not create or change a tiniest bit organically in a living tissue or process, except by destroying something in it or evoking its reactions, which are governed by the paradoxical logic of reversals. Organically integrated improvement of anything living would be as complex as creation of a living tissue.

Yet the modern medicine expects greatest progress through direct improvements in organic functions. Various means, from aspirin and ascorbic acid to MAO inhibitors and biofeedback, have been shown to have clearly wondrous effects—that fail to bring the expected wonders and rather deepen functional disorders.

None of such means change anything organically, and the *organism responds with opposite reactions to all nonorganic changes,* as it restores the normalcy or sameness it inexorably maintains. Even if such normalcy may occasionally look deficient, it still is billions of times superior to anything man-made compounds or artificial intervention could create. Even the lowest living form is ungraspably miraculous in its complexity of multiple details.

Drugs, the main artificial means used, are preposterously crude compounds in comparison with organic forms. But they create wondrous improvement effects, by eliminating restrictions and thus permitting excessive use of functional reserves. No complex skill is necessary to stop, destroy or inactivate anything living. Knocking out one element in the endless organic chain processes can produce a selective effect. But the organism has to restore its normalcy or reserves, therefore imposes above-normal restrictions, felt as worsening.

As René Dubos states, "it is a painfully but richly documented paradox that each and every drug proven worth in the treatment of disease can itself become a cause of disease even when used with understanding, skill and moderation."[18] He points out that these effects are "extremely indirect and delayed."[18] Brian Inglis, in his book on modern medicine says: "To sum up, it can now be asserted with depressing confidence that allopathic remedies are ipso facto a danger to man . . . the public does not have any conception of how many lives have been unnecessarily sacrificed, and how many disorders unnecessarily caused by drugs."[18] He thinks that "the reaction of the life force against the drugs will in time be recognized as the basic cause of side effects; the body is regarding the drugs as interlopers."[18] The "side" effects are, indeed, the countermeasures by the body against the distortions or excessive releases induced by the drugs.

The same is true of all artificial improvement means, physical, chemical or psychologic. They cannot and are not even intended to create organically integrated, structural changes in the ungraspably complex living mechanisms. Therefore the opposite reactions have to follow.

Physical therapy uses outside influences merely to evoke organic reactions, which are followed by opposite aftereffects. *Chemical means,* say, iron or iodine preparations also serve only to evoke stimulating reactions, rather than to reorganize or build organic mechanisms. The organism is too complex and too intricately integrated to be helped by chemical interferences. It builds by use of foods which it finds and assimilates with inventiveness that no scientist can follow or understand. Children may start eating strange things, bits of soil, dirt, plaster, stone or worms, and preganant women may sneak out at night to eat pieces of coal, because their bodies may need something that doctors cannot explain.

Of course, drugs and chemicals are helpful where they destroy pathogens, bacteria and viruses, or supply some simple elements that body lacks, as in the few diseases like phenylketonuria or galactosemia. But here the causes are external and simple, and the disorders organic, not functional. None of the general health problems of the modern men or their functional disorders belong here.

Hormones, of all kinds, are being increasingly used, because they are extremely effective. But the body can always create all the hormones it needs. Hormones are sufficient in phenomenally minute amounts. The pituitary hormone can evoke physiologic response even if diluted to one part in a hundred million. Adrenalin can act in a dilution three times weaker. Prostaglandins produced by the body in one day weigh one tenth of a milligram, enough to cover a printed dot. Moreover, the dominant hormones that determine all other reactions consist of steroids, made of elements most plentiful in the body, and are so simple that they can be produced or substituted even synthetically.

Evidently, the hormones are only signaling devices or triggering switches operated by the whole unfathomably complex organic system. It would be a sheer folly to start managing the signals or switches in such a system, of living processes, that no genius can causally understand, create or direct. In all cases of this kind of artificial, hormonal intervention, bringing "improvement," the organism restores order by opposite processes, felt as worsening.

Psychological intervention, by use of means like *biofeedback, meditation or hypnosis,* can help even less than drugs. Such means, equally, cannot and are not intended to change organically and permanently the biology of the body. The initial effects of relaxation, or stimulation, therefore lead to equal opposite aftereffects as the body regains its structural and dynamical organic sameness.

Even when used merely to calm the body, drugs or other artificial means do more harm than good. When the organism needs peace it maintains it to a more than necessary degree. If a limb or organ is even slightly injured, the whole body is immobilized. And it is the pain, not its removal, that achieves this. Restlessness, when organically permitted, is the best way of how the organism can find new necessary readjustments on all levels of integration. Moreover, the soothing means have to interfere with deeper, controlling mechanisms, that maintain the organic normalcy.

True, the body still functions, on the lower levels, even while consciousness that carries pain is excluded. But the gravest general risks lie in exclusion of this very center of human organic control from participation in important readjustments. As we saw, it is the person's conscious attitudes that determine whether he turns any, even ordinary, functional enjoyments into overenjoyments, which are the causes of all functional and malignant disorders. These attitudes can, evidently, become disordered if the consciousness is so drastically altered.

Doctors are often aware that it is the nature, not any artificial means, that cures. They may differentiate between mere *symptoms,* that might as well be removed, and the cause. But as we saw, the doctor always deals only with reactions of the body or of its organs and tissues. Such reactions, showing as the symptoms on the more general level, are his only possible guides, in dealing with functional diseases, under the right logic.

Nothing is irrelevant in organic reactions. The unpleasant symptoms, much as all "disease" externally, are the organism's reactions for restoration of normalcy. Accordingly, the unpleasant *"symptoms"* are to be kept alive or strengthened, in the functional diseases. They disappear when they have fulfilled their paradoxical role.

But how could one *distinguish between a logically real disease* like an organic deficiency, to be remedied by an improvement, *and a functional "disease"* which is only deepened by direct improvements? The modern medicine is tremendously successful in solving such technical difficulties, once causal understanding is there. Of course, it would have to use here the paradoxical logic of reactions and overenjoyments, as well as methods of relative comparison. The task is not impossible. People recognize when they see effects of overenjoyments, as in intoxication; or their aftereffects, like a hangover. Medicine can be here as much more effective as is a microscope in comparison with the naked eye.

The decisive point would be *the recognition, for the first time, that experimentally clear direct improvements can be sources of the diseases* modern men suffer from most. Then the awe-inspiring skill and power of modern medicine would go into a causally understood combating of these diseases, and not into the enormous "improvement" efforts that create them or make them worse.

Even the vastly expanding use of drugs could play an important role, in new, different treatments. Means like drugs can be used to prevent or counteract overenjoyments on the deeper, physiologic levels, since no extraordinary complexity is needed to disrupt or stop living reactions. We saw that in the recent efforts against cancer, immunotherapy is seen as a possibility, and it uses strong alarm agents on physiological levels.

If overenjoyments can be prevented on deeper biological levels, this together with conscious restrictions can offer complete protection against functional diseases, even cancer—though practically it is very difficult for men to accept the restrictions.

Overenjoyment as cause of functional diseases *should not be difficult to understand.* Enjoyment is man's strongest tendency, and its paradoxical, exhaustive effects can be seen from such enjoyments of the feelings of well-being as the use of drugs. Now the modern medical and general progress has provided man with means to overenjoy his every organic function to similar extent, in prodigiously inventive ways.

Our unique progress and "scientism" have outrun the old restrictive wisdoms. The modern medicine simply does not know any other logic than that of experimentally direct improvements; or of unrestricted normalcy, even though the person has to live subnormally upon functional exhaustion or under any organic weakness he may particularly have.

The modern medicine does everything that can deepen functional overenjoyments to their extremes. If left to themselves, as in primitive or animal adjustment, occasional overenjoyments are counteracted by immediate aftereffects, the diseased aftermaths. The result is absence of functional diseases. But the modern medicine and its supported improvements of modern life enable man to meet every negatively felt afterreaction with still further improvement. Such overriding of aftereffects starts the vicious circle, which is so decisive in causing the extreme functional impoverishment and disease.

In fact, one of the main medical efforts has become the *removal of drug aftereffects,* the "side" effects, since drugs that "cure," temporarily, have already been found for almost every functional disease. The drugs against "side" effects are particularly aimed at mere continuation of functional enjoyments, rather than at rebuilding anything. They act merely through neural and hormonal controls, and only suppress the restrictions, so that deeper functional resources can be overspent.

It is truly ominous that the modern medicine uses its staggering resourcefulness and influence to intensify the "improvements" that are the very sources of functional diseases. *If the direct improvements were the solution, doctors would have merely to prescribe what the person does already* while he deepens his functional disorder. For he knows and uses exactly the means that give him the best, most pleasant relief from the reactions and stress that he is struggling against.

The main, insidious fact about overenjoyments as causes of functional diseases is that the disease is deepened to extremes by means and ways that *seem satisfactory, beneficial or positive* in every logical or experimentally verifiable way. This is the main practical reason why in medicine, or other fields, admitedly nobody has yet discovered the real causes of the functional diseases and disorders.

By the way, *even general, nonfunctional diseases* may become causally confusing if the paradox of reactions, within the organic limitedness, is not understood. As we saw, even in their strict laboratory findings doctors are, actually, dealing only with reactions of organs or tissues. And reactions are governed by the unsuspected opposite causation. An organic disease, disturbance or injury may evoke restrictive, "negative" reactions, as the limited organism tries to establish resources or new adjustments. Such negative reactions, by the organs, cells, or tissues, then may show in the tests and analyses as the immediate causes of the disease. Thus life-saving reactions may be treated as ills to be removed, even under advanced, experimental, laboratory methods. Or, richly wasting, experimentally positive reactions, that ultimately worsen the ill, may be favored in the experimental modern medicine, unaware of the paradox of reactions, that is due to the limitedness of the organism.

In conclusion we may emphasize the inherent conflict between the organic limitedness of man and his uncessant pursuit of increased feelings of well-being or happiness. This is *the greatest danger to man as a conscious planning being.* Because of its limitedness, the organism functions by equal restrictions and releases. But man's striving for the increase in the feelings of well-being or pleasure amounts to constant attempts to remove the restrictions.

Now the uniquely resourceful modern man is finding himself enabled and encouraged to remove all restrictions, in his effort to live by pleasures or satisfactions alone. The inevitable result is, as we saw, the vicious-circle, malignant functional overenjoyment and exhaustion or disease. Is it not revealing that the *peoples having least means and knowledge are free of the diseases of which we are epidemically dying?* We may add that any directly increased enjoyment is felt as such only briefly, at the beginning, since the negative opposite effects take over afterward.

It is almost self-evident that man's excessive striving for enjoyments causes his disorders. Everybody can see that we would be free of most ills if we could stop our indulgences, like overeating, smoking or avoidance of physical effort. But the pampered modern man, in particular, feels that he is endangered by illness when his negative reactions appear, under all kinds of overimprovements. And the modern medicine helps him in his virtually suicidal effort of adding more improvements for more enjoyments.

The blunder of our age is the "scientific" logic that we should increase directly and enjoy as much as possible our feelings of well-being, satisfactions or pleasure releases and freedom from pain, stress or restrictions. Use of all kinds of drugs, is typical here. Such enjoyments always seem, experimentally, beneficial but lead to functional, vicious-circle exhaustion as the cause of the diseases and disorders from which the modern men are suffering and dying at epidemic rates.

The causal paradox here is due to the inexorable organic limitedness of man. But this limitedness is unacceptable in human thinking, or behavior; and its causal logic has not been scientifically understood. The practical result in the field of medicine has been that our self-inflicted, functional diseases now cause three fourths of our deaths and have remained admitted mysteries causally.

IV

ALCHEMISTIC IMPROVEMENT LOGIC IN PSYCHIATRY AND PSYCHOLOGY

In his mental life man could always create more positive ideas and feelings, independently from outside circumstances, if he wanted to, which again is his mental capacity. That is why so many noted experts are advocating more positive inner satisfactions, feelings, thinking and attitudes. Of course, satisfactions or pleasure releases are the sources of all our capacities. So why not increase this most precious human capital by improving our inner feelings? That would be an easy enjoyment. It all would amount to a pure alchemy.

Yet the modern psychiatry and psychology do proceed by the logic that positive reactions come from positive causal backgrounds. Logical, direct improvement of feelings, reactions and experiences becomes the goal in everything psychiatry or psychology does. This logic is evident from every discussion or every page written in these fields. The logic of the opposite causation—of restrictions or seeming worsening providing the real, unreversing improvement or releases—has not yet been heard of. It is contrary to the present beliefs, here as elsewhere. We shall not repeat the explanation of how value reactions can derive only from their opposites because of the limitedness of the organism.

The paradox of mental direct improvements turning into disorders—due to the opposite causation—can be easily observed. *The clearest mental improvements, by drugs, create aftereffects that can not be distinguished from psychoses.* The mentally weak neurotic or the autistic psychotic, having less restraints on the primordial pleasure drive, enjoys similar direct "improvements" in his emotions, and suffers the malignantly deepening negative aftereffects.

Neuroses and psychoses, as such aftereffects, are perfect clues for observing how positively-felt overenjoyments create opposite reactions, which deepen into malignant disorders through the vicious circle. Naturally, *it does not matter,* for the organism, whether an overenjoyment is induced *by narcotics or by direct* psychological means. But neuroses and psychoses have remained admitted mysteries causally[1,2,5]—because they follow the seemingly paradoxical opposite causation.

The fallacy of direct improvement logic is perpetuated by the modern psychiatry as a logical science, without slightest hesitation. Psychiatric treatments are, invariably, aimed at improving the patient's feelings or reactions directly, without their opposites. The treatments become great immediate successes, but lead to general, admitted failure.[1,2,3] In the modern psychiatry "everything works and nothing works."[4]

The modern *psychology* has become a virtual modern alchemy. Our precious psychologic capacities are expected to come from *positively felt background causes, that can be only enjoyable;* or through ideational, perceptual and learning experiences, *which are easy,* and weightless in pleasure terms. The modern psychology totally ignores the pleasure,[1,7,8] by which men live every minute of their lives. The pleasure economy, of equal effort for every gain, is never recognized, though it is the core of our main practical problem, our desperately hard, daily struggles to earn our badly needed positive capacities.

By missing the real source of our behavior, psychology loses itself in endlessly confusing, irrelevant imitation of the exact sciences with their totally different causal logic. The old alchemy was similarly a product of imitation of the contemporary authoritative, but irrelevant, philosophical disciplines.

The Paradox of Mental Improvement

The most concrete mental improvements are attained by drugs, particularly those inducing stimulation and pleasant reactions. Amphetamines are a good example. They are so effective that they have been regularly used in some professions.[5,6] But the after-effects induced by amphetamines are "indistinguishable from paranoid schizophrenia." This has been established since the noted work by P. H. Connell on "amphetamine psychosis."[6] Another good example are the LSD aftereffects.

When the exciting initial effects of LSD first came to general attention, fifteen years ago, they were viewed with remarkable enthusiasm. Revolutionary possibilities for dealing with human problems by use of drugs were predicted by leading scientists, such as Robert H. Felix, then director of the NIMH, Glen T. Seaborg, B. F. Skinner, or Julius Axelrod. But the aftereffects of LSD become a disorder "clinically inseparable from the paranoid types of schizophrenia."[5]

Aftereffects of all drugs used for mental improvement with its pleasant, positive, stress-relieving effect, similarly resemble mental disorders. It can be stated that "if we include all drugs, we could cover the entire spectrum of symptoms encountered in endogenous mental disorders."[5]

Again, for the organism it does not matter whether the "improvement" is induced by drugs or by direct internal enjoyment. Here the special *tendency of the psychotic, particularly the schizophrenic, to live in his inner world* as if it were real, is decisive. As Clifford Morgan points out the psychotic "lives in a world of his own making," a world of "fantasy carried too far."[8] He "gives himself over to daydreaming" which "replaces reality for him," according to Ernest Hilgard.[7] The tendency of the schizophrenic to lose the distinction between his inner world and the reality is generally recognized.[1,3] This tendency certainly enables him to enjoy perfect satisfactions and freedom from any stress, which are what every living being wants. Psychologists have repeatedly shown that daydreaming serves coping with unfulfilled satisfactions or with stress.[1,2]

The point is that the psychotic lives in a world of his own making, *in which he naturally creates every enjoyment for himself.* Unlimited enjoyment of the inner gratifications created in this way then leads to equally unlimited incredibly strong opposite feelings and reactions, through the vicious circle.

In neuroses, the overenjoyment tendency of the neurotic is best evident from the *Defense* and *Conflict,* the generally recognized causes of neurotic reactions.[1,2] The Defense is clearly an *excessive avoidance by the neurotic of the negative reactions* that become inevitable exactly because of such excessive avoidance. The self-perpetuation and deepening of the Defense is generally noticed.[1,2] Various explanations of its insidious nature have been offered. According to Karl Menninger the neurotic chooses the wrong ways for warding off anxiety, because of his various unconscious conflicts, and thus continuously runs into more difficulty.[2] Such wrong choices are generally attributed either to unconscious, irrational and symbolic motivations or to faulty learning.[1,3]

But nobody ever makes mistakes as to what is pleasant or emotionally positive, particularly on the unconscious level; and nobody ever learns what is uselessly unpleasant. On the contrary, the positively felt reactions are the simplest, easiest things for man. Because the neurotic, or psychotic, constantly chooses them, without restraint, as easy immediate improvements, the vicious-circle impoverishment deepens at every turn.

The generality of the theories of Defense merely proves that the excessive striving for improvements is the observed dominant feature in the disorders.

The Conflict similarly grows from the excessive tendency of the neurotic, or psychotic, to avoid negative reactions. As Robert W. White explains, the neurotic is dominated by "over-driven strivings" or "protective traits," and the conflict in disorders implies by its very nature an intense, even well-reasoned effort to solve the difficulties.[4] The source of Conflict is the paradox of worsening through improvement or of stress upon excessive releases.

Without this paradox there would never be any conflict. The neurotic needs only the positive pleasure releases and these are the easiest things to choose—after they have been made available, through restrictions. The paradox turns every improvement attempt into its conflicting opposite.

Whether the Defense and Conflict or other concepts are used, it is generally recognized that an *insidious, self-perpetuating tendency* in the behavior of the psychotic or neurotic is the cause of the disorders.[1,3] It is also recognized that he strives excessively to avoid hardships and stress, or to enjoy perfect security and superiority as well as bodily gratifications.[3,8] Apparently, he is the mentally weak person who is unable to bear restrictions and who yields easily to the pleasure drives.

There is only one way *how the person can bring on himself, in an insidiously persistent way, the deep negative reactions, while striving for pleasures or improvements.* That way is the overenjoyment, creating the vicious circle that can deepen the negative reactions beyond all rational bounds. This has to be stressed here as well as in the etiology of any functional disease.

Of course, one can pursue the enjoyment of having a positive feeling as well as that of not having or avoiding a negative one. Hypochondria is the opposite aftereffect of the overenjoyment of freedom from diseases or of not having them. Phobic reactions grow through overenjoyments of avoidances. Overenjoyments can combine in endless ways. But the simple end result is that a neurosis or psychosis, like an evil mimicry, consists of everything the person least wants to feel or do.

Strange mannerisms and compulsions grow through overenjoyments. If the psychotic, in his easy world, derives his enjoyment by mere snapping of his fingers or avoidance of unlucky numbers, he still suffers full aftereffects. Exactly because he derives real enjoyment with such ease, he drives himself into strong negative reactions in this easy way, as if without real, equal cause. The psychotic, or neurotic, lives with such trivial preoccupations, because greater values as satisfactions grow from stronger restrictions, which he cannot bear.

Moreover, he *cannot abandon the trifling preoccupation,* like the snapping of the fingers. For him it is just as real a means of enjoyment as is heroin for the addict. He can only add to it, which he does eagerly, thus creating a complex system of mannerisms or ideas. If he has built himself up into a Napoleon, he cannot abandon the idea even if it later creates for him only more difficulties. Every step in such buildup brought him real physiologic releases; that is why he pursued the idea. Consequently, every step down, back to his pre-Napoleon level would require equally real, physiologic deflation or restriction.

Finally, we have to point out that without overenjoyment a person can endure severe adversities and still adjust to them normally, by suffering equally severe restrictions in the life flow and thus accumulating the needed reserves. Conversely, one can enjoy every ease or well-being and still drive himself into release impoverishment.

This happens if he *spends more of the releases than the situation warrants*—than is normal according to the complex but precise correspondence between internal releases and external fact values, which is maintained in steady behavior. By attributing precise inner values to fact values motivations are usefully ordered. The mentally unbalanced person tends to attribute, emotionally, higher values to things he wants to enjoy. But he later notices the exaggeration, and opposite reactions arise. If he overcomes them by further exaggeration the vicious-circle disorder starts.

As long as one holds to the "reality principle" and does not improve his feelings above the outside value reality or above his inside normalcy of reactions, he is free of disorders. Yet in the modern psychiatry and psychology, the improvement logic inevitably leads to *promotion of logical, direct improvements* in feelings and reactions. Under the organic limitedness, improvements, as increases in releases, can be attained only by equal restrictions. But now restrictions are viewed as sources of all evil, because they do appear as the diseased reactions, while they restore organic normalcy or release reserves.

The Simple Cause, and Mystery, of Neuroses and Psychoses

Mental impoverishment or exhaustion is the immediate cause of functional neuroses and psychoses. Mental disorder never appears when there is a plenty of satisfaction or pleasure releases. A simple release-increasing drug, like iproniazid or chlorpromazine, can cure, temporarily, a series of mental functional diseases. But, as we have repeatedly explained, only functional overimprovement or overenjoyment, with its vicious circle, can lead to excessive, malignant exhaustion of a function. Neuroses and psychoses are *perfect examples of mental exhaustion through continuously added, vicious-circle overenjoyments.* This explains the incredibly deep, and tenaciously or "ingeniously" self-generating negativity of reactions, revealing the opposite causation. The neurotic or psychotic suffers from reactions which he wants least, which are exact opposites of the feelings that he wants most and that he has overenjoyed.

Of course, all this has to remain incomprehensible in modern psychiatry proceeding by a logic exactly contrary to the seeming paradox of disorders from improvements or of the opposite causation. That is why the functional neuroses and psychoses *have remained admitted mysteries causally*[1,3,9]—or are "explained" by the mystifications about unconscious personified agencies,[2,3] the modern demons of a hidden mental world.

The simple but "paradoxical" opposite causation, as the inevitable reason of the mystery, is evident from all neuroses and psychoses. We may look at their main forms.

ANXIETY REACTIONS. These reactions are the most frequent form of neurosis; and anxiety is a component in all other neuroses.[1,2] This is so because most satisfactions are conditioned ultimately on *the feeling of security or survival.* Therefore overenjoyment of any satisfaction or value in our life has to bring *the opposite feeling, the anxiety.* Since the enjoyment of the satisfactions of security is so general, it is never noticed as anything particular and is merely felt as a pleasure in whatever we do. Overenjoyment of this feeling can therefore be incurred through every one of the improvements in life and is as unnoticed.

Consequently, the anxiety—upon such overenjoyment—seems to appear from nowhere, as a ghost phenomenon, without cause. Hence the endless mystifications about anxiety and its causes.[1,2,9] Hundreds of books have been written about it by various theorists, from Freudians to existential psychologists. No explanation fits, because the logic used is contrary to the actual causation of anxiety.

The opposite causes of anxiety are evident from the simplest facts. Use of drugs and intoxication lead, upon discontinuation, to a virtual anxiety neurosis, but are resorted to for overcoming of anxiety. The most general proof of the opposite causation of anxiety is, of course, our Age of Anxiety itself. Never before have people enjoyed more of everything they have always wanted—of all the values and feelings ultimately aimed at security or freedom from anxiety. But never before have men suffered more from anxiety. As Rollo May points out, anxiety was unknown as a mental problem fifty years ago.[21]

The confusion about anxiety is increased by the fact that mostly ideas and ideational contents appearing together with anxiety are studied to explain it.[3,9] The real determining factor, the economy of feelings, never becomes the object of study because it makes no sense if its opposite causality is not understood. Analyses and psychotherapies of anxiety deal with the ideas or perceptions of the patient.

In truth, the ideas or perceptions in anxiety are purely accidental. Everybody can see that an irritated or morbid person will blame as reason of his irritation or as explanation of his morbidity anything that happens to be in his way. The first thing he accidentally meets with may become, by fixation, the center and the seeming essence of his whole system of preoccupations.

It is not the psychologically weightless ideas, or philosophic existential concerns, but grave and deep organic impoverishment that is the source of anxiety. Psychologists know that anxiety is as physically concrete as asphyxiation or drug withdrawal.[2,9] Deep, vicious-circle overenjoyment, just as in the drug use, is the simple weighty cause of anxiety. But the causal logic that positively felt experiences can be causes of negative reactions is still the last thing a psychiatrist or anybody is ready to accept.

OBSESSIVE-COMPULSIVE REACTIONS. The very essence of these reactions is that the person suffers from feelings and reactions *opposite* to those he wants or strives for most.[1,3] In a typical obsession, the man who cultivates the most loving thoughts about his wife and children is suffering from ideas that he may do horrible things to them.[1] Under the compulsive reactions, the housewife who strives to enjoy perfect cleanliness of her home finds it so unclean that she has to dust it twice a day.[3]

All theories on the obsessive-compulsive reactions try to find explanations for the observed *opposite* emotions and reactions. Oversolicitous love or idealistic perfectionism is assumed to be a disguise for aggressive inner wishes or hidden hostility.[2] Mechanisms of reaction-formation, displacement and symbolism are seen as devices for hiding or abreacting repressed conflicting, opposite drives.[3,9] The child avoiding cracks in the pavement assumedly wants rather than fears to "break mother's back."[8]

Overenjoyment and its aftereffects are the simple causes of the opposite mysterious reactions here. *Every overdriven mechanism supporting the overenjoyed emotion reverses,* in the end, and all the opposite reactions or feelings follow. The "ingeniousness" of these reactions is as great as was that of inventing the overenjoyments. Of course, the feeling of enjoyment is soon lost as the negative reactions become excessive under the vicious-circle.

But, as we saw, the neurotic cannot abandon the overenjoyment effort even if it finally brings him only endless trouble. Also, he becomes compulsively entangled with ridiculously unimportant, trivial matters, because great, important satisfactions, values or releases would require investment of equal nonsatisfactions as needs, or restrictions, which the neurotic is unable to accumulate.

Obsessive-compulsive reactions are perfect examples of how a person overenjoying the reactions or feelings that he wants most ends by suffering the opposite reactions he wants least. Conversely, *if the neurotic can be induced "to do or wish to happen the very things he fears"*[10] *he loses his obsession* or compulsion. Victor E. Frankl has used this method in his Logotherapy. A patient suffering from the compulsion to wink or stutter loses it if he deliberately tries to show how excellent a stutterer he is. Or, obsession with fears of plane crash is overcome by a vivid, fearful reliving, in imagination, of a plane crash.[10]

PHOBIC REACTIONS. Overenjoyment of avoidances is the cause of phobias. It is only logical that overenjoyments can consist of enjoying the positive as well as avoiding the negative. The neurotic overenjoys, in perfectionistic ways, the avoidance of what can be feared or loathed. The decisive factor is not actual danger from the thing feared but *the opportunity to avoid it repeatedly,* so that the vicious circle continues working. The most ordinary things one meets with constantly, like closed spaces, crowds, streets, insects, germs, cats, cars or bridges become objects of phobias.

It is well known that the overprotected child starts fearing, unreasonably, slightest dangers. Such overprotection is intensified by the neurotic many times over, and produces so much greater unreasonable fears. The neurotic may start a phobia by overenjoying the comfort or safety of his home. As such safety is overenjoyed, the unsafety of the street becomes more felt. If this unsafety is then avoided by even stronger enjoyments of the home, the vicious circle is started.

But the mystery here is complete because nobody ever thinks that by securing and enjoying more safety he gets more of the opposite feeling of unsafety. The opposites of other enjoyments of avoidances may be even more unrecognizable.

That is why phobias have remained so mysterious causally.[1,3] *The mystery is compounded as separate causes are sought* for each of the endless kinds of phobias. According to an often mentioned explanation, a woman fears the street because she is afraid to become a streetwalker.[21] Or a man fears "high" places because they symbolize the "superiority of father."[21] Less mysterious explanations, by concepts of learning or conditioning, do not help. Nobody learns or is conditioned to acquire useless fears.

To acquire something so tormenting and useless as phobias in direct "logical" ways would be extremely difficult. But phobias grow with self-enforcing ease, under the strivings of the neurotic seeking the easiest, most pleasant feelings and reactions. The strongest human drive, the pursuit of pleasure excessively exerted becomes a vicious-circle source of the opposite, strangely unrecognizable negative reactions here as in other disorders.

We may note that the phobic patient is helped by treatments like the Behavior Therapy, which force him to experience strongly the fears and aversions he is suffering from. Such therapies have brought complete cures,[1,10] which is unusual for the present mental treatments. *The seemingly absurd improvement by worsening* is evident here.

OTHER NEUROTIC REACTIONS. The most frequent modern neurotic reaction is *Depression.* It is the exact opposite of the excitement and stimulation that modern men certainly are enjoying to excess. Opposite swings in mood are observed as a prominent syndrome of depressions.[1,3] It is noted that "depression commonly occurs at the point at which a person has reached the goals toward which he has been striving."[11] A depression lived through fully brings relief, as Frederick F. Flach shows in his book *The Secret Strength of Depression.*[11]

Because *the opposite causal logic* governs depressions they remain causally unexplained.[1,3] Unconscious complexes, like aggression turned against oneself, are sought as explanations.[1,9] Of course, the overenjoyment of excitement and stimulation always fades quickly and the progressively deepening depression soon takes over. Then the persistence of the depressive reactions may seem to confirm the mystifications that the neurotic, unconsciously, wants such reactions.[1,9]

Neurasthenia consists of reactions of tiredness, irritability and feelings of pain. They are easily understandable as the deepening *opposite effects* of excitement, gratification and avoidance of pain. Since such enjoyments have been more richly available in this country, neurasthenia has been so more frequent here that it has been called the "American disease."[1,8] Theories about unconscious intents and conflicts are used to explain neurasthenia.[3,9] They are clearly incongruous, since the reactions here are physiologically concrete.

Hypochondria is caused by the overenjoyment of being free of diseases. Not having diseases can be a source of enjoyment. The neurotic turns it into an overenjoyment. Then as the *opposite reaction,* of having disease arises, it is compensated for by even stronger satisfaction of not having it. Of course the progressively deepened feeling of disease soon becomes the dominant emotion, while the satisfaction potential has become exhausted.

Then it may seem that the hypochondriac wants nothing but

the symptoms of his imagined diseases. This is a generally accepted view.[1,9] Karl Menninger has said, "hell has no fury like the hypochondriac deprived of his symptoms."[21] The hypochondriac has every reason to be furious about the doctors who believe that he is only imagining his suffering. He feels as concrete and painful reactions and symptoms of disease as were his exaggerated enjoyments of not feeling the disease and not having its symptoms.

Some other forms of neurotic reactions like the *"Christmas Blues"* or *Sunday and Vacation neuroses*[1,21] are evidently after-effects of overenjoyments. Curiously, *Depersonalization Neurosis* has been recently added to the list.[1,3] The reason is that, under the modern theories and fashions, the discovery of Self, Identity or one's own personality has become a strong, continuous enjoyment for followers of the modern psychological movements. The underlying sources of enjoyment here are, probably, the sense of one's own perfection, and an increased recourse to inner releases. Whatever the sources, the feelings of own "identity" can be over-enjoyed, and the strange opposite reactions follow.

THE UNCONSCIOUSLY CAUSED NEUROSES. The only unconsciously caused neuroses are the *Hysteric* and *Dissociative* reactions, while the other neuroses, as we saw, are caused by consciously pursued and planned overenjoyments. It is only natural that there be the two kinds of neuroses. For there are two different ways of how man pursues pleasures and avoids displeasures. The one is by active, conscious striving, the other by passivity, abandonment, or self-paralyzing "freezing," which is instinctive in animals in face of danger.

The theory that all neuroses are unconsciously caused was started by Freud. It has been eagerly accepted because it "explains," by personified agencies, how the person acts so ingeniously and persistently against himself. We saw that the simple, mechanistic cause of this ingenuity and intensity is the opposite causation. But it has remained unrecognized. *Freud accepted hysteric reactions as the prototypes for all neuroses.* In his first case of psychoanalysis, the girl had suppressed her feelings about traumatic experiences and was cured after she was induced to abreact them by painfully reliving them.[4,7]

It is understandable that by straightening out past suppressions normalcy is restored. The Freudian fallacy lies in *not distinguishing between pleasure and displeasure,* the black and white in psychology. Freud assumed that just as the past traumatic experiences are suppressed so are human drives, particularly the libidinal desire, suppressed in all neuroses.

The universal human drives are pursuits of pleasure, libidinal or general. Freudians recognize this, and claim that our drives suppressed in all neuroses are to be released. Repression of libidinal or other pleasure drives is the key concept in the Freudian etiology and therapies.[1,9]

This is clearly absurd. *Just because tormenting traumatic experiences are suppressed, in the dissociative reactions, it is assumed that pleasures are suppressed, by the neurotic, in equally intense ways,* of all things on the unconscious level where pleasure drives alone rule. We know how ingenious and forceful man is in pursuing, not repressing, his universal drives, for pleasure—libidinal, aggressive or general. The neurotic is even more so. He may suppress very *unpleasant* feelings, which are not even unconscious. For they are strongly, traumatically felt, and to feel is to be conscious. What is unconscious is the method of suppressing such feelings.

Hysteric and dissociative reactions are caused by suppression of tormenting past or present experiences. This is attained by a kind of unconscious self-hypnosis,[1,4] that grossly inactivates whole areas of functions. In *Amnesia* or *Fugue* the person forgets a traumatic experience or problem and wanders away. Since all mental and physiologic associations with the traumatic experience have to be suppressed, the results can be peculiar. The necessarily gross suppressions become confusingly extensive. The person has to forget his whole past. Or he has to suppress whole areas of physiologic reactions. Typically, such odd, subjectively or superficially controlled paralyses resemble hypnotically-induced incapacities and sensory distortions.[21]

In *Double Personality* the neurotic suppresses disturbing awareness about his one world while living in another. The two incompatible worlds are developed by him as he lives through periodic mood swings. He exaggerates the reactions during the period of freer releases, and thus brings on himself equally strong restrictive reactions during the opposite period. Thus the two worlds or personalities become strongly incompatible. More than two personalities may develop if the fluctuations in releases affect different functions at different periods.

The point is that the relatively rare unconscious neuroses, caused by hypnotic suppression of traumas, are *totally different in their etiology* from the general neuroses caused by conscious overenjoyments. The unconscious, dissociative reactions are wanted by the neurotic.[1,3] Hence his *belle indifference toward them.*[1,9] But general neuroses are the most unwanted reactions for the neurotic. The hysteric and dissociative reactions are caused by suppression, of displeasures, but the general neuroses by lack of restrictions. Revealingly, the hysteric reactions can be easily cured by hypnotic treatment, by forcing the neurotic to relive the repressed experiences. Nothing of this is true of other neuroses.

The blunder that human drives, for pleasure, are as eagerly suppressed as traumas would have never been committed if it were understood how the intense and "ingenious" neurotic suffering is automatically incurred by equally intense overenjoyments.

SCHIZOPHRENIA. The overenjoyment etiology is particularly clear in this gravest and most frequent psychosis. As we saw stimulation drugs lead to reactions that cannot be distinguished from schizophrenia.[5,6] Of course, the same drugs, like LSD and amphetamines, can relieve schizophrenia, and have been tried in its treatment.[6] The tendency of the schizophrenic *to live in the world of his own imagination can certainly lead to overenjoyments as intense as could be induced by drugs.* Even if such tendency is weak, the overenjoyments can still accumulate to excessive degree through the vicious circle during years.

It has been argued that while fantasy is a "harmless device for satisfying needs" for normal people, the schizophrenic carries it too far;[8] or that the unreality becomes too real for him.[1] But logically, the more extensive and real such satisfaction, the more good it should do. The fantasy world suits the schizophrenic very well. He has low tolerance for unpleasant realities or hardships of life, and lacks inhibitions.[1,4] The absence of restrictions is apparent from his lack of shame, his exhibitionism, looseness in sexual behavior, fantasies of grandeur and lowest personal habits or moral controls.[1,7,9] Already as a child he is seclusive, unsociable, untidy and secretive, withdrawn in his own world.[1,7]

Since in his own world the schizophrenic overenjoys everything he feels or does, he ends by suffering every reaction of anxiety, obsession, "tic," phobia, hypochondria, depression or fear, to a progressively deepening, excessive degree. He has not lost his mental capacities, as several studies have shown,[1,12] and a simple release-increasing drug can restore, temporarily, his normal reactions.[14,15] His extreme mental impoverishment is emotional. With all the above anxieties, compulsions and fears even a normal person would behave in schizophrenic ways.

But the general negativity of reactions in schizophrenia is only the effect, not the cause. As in all functional disorders, *the "disease" here, as organism's extreme restriction, is rather a pressure back toward normalcy.* Experts have, logically, tried, in various ways, to get the schizophrenics to free or enjoy themselves more.[18] The efforts have been as futile in practice as they have been promising in theory.[1,21] The pressure, in schizophrenia, back to normalcy can have bizarre effects.

In some cases the excessive-release drives may be physiologic, contrary to the person's intentions. To suppress such excessive overenjoyment drives, the person may resort to some equally excessive contrary effect, like one obtained by smearing himself with faces. His other negative reactions, like stupor or the "waxy flexibility," may serve similar purpose. Corresponding internal reactions, like the production of the taraxein, are equally part of the "disease" as pressure toward normalcy.

As in all functional disorders, *this role of the natural "disease" as organism's remedy is totally confusing* here for the experts seeking "logical" explanations. That is why even the clearest factors, like the taraxein, only lead to more confusion.[1,3] And the "weird" behavior of the schizophrenic is invoked to support mystifications about sinister forces in his psyche.

Sometimes it is recognized, though only indirectly or intuitively, what the role of schizophrenia as "disease" is. Hence the popularity of the writings of Dr. R. D. Laing, who has demonstrated, supposedly from his own experience, that schizophrenia performs an important role for the psychotic and should be let to run its course. In his numerous impressive books he shows how completely misdirected and confused modern psychiatry has become in its efforts to suppress psychoses directly.

The modern psychiatry has *no causal explanations of schizophrenia,* in spite of enormous efforts to understand it.[1,3,9] Psychiatrists themselves are puzzled by the increasing confusion.[8,16] Thus probably the most clearly physiologic mental disorder seems to arise "without any known physiological basis,"[1] and no accepted conclusions about the biochemical processes involved have been reached.[3,16] All the physiologic factors have been discovered and endlessly analyzed. But nothing fits in causally. The reason is the opposite causation.

At every step the research, logically, shows as cause of schizophrenia what is actually the organic reaction toward recovery from it. Or it *shows as means of remedy the very factors that increase the disorder* in the end. This reversed logic can lead to incredible confusion because of the endless complexity and multiplicity of the organic processes involved and governed by the "reverse" logic.

Understandably, *mystifications* about unconscious complexes, hidden agencies and symbolic causes have flourished.[1,9;13] The theories are too many even to list. Psychotherapy and psychoanalysis are widely used to deal with the hidden mysteries.[3,12] One can only wonder how such unconscious and symbolic factors that, necessarily, have not been felt, can cause the gravely emotional, physiologically deep changes.

More sober theorists may seek explanations in learning and conditioning.[1,7] This implies that somehow the schizophrenic learns or is conditioned to torment himself uselessly. The same can be said of ideational factors, like associations, perceptions or wrong beliefs and ideas. They all are psychologically weightless and could be changed by brief explanations. Of course, emotional factors are often subsumed under these concepts of ideational causation, which increases the confusion.

All in all, schizophrenia is presently theorized about and treated *under the direct "scientific," inherently alchemistic logic, and under the assumption that man somehow learns or creates ideas for tormenting himself,* or that experiences which have never been even felt, become weighty causes. The alchemistic logic is inherent in the assumption that negative, stressful or restrictive factors are causes of schizophrenia. This implies that by enjoying himself more and freeing himself from restraints the schizophrenic could overcome the disease. What could be easier? In truth, he already has done that to excess.

But the "scientific" logic is based on the experimental proofs that schizophrenia consists of extreme restriction, stress and emotional negativity. The real explanation, the simple opposite causation, due to the organic limitedness, is not yet recognized.

PARANOIA. In paranoia the opposite causation is even clearer. The paranoiac feels he is persecuted, vulnerable and hated, while he has sought to enjoy excessively the sense of personal grandeur, of being loved, and of love in various forms—as is generally noted.[1,9] Naturally, one's own power, and love by others are the most enjoyable values, totally ensuring survival and security. The opposite reactions from their overenjoyment emerge when further increase in it fails due to some physiologic setback, exhaustion through illness, use of drugs, psychologic defeat or age, which have been observed to precipitate paranoia.[1,3]

The opposite reactions here are the feelings of threat to survival and to security. *The opposites of the sense of one's own power and of love by others are the fear of persecution, sense of hate by others, jealousy* and similar negative reactions. They all constitute the recognized syndrome of paranoia.

Of course, the enjoyments of sense of superiority and love start vanishing as they continue, or become usual and therefore little felt. Moreover they, directly, contribute to a very "normal," accumulated overenjoyment background, against which the opposite reactions, when they start emerging, are felt very strongly. These feelings, of persecution, hate by others and jealousy, then may seem as coming from nowhere, for some mysterious reason.

Causal explanations of paranoia are, admittedly, missing.[1,3] The most frequent speculations center on unconscious, homosexual conflicts, mechanisms of projection, hate turned against oneself, symbolism, or wrong learning and ideas.[21] Homosexuality is easily inferred from the paranoiac's excessive need for general love. We do not need to repeat that unconscious conflicts, symbolism or ideational factors are weightless and that nobody learns or creates ideas to torment himself.

If the paranoiac does something to himself, as all the theories imply, it is a thousand times more certain that he will strive, particularly on the unconscious level, to have the most pleasant feelings, of being secure, superior, or loved by others. Which is exactly what he does, to excess. But only the opposite causation can explain how the overenjoyment of such feelings can bring their unrecognizable opposites, which constitute paranoia.

MANIC-DEPRESSIVE REACTIONS. The very essence of the manic-depressive reactions is the change of one psychic state into its *opposite*. It is revealing, in practical terms, that the remarkable, lithium treatment prevents the depressive stage by first suppressing the manic stage. The alternation of the opposite states would be even clearer if psychiatrists paid more attention to the real causal factors, the emotions, rather than to external reactions. Evidently, a person may appear "manic"—excited, overactive or eccentric—under an acute distress as well as under strong enjoyment.

Further, *the exaggerated positive states are often not noticed* because intense positivism may appear as very normal adjustment. Also, the positive state rarely comes with suddenness, because its causal source, the negative background is accumulated only very slowly or reluctantly. But the depressive state always breaks out with cataclysmic suddenness, for the converse reason. This is why clinical observations and statistics show, misleadingly, that there is less of the manic and regular cyclothymic cases, or that the manic states are milder.[1,3]

Mystery is increased by the *absence here, as in all psychoses, of logical experimentally correlatable physiologic changes.*[9,12] The reason is the paradox of initially negative, restrictive factors bringing positive effects, and vice versa. Also, a stimulant in the organism has a lesser effect as it has become increased. Thus the drug user or psychotic may have more than usual amounts of stimulants in his blood and still be understimulated. Manic-depressive psychosis is found to resemble the syndrome of morphine effects, and no logically explainable physiologic changes are discovered for either.[1,16]

The absence of physiologic explanations here is found puzzling;[1,4,10] and numerous theories have been advanced, about self-punishment, unconscious mechanisms and conflicts as causes. Restrictive attitudes of the person are, logically, blamed.[2,3] Entertaining, enjoyable diversions are sought for the depressive, though they rather exacerbate his depression.[1,9,11] *An exactly contrary treatment,* the shock therapy, is uniquely successful in curing depressions. It is the opposite of everything psychiatrists believe about helping the psychotic through more positive or satisfying, soothing and reassuring influences.

Involutional Melancholia is mostly recognized as a "unipolar manic-depressive" reaction.[1,8] It is to be expected that in many cases the overenjoyment phase remains completely unnoticed for reasons we explained. The same mystery and confusion that persist in the explanations of depression are found here.[9,12] The paradox of overstimulation applies here as well. A drug user put on a lower dosage that would be still high for a nonuser would feel low.

To conclude, in all neuroses and psychoses, as we saw, *the opposite causal backgrounds,* of overenjoyment or emotional overimprovement, are almost self-evident. But psychiatrists as "scientists" cannot recognize the paradox of opposite causation—though the drug effects, which so closely resemble psychoses, offer a simple, clear proof.

Psychiatrists proceed by the exactly contrary logic, of negative reactions deriving from negative causal backgrounds. This, of

course, *implies the alchemy* that by pleasant addition to our positively felt reactions our capacities could be increased or maintained.

The "Improvement" Fallacy in Psychiatry

Though inevitably alchemistic, the logic of mental improvement
through direct increase in the positively felt reactions governs in
all psychiatry. If everything worked the way psychiatry sees it, the
mental patients would be directly provided with the more enjoyable
positive satisfactions, which do constitute our positive capacities.
Not effort or restriction, but ease and pleasure releases would be
increased for the patients. Modern psychiatry still wants to *remove
directly the restrictive "disease,"* which is the organism's natural
effort to restore release reserves or normalcy.

DRUG THERAPY. This is the most typical main psychiatric treatment, aiming at direct, easy relief from mental disease. Drugs can
provide miraculous improvements, by removing the restrictions and
thus increasing the releases. But the organism has to restore its
normalcy, by opposite processes. Every year new wonder drugs are
promoted providing direct effects that could wipe out all mental
disease; but the end result is that mental diseases have increased
fourfold, as we saw, since the "wonder" drugs went to market,
in the mid 50s.

By the way, drug treatment enthusiasts like to refer to the decrease in the number of patients in state mental hospitals, which
was a half million in 1955.[15,17] But this decrease is due to a general
policy of reducing the use of these hospitals. Now only one-fourth
of inpatients are held in such hospitals.[1,9] Other facilities are increasingly used, and in the general hospitals alone mental patients
now occupy more than a half million beds.[1,9] Above all, the out-
of-hospital treatments are the new big trend[1,10]—as the previous,
institutional methods are found disastrous.

Every authority recognizes that drugs provide wondrous relief,
temporarily curing the disorders, but that no permanent cure is to
be expected from drugs.[7,8] The initial effects are spectacular.[5,15]
Yet in the end "drugs do not offer a solution to the problems of

emotional illness but rather add to them."[15] *The more effective a drug is the more dangerous its aftereffects.*

The most popular, meprobamate drugs, providing miraculous relief, had to be condemned by the FDA as dangerous.[9,17] Another virtually miraculous drug, the chlorpromazine, has similar after-effects.[9,15] Iproniazid, considered as a treasure, in an "acres of diamonds" story, by Nathan S. Kline,[17] had equally to be prohibited by the FDA.[15,17] The later MAO inhibitors, in particular, have spectacular initial effects, that lead to even worse "side" effects.[15,17]

The simple rule is that *the initial improvements induced by drugs are followed by exactly equal aftereffects.* As T. H. Greiner of the AMA Council on Drugs states, "tranquilizers have caused about as much trouble as they have abolished."[5] Or, as Robert de Ropp writes, "the same tranquilizing drugs now commonly used to relieve the so-called anxiety of violent restlessness of schizophrenic patients are capable of temporarily inducing identical symptoms of this common malady in normal patients."[21] Similar effects and aftereffects are found for stimulants.[5,6] Paradoxically, barbiturates are found to produce overexcitement, and amphetamines depression, as aftereffects.[1,5]

Various explanations are offered for the disappearance or reversal of the initial drug effects. Walter Modell has argued that drugs act only as placebos, therefore have no real biochemical impact.[18] Yet experimenters find that biochemical changes induced by drugs are astonishingly concrete.[5,15] Modell also blames drug abuse and their complexity.[18]

But the striking fact about the wonder drugs is that they work as perfectly in every way at the beginning as they are "abused" or become too "complex" later. Actually "in the beginning, every potential abuser comes to feel that the effects of the drug he is taking are desirable and/or necessary for his well-being," according to G. Johnson.[15] Surely drugs are "abused," when they start losing their effects and have to be increased.

We saw the curious *confusion, in the modern science, about addiction* which is actually due to the simple opposite causation. Even best authorities have sought explanations for it in specious conjectures. J. Harold Burn has argued that the habit of smoking may be due to the need of keeping hands busy, or to its air of elegance, or to the fragrance.[14] Walter Modell has sought to explain the addiction to alcohol by such vague factors as "essentially a psychological compulsion" or "the circumstances under which it is consumed."[18] Also, most of the addictive means, even amphetamines and cocaine, are not addictive but only "habit forming" according to drug experts,[5,18] as we saw before.

Explanations of the negative aftereffects of drugs are usually sought in "toxic" agents as harmful residues left by the drugs.[5,8] But the sickening, death-like, withdrawal reactions, negative in every respect, appear exactly to the extent the body is cleaning itself of narcotic, toxic substances. Is not this revealing for the paradox of organic improvement and worsening? By the way, even placebos, when effective, can produce negative aftereffects.[1,5]

The confusion about drug effects is so general that it may seem as if "an unbelievable fraud has been perpetuated on the public," writes G. Johnson.[15] According to him the "passion and letdown that drugs inspire in one after another person" look like results of a hoax.[15] The attitude of modern scientists is incredible. Having discovered a couple of organic chemicals, like the epinephrine or serotonin, they want to control them,[1,5] without regard to the innumerable other, ungraspably complex, purposive processes involved—and in spite of the obvious confusion of the present explanations.

Many drug experts are claiming that drug effects vary depending on the circumstances and mental condition under which the drug is used. Of course, if the paradoxical reversal of effects, at every step, is not understood, everything seems to vary unpredictably. The effects on the complex higher mental processes, in particular, can become confusing. That is why LSD, affecting them, is becoming so controversial.[5,15,18]

Among the scores of drugs used in therapy, *some may happen to have restrictive overall effect,* therefore help the organism to restore normalcy or the release rseerves. They may be continued to be used upon incidental discovery of their practical success, though their action may not be understood and may be counteracted by the rest of the treatment. Shock therapy shows what such treatments can do.

SHOCK THERAPY. The improvement logic is reversed in the shock therapy. The shock amounts to infliction of extremely negative, almost death-like stress, as restriction, on the organism. Schematically, by such repression of the organism onto a lower level of adjustment, room is gained for new, normal movements up, and down.

Shock therapy is *contrary to the present, improvement logic* in psychiatry. But it is the only treatment that cures, definitely and without side effects, the disorders to which it is applicable in its present form. Such *success is unique* in psychiatry. It should be noted that in its present form, of a merely physiologic "stab in the dark,"[4] the shock can be properly used only for treating physiologic depressions, which it cures without exceptions. Because of this unique success, it is then, improperly, used to treat other disorders.[1,9]

Still, it is found to provide "one of the most spectacular therapeutic responses in medicine."[1] For the proper patients it is "the fastest, safest, least expensive and most effective form of treatment."[9] It is of "unsurpassed clinical effectiveness in the treatment of patients with depressive illness."[10] And this success is attained in spite of the fact that nobody is enthusiastic about it.[10]

Thus we have here a treatment that is uniquely, practically successful, probably the only one in psychiatry that really cures. But it works in ways opposite to every tenet of modern psychiatry or its very logic of direct improvement. As Robert White points out it is contrary to existing theories and to everything believed about therapies.[4] He concludes, "we are truly without a theory of the shock treatment."[4] Similarly, Karl Menninger states that "we have no definite knowledge as to why it has a therapeutic effect."[2]

The present shock as extreme physiologic stress or restriction cures completely the physiologically caused mental impoverishment. *All mental disorders could be similarly, completely cured* if expanded and adapted forms of "shock," particularly psychological stress, were used in treatment. Even chronic, "incurable" schizophrenics have been observed to recover when in danger of death, grave operation or fatal disease.[1,21] They relapsed when the danger was over.[1,21] Imposition of continuous restrictions should be possible, as we shall see in a moment.

Psychiatry could find and perfect diverse means and ways of adapting the "shock" to various disorders. Drugs could be one means. Lithium treatment already shows that by suppressing the mania, as the overenjoyment, the depression is prevented. Dr. W. H. Stewart, as U. S. Surgeon General, reported that "lithium appears to be the best specific agent yet found for the treatment of any mental disease."

The point is that by using extended and adapted methods of imposing stress or restrictions, contrary to the present improvement logic in psychiatry, all mental disorders could be cured, or prevented, as fully as now the depression is by the shock therapy, or by the lithium treatment.

PSYCHOTHERAPY. The most widely used but practically useless form of treatment is psychotherapy. It deals with ideas, perceptions, learning and reasoning, all of which are psychologically weightless and easy. But people believe that they behave according to their reasons. Psychotherapists want to deal with such ideational causes, particularly since the neurotic clearly acts most irrationally, against himself—and the real, emotional cause for it is not seen. The confusion is evident from the endless controversial, conflicting forms of psychotherapies of which there are hundreds.[1,10]

For curing the patients *psychotherapies are useless.* In their book on scientific findings, B. Berelson and G. Steiner state that "psychotherapy does not improve a patient's chances of recovery beyond what they would be without any formal therapy whatsoever."[21] The best compilation of statistical studies here is probably that by H. J. Eysenck. It shows that 72 percent of patients recover by themselves, but that only 64 percent recover with psychotherapy and a mere 44 percent with psychoanalysis.[3,21]

As Dr. B. A. Maher states, we are "compelled to draw the conclusion that psychotherapy is associated with lower rate of recovery than no psychotherapy at all!"[16] O. H. Mowrer concludes, on basis of studies by Ausubel, Cartwright, Dollard, Eysenck, Massermann, Moreno and Ubell, that for all forms of psychotherapy "the accomplishment is, in fact, nill" and that "untreated controls seem to fare as well as the treated groups."[21]

Psychotherapies are popular because *they offer immediate relief,* actually a delay in the organic restrictions pressing toward normalcy. The patient is permitted more reasoning and a continuation of overenjoyments, in new ways. That is why the Transference, as patients' attachment to the therapist and to what he is doing, has become the main achievement and, admitedly, the very core of analytic psychotherapies.[3,10]

Some therapies work, for reasons different from the "improvement" logic of therapists. For instance, in group therapies, as well as in the Synanon or Alcoholics Anonymous, the patient finds himself compelled to accept restrictions, through a curious rebound effect. As he observes the detestable behavior of others, he hates it with deep emotion, which later compels him to detest and abstain from his similar own behavior.

All in all, the modern psychiatry, with its direct "improvement" logic, has helped to create *the modern trend of progressively increasing mental disorders.* At the beginning of this century there were 130,000 patients in mental institutions in this country. Now the number has increased to more than 1.8 million inpatients and 4.9 million outpatients. According to E. R. Hilgard, "now it is estimated that one out of every ten babies born today will spend some time in a mental hospital; community studies have shown as many as 30 percent of the population as having clinical symptoms of personality disturbance."[7]

Of all human problems, *mental disorders should be the most easily controllable,* by the use of the capacities of the mind itself. Psychiatry, dealing with such capacities, should be the most successful field, and the problems of mental disorders should long have been solved, with our unique means and skills. But the reverse is true. And mental diseases have become increasing mysteries causally.[1,2,3] Apparently, the very direction in which psychiatry is moving—by its direct improvement logic—is totally wrong.

The modern psychiatry and the trends created by its approaches are doing more harm than good. Dr. S. Kellam of the NIMH has stated that the "major effort in psychiatry today is to reduce the degree to which the physician and mental hospital stand in the way of patients' own capacity to get better."[7]

It is self-evident that *the psychotic has to be forced to live through the feelings and reactions he has avoided most.* The "disease" here, as in all functional disorders, is already the nature's way of doing this. Psychiatry should help here, instead of standing in the way. Restriction or stress, presently viewed as cause of disorders, can make releases of mental energy available. Karl Menninger writes about unexpected recoveries by patients upon their placement under harder conditions, worse treatment, or upon "most unlikely" event, including intercurrent illness.[2] He concludes that "worse added to worse often works."[2]

We saw that "shock," if flexibly adapted with causal understanding and present extensive means, could cure all mental disorders as it now cures depressions. Of course the shock, as extreme stress, should be mostly psychologic. We mentioned that *even chronic psychotics can be cured* by such shock. In a classic case, 153 incurable mental patients fled, under the fear of advancing Germans in 1940, from the hospital La Charite sur Loire in France. A special commission found, after the War, that 57 percent of them had established themselves in surrounding communities as fully recovered.[2]

Psychiatry as science could do enormously better than what now happens to mental patients recovering by themselves as they live through their "disease." Over 70 percent of them recover in this way, if not "helped" by the present psychiatry. It is evident that our uniquely progressive increase in mental disorders is due to our equally unique improvements of life, in which avoidance of stress is the first goal. The obvious countermeasure is imposition of restrictive, negatively-felt reactions of stress, now viewed as the very cause of mental diseases.

Practically what is needed here is the reversal of the inherently alchemistic improvement logic of thinking. Psychiatry, with its tremendous skills, then would easily find the right means and ways.

Such *reversal in our very way of thinking or attitudes* is required because the direction of our culture itself has to be changed; and presently only science has enough authority to do it. Imposing restrictions above what is "normal" in our present culture would only lead to opposite reactions. Mental disorders and moral license in a society have always shown to come together. Our "scientism" has brought us the beliefs in more satisfactions, favoring enjoyment and license. Science, through psychiatry, now has to reverse the trend.

Psychology as a Modern Alchemy

We may look, very briefly, at those aspects of modern psychology which represent its virtually alchemistic logic of thinking that has become the central fallacy in our human or behavioral sciences. Psychology is, or should be, the key science. For in the world of man everything depends on how he manages his psychological capacities and motivations.

The alchemistic thinking lies in the belief that these precious capacities can be attained by direct increase of our positive satisfactions or releases, and by way of our thoughts, ideas, insights, perceptions, reasoning, learning or other ideational factors. Of course, increase in satisfactions can be only pleasant and the ideational solutions are as easy as logics or all reasoning.

But the "scientific" *belief in direct increase of the positive capacities,* which certainly are satisfactions or releases, is the universal and perhaps the only generally accepted certainty in psychology. You cannot read any book in psychology without being assured that our positive reactions derive from positive causal backgrounds. The like-from-like causal logic is simply the only one known to psychologists as scientists, imitating the exact sciences. Anything resembling the actual, opposite causation of value reactions has not yet been mentioned in any form.

As general is the *belief in the ideational causality* in psychology. We have seen repeatedly how this belief, rooted in the modern psychological theory, governs the thinking about what men do or want[8,12,13]—about "rational" behavior, or "irrational" reactions. Even such factors as the "learning" through hard conditioning, and attitudes, like the Alienation, are viewed in terms of ideational insights, perceptions, skills, reasons, ideas, identification and concepts of "identity" or self.[8,12,13] All the modern psychological movements, from that of "discovery of self" to the transcendental meditation, perpetuate the belief in the ideational insights, and in the direct increase of our satisfactions or releases.

We are explaining the fallacies about direct increase in satisfactions and about ideas as causes throughout this book. We shall not repeat here the explanations or the "logical" scientific reasons behind these virtually alchemistic beliefs. We shall look only at the central cause of these fallacies and some of their main consequences, in psychology.

The modern psychology has grown as an imitation of the exact, experimental sciences, with their like-from-like logic and nonmental concepts. *But men live, every minute, for and by the pleasure,* as a mental value reaction governed by the *opposite causal logic.* Pleasure is, as we saw, the expression of the selfrealization of the life force itself, as well as the miraculously complete, mechanistic "explanation" for man of his otherwise unfathomable inner causal processes. Yet the modern psychology has no place for the pleasure concept in any form.[7,8,12,13]

The reason for this *unbelievable disregard of what makes man tick and understand himself* is the above imitation of scientism. Pleasure is certainly "mental," different from anything in physical or experimental sciences. Moreover it follows the opposite causal logic, contrary to that of exact sciences. Everybody, including psychologists, can see that the people adding or enjoying pleasure most, have least of it. The pleasure, in all its aspects, simply makes no sense without the insight in the opposite causation with its reverse logic.

In practical terms, *the central difficult problem for man,* in his behavior, normalcy and health, is the requirement of the positive capacities and motivations, to be attained through constant hard effort. The reason of the difficulty is the strict pleasure economy of obtaining only as much of the positive gain or release as is "paid" by the negatively felt effort or restriction. The ultimate reason is, of course, the limitedness of the organism. But for psychologists, proceeding by the scientific logic, of satisfactions deriving from satisfactory causal sources, this difficulty, the core of our above central problem does not exist.

The modern psychology is seeking its explanations through *experiments and experimentally logical observations*. But it is ridiculous to think that experiments could account for the determining factors in the living, value reactions, by which we psychologically exist. These reactions are determined by your countless past experiences, much as your satisfactions are by your past needs. Also they are determined in their myriad details by your whole, million-year evolutionary past.

When you deal in terms of feelings or pleasure you account for all these countless determinants, in the virtually miraculous, integrated way the pleasure works. In contrast, experiments neither could nor are intended to take into account such countless determinants. But an experiment that does not account for most of the determining factors involved is useless, to say the least.

Further, *the logic of increase of values by addition* is applied in every experimental calculation, comparison, reasoning, finding or conclusion. But a value, like satisfaction, is decreased by addition. The highest total of satisfactions results in extinction of the potential of satisfactions. All value reactions are governed by this, opposite causation, and they determine our feelings, inner values or behavior. We saw how disastrously misleading are the experimental observations about the direct "improvements" through increase in satisfactions or releases.

Also, experimentally, or purely externally a similar reaction, response or even brain wave may come with totally different, causally contrary events—with an exciting satisfaction, or a tormenting nonsatisfaction.

The results of confusion in psychology are best illustrated by the central tenets of the main schools of psychology. *Behaviorism,* probably the dominant school, imitates most closely the experimental scientism. It excludes completely the "mental" factors and tries to deal only with experimentally registrable facts, like stimuli and responses.[8,12]

Behaviorists could not recognize mental images, feelings, consciousness or any value experiences, by which we simple mortals live. They had to construe emotions as visceral reflexes and the thought as a form of speech consisting of movements in the larynx. [12,13] Why? Because the *real,* myriad processes of feeling or thought are graspable and explainable, mechanistically, only in terms of the "mental" pleasure, the source of value experiences.

The direct, experimental logic is never doubted by behaviorists. They have held that even the behavior of a nation could be predicted by finding out the total of stimuli it has been exposed to.[12] In truth, a people or an individual exposed to extensive stimulation ceases to respond to it, so that when the stimulation has reached its fullest extent or become omnipresent it psychologically does not even exist.

On the practically most important problem, on the *conditioning* by which we are made cultural beings, behaviorists have equally held to experimental concepts and logic. In the "epoch-making" theory by John B. Watson he showed that an infant can be conditioned to fear furry objects by being scared with a noise; and he declared that by such conditioning men can be turned into doctors, or thieves.[8,13]

In truth, this kind of conditioning would be a self-defeating farce. A child growing up, under the real, value conditioning, would evolve rather particularly strong adjustments for counteracting such silly interferences as the "frightening" noise.

Under the experimental logic, conditioning can be attained only by offering satisfactions, like food, to experimental animals. Understandably, the noted, best theory on conditioning, by B. F. Skinner, stresses that only satisfactory reinforcements should be used. But there is not much of direct satisfactions that could be used to condition man, while cultural conditioning requires an extensive amount of them. You cannot condition humans with food, and if you give rewards like money to children you would have to make them millionaires before you got anywhere. Only by dealing with "mental" values, of security or growth, you can create unlimited potential of satisfactions or releases, by first imposing equal nonsatisfactions or restrictions.

Gestalt Psychology, the next most important school, grew as an opposition to behaviorism. Gestaltists proved that no stimulus or object has a logical constancy and that its meaning or value depends on the whole of which it is part. In effect, Gestaltist proofs are unintended demonstrations of the *relativity of values* or meanings, of their dependence on value opposites.

In the visual illusions, as the main proofs of Gestaltists, a line appears shorter when placed along a longer line, or a circle smaller amidst great circles.[12] A person in an artfully tilted room sees his body curiously tilted the opposite way.[8] All forms, sounds or smells acquire opposite value against uniformly distorted or exaggerated backgrounds. [12,13] Even ideational meanings reverse under exaggeration—which reveals them as value processes. A drawing, that could be seen equally well as a rabbit's head turned left or as a duck's head turned right, switches in your perception between the two in a way you cannot control.[13] Here the "exaggeration" consists of attributing only one meaning, at a time, to something that has an equally good second meaning.

Gestaltists did not realize that far more important "illusions" or distortions result, as mental disorders, from strong emotional exaggerations. Nor did they recognize that their other Gestalt principles, like similarity, proximity, "pregnance" or perceptual self-organization are due to our value preferences or value "prejudices". *Gestaltists as "scientists" avoided dealing with mental concepts or values* which explain the illusions and the Gestalt principles by simple, relative, value causation.

Gestaltists had to formulate, instead, laws for each of their more than hundred principles and to endow each of countless Gestalts with its own causal essence.[12,13] For indeed each Gestalt is a curiously unique phenomenon irreducible to anything else[21]—if the simple but paradoxical, relative value causation is not seen.

The Gestaltist world of multiple causal principles and meanings required a miraculous agency or intelligence behind the visible things. The leading Gestaltist, Wolfgang Koehler has expounded, in his book *The Place of Value in a World of Facts,* a theory of transcendental values and meanings inherent in the physical world. He admits that such views go against the whole mechanistic thinking of sciences, which therefore "should be turned around." Gestaltism now permits every kind of esoteric mystification. The Gestalt therapy becomes an alchemy of trying to gain capacities by mere formulistic and symbolic performances.[1,10]

The other, older psychological schools failed. The reasons are obvious. All the schools proceeded by the direct "scientific" logic, of ideas, reactions and feelings deriving from similar or like past experiences and backgrounds, as in associationism or parallelism.[21] But experimenters in dozens of fields proved these basic assumptions to be wrong.[21] The old schools also missed the most universal causal backgrounds, like the ultimate organic needs, the pleasure drive and the conditioning of all of us, which are as universal as the atmospheric pressure, therefore as little noticed.

But the old schools were dealing with psychologically relevant, mental and value problems. Their fallacies therefore became grave, conspicuous mistakes. As a result the *experimentalism and behaviorism have taken over;* and they have avoided completely the inner mental or value concepts. Consequently, no important mistakes can be made, because *nothing psychologically relevant is dealt with.* For only the inner mental and value experiences constitute psychological life. What now remains is a colossal, psychologically irrelevant effort leading nowhere. Not a single generally accepted principle about human behavior has been established, though we are governed by conspicuously uniform mechanisms of organic value reactions.

Schools opposing the experimental physicalism have persisted. In psychology everything is controversial. *The organismic and personalistic theories,* supposedly best represented by Adolf Meyer, Kurt Goldstein or William Stern,[13] are often mentioned. They have tried to emphasize man's integrated development and his individual values. Again, dealing with relevant factors brings only graver mistakes under the wrong causal logic.

The organismic approaches have perpetuated the fallacy that negative reactions originate from negatively felt causal backgrounds.[1,12] The personalistic theories have stressed the logically direct formation of what is "salient" or typical in a personality.[1,13] This is causally misleading. The man with the most salient traits of insecurity is the one whose personality has been formed under the greatest security or overprotection.

The *humanistic psychology,* with its various groups, claiming as its exponents authorities like Gordon Allport, Abraham Maslow, Henry Murray or Carl Rogers,[3,10] is now flourishing. It perpetuates all the humanistic value delusions, which become here causal concepts contrary to what is practically right.

Typically, the most misleading philosophical movements, *phenomenology and existentialism* have been adopted as guides.[3,10] The first stresses the inmost awareness as a direct source of truths, thus favoring direct-value, nonrelative convictions in psychological theory. The second represents the typical value attitude of the modern man, which is an extreme of negativism exactly because of his positive overenjoyments. Evidently, it can only deepen causal misunderstandings, however sophisticated its presentations.

The Freudianism, of course, has influenced the modern psychology most, and deserves special attention. It offers the only "logical" explanation of the foremost problem of how man acts against himself. If the opposite causation, with its "ingenious" opposite effects is not understood, a clever agency hidden inside the person and acting against him is a logical explanation. The Freudianism becomes a pure alchemy, because the causes here are unconscious experiences that by their very definition have not been felt. Unconscious feeling would be a contradiction in terms.

The Unconscious is a prescientific personification, that can serve to explain everything, as could demons. It supposedly proceeds by perceiving inner conflicts, rationalizing, disguising or symbolizing them, making other decisions, and scheming their involved execution. It all amounts to varied forms of thinking, and thus requires, absurdly, the existence of a person as an integrated organism within the person. For all thinking is an experience by the organism as an integrated whole. That is why nobody can think of two things at the same time.

In the truly unconscious disorders, like the amnesias and paralyses, the conflicting thoughts are totally, and crudely, blocked so as not to interfere with thinking, which can be only one for the whole person.

The Freudianism has become so influential also because, beside the perfect explanations, it *offers everything men love to wonder about:* mystery, hidden agents inside us, horrible inner drives, weird secrets of sex, dreams, symbolism or magic, in dramatic forms. An idea gains attention and becomes institutionalized, by fixation, to the extent people talk about it. Freud saw as important everything that is strange, sensational, dramatic, or unusual—therefore only exceptional and causally least valid.

His sensationalism was rather naive. He did not realize that the horrible drives, like the Oedipus complex, would be seen as normal if they were really general. If the lust for mother and the wish to kill father were general, then it would be felt as horrible not to have such desires.

The serious influence of Freudianism is the *scaring of people that repressions or restrictions can cause disease.* We saw how Freud failed to distinguish between pleasure and torment when he claimed all neuroses to be caused by repressions. But the repression theory fits the modern logic that negative reactions derive from negative causal backgrounds. Moreover, experimentally or clinically mental disease is, indeed, an extreme restriction—for restoration of normal release reserves.

It is most significant that *Freud himself rejected in the end the theory of repression,* though it had to and did remain the basis of psychoanalysis. He rejected it in the last revision of his theory, in *Problems of Anxiety.* He had become puzzled, noticing that "what was repression appears later as gratification."[19] He then replaced repression as cause of anxiety by nongratification or Unlust, also termed as "object loss."[19] As White explains, Freud's new theory stressed "increase in tension arising from nongratification of child's needs" and the fact that "the child appraises as danger a situation that is not gratified."[4]

The whole Freudian invention, of personification and mystery, would be seen as unnecessary if it were understood how we act against ourselves, by "ingenious" reactions, through the simple and mechanistic opposite causation.

For instance, the often invoked *Ferudian slip is simply explainable.* Your friend may react or say something in a way contrary to what he feels and wants to feel, because he *exaggerated* his feelings of friendliness, and the opposite reaction had to break out. He still feels friendly, though not as friendly as he exaggeratedly wanted to feel. There is no need to assume hidden hostile Freudian agencies inside him. The same applies to anybody wanting to feel, react or say things in positive ways far above his actual positive feelings or reality.

Freud had the genius of turning the existing confusion in psychology into a dramatic mystery. *He had little of real, practical intuition for psychological causation.* Such intuition is the only useful guide amidst the theoretical confusion and controversies. Freud lacked it so completely that he was continuously suffering from anxiety, phobias, mood swings, fatigue, obsessions, hypochondriac fears, "self-torment and superstition."[20] He not only used drugs, notably cocaine, but was unaware of their connection with the aftereffects and advocated their use among his friends.[20]

The schools and theories of modern psychology exemplify its unbelievable confusion. The only certainty seems to be the clearly alchemistic logic that positive capacities derive from positively felt, necessarily pleasant backgrounds or from the weightless, ideational and unconscious factors. The rest is an endless, increasing confusion. In a real science, like physics, a discovery of a new force beside, say, electricity or of a new law, of dynamics would cause a world-wide upheaval. But in psychology new forces and principles are expounded daily, and psychologists, resignedly, see no point in contesting the conflicting discoveries.

Psychologists know that a central causal law should be discovered and each of them tries to establish his own central principle. After the discovery of the central causal law the *present psychology could be forgotten* and a new unified science based on such new law be started. Such law should, and does exist. Men, as *organisms* live in self-evidently *uniform* ways; and the all-determining, value reactions as the nature's *uniform* device of preserving these ways can be governed only by simple laws. Nature's causal principles are never complex—whatever the philosophical explanations for it.[21]

We have seen that, indeed, *such a simple law exists,* and governs the organisms, limited to their sameness. It is the causal law of organic value reactions, which determine everything man feels, does or even knows. But this law is exactly contrary to the alchemistic logic of present psychology. No wonder that only more confusion and complexity results as the psychology "progresses," in the diametrically wrong direction. The theorization in psychology and psychiatry is already colossal.[1;8;21]

V

ALCHEMISTIC CONFUSION IN EDUCATION, BEHAVIORAL THEORIES AND SOCIAL SCIENCES

Education should be a practically most important science. For we are how we are brought up. Such science presently does not exist; education remains an intuitive art. The determining factors in education, as in all human sciences, are value reactions or satisfactions, like love and interests. These are, in themselves, pleasures. But they derive from their hard opposites, conditioned nonsatisfactions or restrictions. Not to see this opposite causation amounts to an alchemy of expecting to increase these precious capacities by their increased enjoyment.

It is also alchemistic to believe that such capacities can be created by cultivation of ideas, insights, value truths or ideational learning. We saw how easy and weightless such factors are: all the great ideas necessary to have every success and a perfect world could be learned in one hour. Yet educators still believe in ideas, truths and ideational values—learned from treasures of thought, or great books—as the determining causes.

Behavioral theories should be equally important in providing us with causal inderstanding and detailed ways for managing our behavior. But the present behavioral theories are, again, alchemistic confusions. The positive capacities and motivations are here as well expected to come from positive, enjoyable causal backgrounds, or from the weightless ideational, cognitive, perceptual or unconscious causes.

Social sciences could provide us with guidance, causal understanding and solutions, for some of our behavioral problems. Our practical, everyday behavior depends, to some extent, on what social aims we have and what influences we get from the social environment. The present social sciences, though, cannot offer much practical help. They are still at the stage of confused, endless theorization, as social scientists themselves admit.[17]

In fact, no exact social science yet exists, because there are no causal laws or principles it could use—to determine what happens or what comes from what. Social phenomena, viewed in themselves, as they presently are,[17] never follow any causal laws. For they are creations of men with their free, ever-changing intents and ideas. *Only individual, not any "social," behavior obeys causal laws,* which derive from the never-changing preservation of sameness by the organism. Social phenomena should be studied as products of individual behavior. But social scientists deal only with "social" concepts. The result is an accumulating confusion instead of science.[17]

Even apart from this inherent fallacy of social sciences, *the present theorization by social scientists is useless because it is alchemistic.* In social sciences in particular, ideas, ideologies, philosophies, perceptions or other ideational factors are viewed as the causal sources. The real causes, the value reactions behind the weightless, easy ideas, are not recognized, or are totally misinterpreted by social scientists because the actual, opposite causation is not seen.

Wherever social scientists deal with the determining, value reactions or feelings, and with factual conditions, they never depart from the belief that positive reactions follow from positive causal backgrounds. This, of course, amounts to an alchemy, as we have explained. But this logic is stronger in social sciences than in other fields, where it is at least practically known that best conditions can lead to negative effects, and that ideas are powerless.

Education in Practice and in Theory

In practice education is successful because it works under the simple but powerful instincts that bind the child and the parent, or educator, together. The parent and the child feel like they are part of each other. The parents simply want the child to be as they are. He is to find happiness or pleasure where they find it, and to see the dangers where they see them. The child fears to be separate or different from them or to lose their favor and care. The result is effective *education through simple, natural, reciprocal love.*

Thus under the instinctive drives, cultural conditioning by which the parents live is transferred to the child. By treating the child as they would treat themselves the parents and educators impose on him all the conditioned needs or nonsatisfactions and restrictions, as sources of satisfactions and releases that become his positive motivations and capacities.

The cultural conditioning may be very complex and subtle, as the restrictions are accepted by pursuing rewards or satisfactions. But it all is acquired by the child as an assimilation of the whole way of life of his educators, with all its contradictions. It is a *conditioning as universal as an atmospheric pressure, under which the child lives every minute.*

Moreover, the conditioning increases by itself. As the love or dependence between the child and the parents or educators is enjoyed, slightest disturbance in it is strongly felt. To avoid that, the love is intesified, which only increases the child's fears of losing the love if he is not good enough or does not comply. All overenjoyments and overprotection create such anxieties. Here they serve educational goals. *Thus a perfect, refined love, not punishment, becomes the most effective means of conditioning.*

The point is that love, as instinctive unity between parent and child brings about the complex and subtle educational conditioning, which imposes the restrictions in the name of satisfactions. That is why *children cannot be brought up without love,* and why *the same level of culture persists in the families through generations.* Nothing can replace the love; and all educational efforts to change quickly cultural levels of population groups have little success. A noted study, by Christopher Jencks, shows that our schools add nothing to the motivations or abilities that the students bring in from their homes.[1]

The overprotective closeness between parents and child requires that the child grow up closeted in the atmosphere of his home—

like a plant in a greenhouse. That is why street influences are so devastating. Such constraining atmosphere of homes is, of course, deplored by psychologists and behavioral scientists.

Smothering restrictions by parents are blamed as causes of disorders.[4,6] The often discussed stressful *double bind* rseults mostly from parents' wishes to make the child happy while restricting him.[4,6] Under logical or behaviorist views, the limiting and contradictory conditions of family or home make it unsuited for raising children, as B. F. Skinner makes clear in *Walden Two*.[21] We explained that exactly to the extent the conditioning is as tight and general as an atmospheric pressure it is most effective, and least felt, or even noticed by psychologists and educators.

In the logical "scientific" theory the positive motivations and interests, as satisfactions that they are, become the factors *to be increased directly, by their greater enjoyment.* Their opposite causal sources are never recognized. The idea of such satisfactions deriving from the nonsatisfactions or restrictions would be, rather, found abhorrent.[21] Every theorist sees the direct satisfactions, furthest away from any nonsatisfactions, as the source of the positive motivations and interests.[5,6]

According to a generally accepted theory, promoted by such authorities as Abraham Maslow and Carl Rogers, the higher satisfactions, of self-actualization or of need to know, arise after all lower needs have been satisfied.[4,6] Thus only satisfactions, never any needs or nonsatisfactions, are to be cultivated. We agree that needs of food, shelter or physical well-being have to be satisfied first. For they as natural drives that are not conditioned would overrule any conditioned, refined and weaker needs.

But the great lower, basic needs, of survival, growth or superiority, the sources of all other needs, have to be conditioned, by nonsatisfactions, into the higher needs. In simplest terms, the child complies, imitates or competes by striving for security or love, for growth or attainment of the status of grownups, and for superiority. Of course to the extent the basic needs are satisfied, there is nothing left to be conditioned. In any case, psychologists and educators—as we explained before—do not recognize the experimentally undefinable, and unnoticeable *universal needs and the continuous conditioning, which are like the atmosphere.* They rather assume that the higher satisfactions of "self-actualization" or interests to know are somehow already there to be released by satisfying the other needs. [3,4,6]

The reality is completely different. Children do not become intellectually interested or culturally motivated without hard effort as constant restrictive conditioning. The higher interests are not there to be merely released, by increased satisfactions. *If they were, perfect education would come like an orgy of natural pleasures* between the child and the educator. For they both like nothing better than to give and receive satisfactions. Actually, satisfactions are the last thing that education should aim at, because *needs that are satisfied cease to be operative.*

Still, the modern educators see only the satisfactions, the pleasant positive feelings and reactions as the things to be directly increased. Happiness, contentment, joy, pleasures, hope, feelings of success, enjoyments of rewards, and all other satisfactions are shown to be of highest educational value.[5,6] The opposite feelings, of nonsatisfaction, worry, frustration, anxiety, stress, fear or concern are condemmed as detrimental.[3,5,6]

It is not realized that satisfactions cannot exist without operative needs, which are conditioned nonsatisfactions, practically felt as frustrations and anxieties; that success, praise or reward has only as much value as was previous worry, fear or concern; and that any pleasure or relief in education derives from previous restriction or stress, particularly since the educational pleasures are not naturally given but have to be created, by conditioning.

The practical education has to impose all these conditioned nonsatisfactions and restrictions, as the sources of the desired satisfactions and pleasures. This is done in all education, in all cultures. In fact, it is the very reason why education is and has always been necessary and important. For, if the educational satisfactions existed by themselves they would break out irresistibly and no education would be needed.

Of course, the nonsatisfactions are imposed by way of pleasant inducements, rewards, praise or anticipation of future pleasures. The educator wants the children to be happy in the way he is

himself, with all the pleasant expectations from the "good," conditioned behavior, as well as fears of a different behavior. We saw
that such heightened, refined love, not punishment, becomes the
compelling force behind the conditioning. Educators, however
restrictive, have always known that love and pleasant inducements
are the ways to educate children.

But, in essence, practical education always amounts to imposition of the nonsatisfactions, needs and restrictions, the very opposites—and causal sources—of the educational satisfactions and
pleasures or interests and positive motivations. We are repeating
this because it is crucial. Thousands of volumes, and of misunderstandings, by persistent critics, from Rousseau, John Dewey or
Whitehead to the more radical progressive modern reformers,[2,5]
could have been spared if this simple causal truth were recognized.

Because the paradoxical causation here has never been understood, no educational science exists. The logically or "scientifically"
minded theorist sees that the negatively felt rather than positively
enjoyed experiences are fostered by education. Some of our best
educational and social critics—Charles Silberman,[2] Ashley Mon-
tagu,[21] or Jules Henry[21]—have exposed, with righteous incompre-
hension, *various seemingly totally negative attitudes in the traditional education.*[2,21]

In fact, the radical educational reformers have only to describe
the practical traditional education to prove how shockingly education suppresses all pleasures, freedoms and values that any enlightened man accepts as goals of education. Every aspect of our
traditional education has been found outrageous under the criticism
by our leading progressive educators—A. S. Neil, Reston Wilcox,
Ronald and Beatrice Gross, Sylvia Ashton Warner, Edgar Z.
Friedenberg, Kenneth Clark, Jonathan Kozol or Herbert Kohl.[3,4]

The whole past education and culture could not, possibly, be
so totally wrong. Practical life and cultural selection would not
permit it. But logically and "scientifically," even in experimental
terms, the *practical education does seem to be repressive rather
than productive* or positively attractive. Even children themselves
may testify to this.[5,7] For they as well see only the pleasant satisfactions as the reasons of their positive interests and hail the events

that permit the releases, while hating the restrictions, which actually make the releases possible.

Children, as all men, always follow only the satisfactions or pleasure releases, without ever recognizing their opposite causal sources. The permissive educator is, easily, more liked and better followed. He can therefore show greater success, while he actually depletes the sources of the motivations. To sustain his success he has to go down, to offering more and more permissive pleasures.[21]

The "free" educators show great initial success but fail quickly. More than two thousand "free" schools have been successfully started, in a period of five years, in this country, but have lasted in the average only eighteen months.[8,21]

Yet the logic of more freedoms and satisfactions as the positive causes is the dominant modern tenet. Hence the popularity of studies like that by Margaret Mead, on Arapesh and Mundugumor tribes, which tends to show that permissive education produces better people. Such studies, conducted without insight in the paradox of values and adjustment, are as far from being scientific as are presently all fields dealing with man. The result is rather a confusion. In fact, other studies, on Navajo and Hopi Indians and on Kaska and Haitian personalities as well as on other tribal customs have led to contrary conclusions.[21]

The logical theory becomes different from practice everywhere. The most popular experts on education of children, like Benjamin Spock and Haim Ginott have been, rightly, criticized as permissive and liberal in their theories.[9,21] But they have shown, particularly in their later books, to be conservative when it comes to practical discipline and morals.[9]

They have, though, defended the value of discipline still with the direct improvement logic. Children, supposedly, reason that the parents who punish them love them.[21] Also, the parents are assumed to be more relaxed when they can freely discipline their children.[9,21] In truth, reasons depend on emotions, particularly for children. And parents who derive relaxation from punishing children must be sick. A healthy parent when he disciplines his child feels as bad as when he has to restrict himself.

The problems that the modern liberal education has created are as unique as is its permissiveness. The whole generation of our young seems to have nothing but irrational hate and disdain for their parents. The universal "generation gap," as well as the student riots of the pre-recession period, show the unique extent of the disorder. We have produced the most spoilt children, because we have lavished on them the greatest, most unrestrained improvements of satisfactions and freedoms.

Spoilt child is always the one who has enjoyed the truest natural love—even the natural selfish and biologic freedoms that are presently claimed to be so important. To explain *the inherent paradox of spoilt children,* modern theorists argue that the excessive love here is hidden hate. This is one of the most frequently invoked explanations of our parent-child relationship problems.[4,21] By arguing that the great direct satisfactions are not what they are, the theorists can proceed with their "scientific" logic.

Educators have always believed in *ideas, insights, reasons and understanding as important causes.* We do not need to repeat how alchemistic these general human delusions are. Yet the most noted modern educators have argued that the higher general education should consist of the study of treasures of thought and ideas.[21] A university should be "a kind of continuing Socratic conversation on the highest level."[21] The Great-Book method, promoted by best authorities, notably by Robert Hutchins and Mortimer Adler, is a good example.

Reason and perception as causes are accepted also in the approaches emphasizing the development of thinking in children. The famous studies by Jean Piaget[10] are, probably, the best examples of such approaches. Understanding of child thinking may be important in dealing with abstract and perceptual learning, which in itself is weightless against value reactions, the real sources of motivations and behavior.

The pathetic dictum "knowledge will make you free" is as frequently cited as it is fatuous. In practice, hardly anybody is morally more obnoxious than a rationalist, particularly one asserting his freedoms in the name of reason or knowledge. Socrates is the classic genius of rational education.[2] He had to be condemned for corruption of youth by the Athenians, who were very tolerant in matters of ideas. A stubborn rationalist can become a morally dangerous pest. Practical education is as contradictory or seemingly paradoxical as are all human strivings and happiness.

The second most extolled goal of higher education is the *appreciation and enjoyment of esthetic treasures.*[4,7] This attitude is due to the influence of the humanistic beliefs in the verity of our deepest values. We shall explain later the humanistic value delusions and our self-enslavement into senseless fixations in esthetics or culture.

Enjoyment, in whatever form, exhausts rather than contributes to our capacities and positive motivations. No wonder that the more educated people suffer more from behavioral problems. Cultural and esthetic refinements play important role, as inducements, in educational conditioning. But it is not their enjoyment, extolled by the humanists, that should be the goal.

Neither our great ideas and wisdoms of thought, nor our precious, enjoyed treasures of esthetics and culture are educationally important, in themselves. They all could be forgotten today, and it would make little difference. *Completely different, contrary, wisdoms and treasures are taught and enjoyed in different cultures,* and the educational result is the same. It is mere fixational tradition that has determined our higher Learning, much as the medieval learning was constricted by similar fixations.

Intellectual, abstract training is enormously important. But it could be best attained by study of sciences, or of professionally useful as well as theoretically intricate problems. The scientific study would, eventually, include that of values. This would offer real, causal understanding, instead of philosophical and humanistic confusions, about man and his behavior which then would become a field of science worth studying.

As to moral education, it cannot be helped by the present rationalistic and liberal learning, of the treasures of thought and art, anyway. *Practical moral, restrictive conditioning is the only way.* Hopefully, the future sciences of man will help it, in the surprisingly effective ways that true sciences always invent. In the meantime, moral education would be best achieved by practical work for moral goals that we all know intuitively—and that the moral, restrictive tradition embodies. There is a lot that can be done, like helping the disadvantaged groups, building things and working—instead of organizing protests or seeking "identities."

The general, immediate problem at schools is how to teach the students the reading, writing, mathematics and other *abstract knowledge*. The great modern "discovery" has been that students are more interested if the tasks are adapted to their natural interests, as in the learning-by-doing, or by use of games, pictures, toys and gadgets serving immediate curiosity or gratifications.[2,7] Surely, motivations are increased when more natural pleasures are aroused. One can only agree here with the great reformers, Rousseau, Pestalozzi, Montessori or Dewey.

But the goal of school education is the development of abstract interests and capacities. When these are attained, everything else comes by itself. *And they are furthest away from the natural interests.* Think of mathematics, the queen of sciences, or of scientific work best performed in barren isolation. The pleasant natural interests may be used as stepping stones for children if they are incapable of abstract thinking, but should be avoided as soon as possible.

New gadgets, computer games, TV shows or similar aids have been demonstrated to bring revolutionary success, when first introduced. But the novelty soon wears off, for the students, and the enthusiasm disappears. *None of the gadgetry has really brought the promised revolutions.*[2,5] What remains and really matters is the conditioned motivation of each student to learn what always is hard and abstract but becomes interesting or pleasant as a satisfaction of conditioned needs. The key is "to develop the motivation to study, but the student must somehow supply it himself," as Clifford T. Morgan points out.[21]

This, the only, practical source of success, the conditioned motivation, is not helped by the modern improvements at our schools, but is created at home. We saw how simple but total, like an atmospheric pressure, the restrictive conditioning in a good home is. The most extensive, best studies, by Jencks, Silberman, Coleman the author of the famous report, and by others have revealed that the modern improvements at our schools had almost no effect on the success of learning.[1,2] *The only thing that mattered was the higher motivation of students, brought from their middle-class homes.*[1,2] The restrictive, traditional conditioning is preserved best at such homes.

Still, the educators see only the direct motivations, the pleasure releases, as the goals. Perfect education is seen as a pleasant adventure—though even in a fantasy world of a novel the exciting pleasures derive from the anxieties and troubles of the hero. It is constantly argued by progressive educators, as was notably by Dewey or Whitehead, that subjects taught should be made as interesting as life.[2,3]

Actually, to have an enriched experience, first backgrounds for it have to be created. Historical events become as interesting as real life adventures after you see their background, which you build up gradually by learning dull details. In every subject, *the drilling in of hard, tedious detail or of difficulties to be solved is the source of the "adventurous" pleasures.*

The general, underlying motivation is, of course, the conditioned needs to learn or succeed. The conditioning is, inevitably, hard, actually, nonsatisfying or "frustrating." It can always be proved that any reward system, of grades, exams or punishments, has negative effects.[3,4] The students gain from it no direct satisfactions, or pleasure about the subject. Rather the grading marks in themselves, or efforts to please the teacher, are shown to become the goals.[4,7]

But all conditioning, by parents, or by teachers as their substitutes, imposes only nonsatisfactions, as needs, from which the satisfactions then derive. And it is always the signs of personal award or punishment that serve as means of conditioning, however vast the love or system of motivations that grows from it. After all, there are no natural or nonconditioned cultural and intellectual needs or interests.

The middle-class atmosphere of conditioning, perpetuating the restrictive cultural tradition, is the highest creative source in education. *That is why integration is important.* As that atmosphere is brought to the school the students from lower classes improve, regardless of race. Mere mixing of races from lower-class backgrounds has no effect.[1,2] We explained why value atmosphere, not ideas or philosophies, is decisive. Of course, that atmosphere at a school declines to the extent lower-class students are admitted. This is the price we have to pay for a better society. But the parents who object to integration are not merely irrational bigots. They intuitively know what happens in practice.

The middle-class cultural atmosphere is, of course, regularly exposed as a repressive or superstitious backwardness, by most of the rational and "scientific" reformers. It also is so hard and, it seems, uselessly restrictive that the lower class prophets mostly oppose it as a stultifying influence.[7,21]

In conclusion we may point out the paradox that educational interests and motivations to learn or to know are *pleasures or satisfactions* but that they come through hard, boring work, preparations and anxieties, *the very opposites of pleasures or satisfactions*. The only sources of educational satisfactions are conditioned needs, which are created by nonsatisfactions or, practically, frustrations. And pleasure releases without accumulated restrictions bring exhaustion.

Within the organic limitedness, the nonsatisfactions and restrictions have to be created first. Then the satisfactions and pleasures break out by themselves. Who in the world would need education or help to enjoy already existing satisfactions or pleasures?

The "Alchemy" in Behavioral Theories

The modern behavioral theories are built on the like-from-like logic, of the exact sciences. Our positive motivations and capacities, which are satisfactions or pleasure releases, are believed to derive from satisfactory or positively felt causal backgrounds. This is the only logic one finds in everything said or written about behavior. But it, evidently, amounts to the alchemy of expecting our precious, positive capacities to come with the ease of added enjoyments.

Since the requirement of the causal value opposites, the needs and restrictions, is not recognized, the *behavioral theories are never limited by the considerations of equal effort for equal gain*. They accept all kinds of emotionally weightless, or positively-felt means and methods, like the discovery of self, identification, role enactment, meditation, awareness or consciousness exercises, as ways to better adjustment. This is the modern alchemy in practice.

None of the causal concepts of behavioral theories are free of implied alchemy, for the same reason—the disregard of the rule of equal hard "payment." Ideational and intellectual factors are viewed as important,[14] though they are psychologically easy. Or, unconscious and nonconsciously instinctive causes are accepted, without regard to the decisive, weighty economy of conscious pleasures, and displeasures, by which men live.

As to the logic of *satisfactions from satisfactory causal backgrounds* it rules supreme in all behavioral theory.[14,21] This cannot be overemphasized. Every book or discussion implies, in one way or another, that a satisfactory, positively felt behavior was due to a causal experience of the same, satisfactory, positive nature. Behavioral scientists are discovering, under various concepts, that our capacities and motivations are pleasure releases or satisfactions. Then why not increase them directly, logically, by their greater enjoyment?

It is indeed remarkable how every noted author or expert has advocated, in some way, the increase in satisfactions, positive reactions, pleasure of doing things, interests, satisfactory attitudes, "positive thinking," faith, love, or joys of life.[11,14] According to a much quoted saying by Bertrand Russell,[11] all that men now have to do is to learn how to open their hearts to joy, in order to attain everything they have always wanted.

The concepts of *Self and Identity* are widely accepted in behavioral theories. Evidently these are cognitive or perceptual phenomena. Theorists talk about Discovery of Self, or Loss of Identity, in arcane speculations.[13] Solutions through the formula "Know Thyself" are recommended by modern theorists, as they were by the Delphi oracle.[21] In practice, the finding of Self or Identity becomes only a more complex term for increase of satisfactions or pleasure releases. Alienation becomes a similar term for their impoverishment.

It is always the *positive, pleasant experience* that is viewed as the discovery of self.[12,13] This is understandable. One's ego or self is the source of all pleasure releases, which are found ultimately inside oneself. Conversely, in case of release impoverishment one tries to avoid his "self" or the demands of his organism for restoration of normalcy through restrictions. This looks like an alienation from self, and from the reality, which is distorted to avoid such return to normalcy.

Of course the most perfect discovery of self is attained by the schizophrenic. With his autistic grasp he reaches and enjoys most directly and fully his inner releases—and exhausts them. Writings by R. D. Laing about the deep experiences of schizophrenics in search of self or identity are enlightening.

The best authority on Identity, Erik Erikson, sees *only satisfactions*, like trust, pride, freedom, sense of adequacy, self-acceptance, enjoyed intimacy or rejection of despair, as requirements of successful development through his "eight ages" of individual.[12] Any satisfaction or sense of fulfillment can be attained by increased enjoyments, even through drugs. But the end result is the opposite of healthy development.

In still more arcane theories about the Self or Identity *its discovery is viewed as the highest satisfaction* and avoidance of deep existential negative feelings. This is expounded in the humanistic psychology, best represented by Abraham Maslow, and in the existential therapies, advanced by Victor Frankl or Rollo May.[13,21] The attainment of the "cognition of being" or of the ontological self is viewed as an ecstatic insight. It is compared, by Maslow, to his concept of "peak experiences," or "growth-through-delight" shown to be accepted as the royal road to Self by tens of psychologists.[13]

One can only wonder why people have not rushed into discovering their ontological selves. Of course, psychologists blame the fear of horrible inner instincts or the still more mysterious ontological fear of knowing oneself. The fear of inner horrible drives is an explanation used in various behavioral theories. In truth, all hidden evil drives are only pleasant to the person himself, however shameful they may become when uncovered by others.

Emphasis on self-discovery and identity often amounts to urging people to *enjoy the pride* of themselves. Adjustment problems, say, of persons from a minority group, are to be helped by feelings of pride or identity. Pride can be creative when it is a positive capacity as a satisfaction of the conditioned need to be good or to avoid shameful, guilty behavior. But enjoyment of pride in itself can lead only to a demand for more praise from others whether it is deserved or not. The end result is bitterness and antisocial attitudes.

Further, the lack of *identification* with personal models is seen as decisive. But identification is a perceptual or cognitive act. One could therefore easily identity himself with the President himself and all the best qualities, even while living in culturally low or delinquent environment. When delinquents "identify" themselves with criminal models they simply want the pleasures, money, power or prestige they see criminals enjoy. All this is determined by the pleasure causality, totally different from exact identification concepts.

Of course, the main problem behavioral theories have to explain is why and how people act against themselves. The most popular concept here is, probably, that of *self-punishment*. It has been notably promoted by best, classic authorities, Franz Alexander, Theodor Reik or Karl Menninger. Almost anything negative can be explained by self-punishment.

A wide variety of maladjustments, including professional failures, eccentricity, repeated marriages, delinquency and recidivism have been explained, by Alexander, as results of self-punishment. He holds that criminals leave clues so that they can be caught and receive the desired punishment. Or, alcoholics drink because "the adverse consequences of drinking replace admirably other forms of self-punishment."[21] The best theory on self-punishment through crime is that of Reik. He explains that punishment of crime may become the main incentive for criminals to commit crimes.

The classical authoritative work on self-punishment is Menninger's *Man Against Himself*.[21] Menninger shows how almost every maladjustment or disorder, from failures in life or addictions to mental and organic diseases, is a form of suicide. Other important behavioral scientists have accepted the theory of self-punishment.[14,21]

This only reveals how general is the fact that men act against themselves, in endless ways; and how absurd are the theories trying to explain it with the direct logic or "scientifically." If anybody wanted to punish himself he could kill or cripple himself in the next twenty minutes, by merely neglecting any of the hundreds of precautions by which we survive.

The theories of self-punishment or death wish can be dramatically interesting and popular, exactly because self-punishment is an extraordinary idea. Men do "punish" themselves, but the natural striving for pleasure, to excess, is the cause.

Very widely accepted are the concepts of *mechanisms like Identification, Projection or Substitution*. Every kind of negative reaction can be explained by arguing that the person unconsciously or consciously substituted one system of feelings for another, or identified himself with somebody or something.[14] The central problem of how we act against ourselves thus can be easily explained. The alchemistic logic of these concepts is apparent. By a mere ideational or perceptual switch of directions in your reactions, through substitution or displacement, you supposedly can change your behavior from positive to negative, or in any other way.

But these mechanisms are readily accepted as causes even by sober scientists,[14;21] because they can be easily observed in human behavior. People do substitute something for something else, or identify themselves with somebody. What is, absurdly, overlooked is that they do so by their constant striving for satisfactions or *pleasures*, whereas the above mechanisms are invoked to explain negative behavior or disorders which are highly *unpleasant*.

Identification is, probably, the most frequently invoked mechanism. It is inferred from the common, *pleasure*-dominated forms of behavior, such as wanting to be like somebody else or to do as somebody else does.[14] Identification with things is inferred from person's boasting about his car or clothes.[21]

But then identification is used to explain the *unpleasant* behavioral reactions or disorders. The manic-depressive, supposedly, identified himself with a dead relative, the paranoiac with a persecuted group, or the sick person with some sick or handicapped person.[21] Similarly aggression is blamed on identification with an aggressor, or homosexuality on identification with mother.

Projection is another often invoked mechanism. Again, it is inferred from usual, pleasurable behavior patterns, of people assigning their own faults or undesirable qualities to others.[14] But then projection concept is used to explain the most unpleasurable, tormenting reactions, even paranoiac fears. It is argued, in well reasoned ways, that by projecting his own hostility onto others the person logically starts seeing them as hostile. In reality, no logic or reason can induce us to feel one way or another, still less to create for ourselves torments or fears.

The person who eagerly resorts to "projection," who overenjoys his own superiority and sense of power over others, is bound to suffer from as excessive opposite feelings and reactions, including irrational fear of the power of others over him. Thus the disorder here, as in all cases, is caused by the striving for pleasure, not by any logically reasoned projection.

Substitution and *Displacement* are very comfortable concepts for explaining anything in behavior. For, purportedly, the very gist of these mechanisms is that something can be substituted by anything else even its opposite, often in a deliberately disguised or distorted way. Usual substitutions and displacements are certainly frequent. People substitute one pleasure by another, or deliberately distort reality to permit themselves greater enjoyments.

But behavioral scientists see these mechanisms as ways by which people incur their *unpleasant,* negative reactions and behavior disorders. In truth, man never gets confused about his satisfactions or pleasures, which are the simplest, easiest things to know and enjoy. Conversely, he never would incur the unpleasant negative reactions or disorders by any substitution or displacement. Invoking the Unconscious does not help, because on the unconscious level in particular only the simple, easy pleasure drive rules.

Behavioral scientists have accepted as causes of disorders similar other mechanisms:[14,21] Negation, Dissociation, Symbolization, Compensation, Introjection, Regression, Isolation, or Reaction-Formation. All such theories imply *the absurdity that men somehow, confusedly, torment themselves as easily or ingeniously as they enjoy their pleasures.* Such mechanisms would be used inordinately only for enjoyment of pleasures—which then can lead to disorders, by the opposite causation.

Also generally accepted are the recently flourishing *inner awareness, consciousness, meditation or "human potential" movements.* [15,16] They are promising unlimited capacities through discovery of inner, transcendental forces, by the right formulas or methods. These range from Oriental rituals, yoga or transcendental meditation, to the Esalen treatment and encounter groups, to bioenergetics, psychosynthesis, Arica or est, and to various newfangled consciousness expansion methods. [15,16] As Theodore Roszak concludes, we are on "the biggest introspective binge any society in history has undergone." [16]

Movements of easy behavioral enrichment have become a trend. Maharishi Mahesh Yogi promising transcendental regeneration by a shortcut had 350,000 followers, at one time, from the best-informed people. The movement of Guru Maharaj Ji had attracted, at its peak, four million worshipers expecting similar enrichment. It is amazing how easily movements and schools of meditation and Eastern rituals mushroom, as can also be seen from the successes of Chogyam Trungpa, Swami Muktananda or Yogi Bhajan. Says Harvard Psychologist Gary Schwartz: "TM is no longer just a movement, but an industry." [16]

Actually the trend should not be a surprise. Modern psychology, as we saw, is a virtual modern alchemy. Already William James, the genius of our early psychology, taught that we have unlimited forces hidden in our consciousness. The above movements are typical of the general alchemistic confusion about human behavior. There are, supposedly, some 8,000 methods offered by the consciousness experts. [16] The belief in easy enrichment through the right formula or technique dominates everywhere.

Another typical trend in the behavioral theory is the emphasis on roles and role playing as determinants of behavior. The best-sellers, by Eric Berne, *The Games People Play,* and by Thomas A. Harris, *I'm OK—You're OK,* are good examples. These authors are the founders of the widely accepted Transactional Analysis, which views enactment of roles as the decisive ways in behavior.

Recently the theories of Erving Goffman are becoming popular. He sees men in their behavior as actors and the world as a stage.

A person's behavior may, indeed, appear as capricious as a game. The reason is the never suspected, seemingly paradoxical opposite causation. The forces behind any behavior are anything but a game. They are desperate, dead-serious efforts by the person to have more of satisfactions or pleasures, as positive motivations or capacities, in a constant struggle with their imminent exhaustion. Role enactment, offered by the Transactional Analysis, Gestalt therapy, Esalen Treatment and other methods, is *a farce in comparison with the weighty and hard effort needed in our behavior.*

Certainly, people constantly pretend or want to be different from what they are, as Goffman extensively demonstrates. But that is effect, not cause, of behavior with all its difficulties, complexes or disorders. The causes are, here as elsewhere, weighty and strict, different from any playing. Sometimes, overplaying a role may bring a complex. But the causal force behind such overenjoyment is the pleasure drive, with its inexorable, grave economy, totally different from capricious role playing.

Modern people, in their confusion about the real causes of behavior, find the role theories interesting explanations. They are thus further misled in their belief that behavior is a result of curious coincidences or gratuitous, organically weightless acts.

Also popular recently have been the *theories of ethology and sociobiology.* The best known ethologists are the Nobel Prize winner Konrad Lorenz, Robert Ardrey, Robin Fox, Desmond Morris, or Lionel Tiger. They hold that human behavior is determined by instinctive patterns. The sociobiologists, Edward Wilson or Robert Trivers, see genetic patterns or genes as the determinants of human behavior. These theories are intriguingly fascinating, because they claim discovery of hidden, nonconscious forces mysteriously ruling over us.

In practical reality, only the *conscious pleasures* or feelings determine our behavior, every minute of our lives, in our pursuit of happiness. Surely, everything in the organism derives from the lower evolutionary mechanisms. But, as we saw, the conscious pleasure integrates, with ungraspably miraculous precision, every evolutionary cause or mechanism. It becomes for man the only, all-determining drive, as anybody can practically see.

Any nonconscious, therefore nonpleasurable, instinctive or genetic interaction would be completely overriden by *man's intense, exclusive drive for conscious pleasure.* If an instinctive drive gives pleasure it has already been eagerly integrated into man's conscious pleasure system.

Above all, man pursues, manages, conditions, and restricts his conscious pleasures by use of his awesome intellect that makes the creations by man gigantically more powerful than instinctive patterns. One can think here of an industrial complex, and a beehive. Our pleasure drives have been evolved into systems of cultural values so vast that beside them an instinctive satisfaction like kicking the fellow next to you or protecting the territory of your corner of the room would be ridiculous. Under such enormously efficient, vast, *all-inclusive and intense drive for conscious pleasures* any nonconscious intervention has as much chance of subsisting as the proverbial snowball in hell.

Exactly because man pursues, manages, manipulates and "improves" his pleasures so completely free of limitations by any instinctive or genetic patterns, he overenjoys them. He thus incurs the "beastly," irrational, unexplainably ingenious negative reactions —which then may seem like surging from man's animal past, from his deeply hidden nonconscious instinctive or genetic self.

Intellect, instead of instinct, has been viewed as the determinant of behavior in other—and not only the traditional humanistic— theories of behavior. All psychological theories accept reason, ideas and learning as causes and thus imply a decisive role for intellect. [10,14] The recently popular humanistic psychology stresses free will and intellectual choices as decisive.[13,21] Intellect is, indeed, a prodigious tool by which man has built his awesome, gigantic civilization.

But intellect is only a tool, that men can use for good and bad. In fact, men become irrational and self-destructive through disorders and diseases originating from the progress brought exactly by the intellect and used with the wrong, direct-improvement logic, sustained by the intellect.

Ultimately, the only thing that matters for human behavior, and health, is *the availability of satisfactions or pleasure releases*. These cannot be provided either by the intellect or through any of the virtually alchemistic factors we have discussed. Pleasure release, as we saw, is equivalent to the release and self-realization of the life flow itself. That is why pleasure or satisfactions are what make man tick—move, act or behave. They are his positive motivations and capacities in everything he feels, does or even thinks.

But the causal law, of the opposite causation, which determines how the pleasure or satisfactions work—within the limited organism—is contrary to the very logic of thinking used in the present theories of behavior or motivation.

Before we conclude, we have to mention some effects of behavior which *may seem to contradict the creative function of restriction*. People having enjoyed more freedom or relaxation, during a vacation, often return to work with more energy. Children permitted an hour of free play may resume their tasks with a greater sense of duty. In all such cases, the determining cause is the conditioned, moral normalcy of duty or security.

While the person vacations or plays he accumulates the feeling of continued deviation from such normalcy, therefore returns to it with accumulated zeal. The boy having spent an afternoon on forbidden loafing returns home with greater sense of consciousness. *This does not mean that the sense of what is right is increased by doing wrong.* Our conditioned moral normalcy, of diligence or duty, is carefully created, by restrictions, and can be gradually effaced, not strengthened, by enjoyments of freedoms, leisure or license.

Conversely, a person living through a hard period of restrictions may still experience psychic impoverishment, not enrichment. The reason is that he may have compensated, for the hardships of restrictions, by inner overenjoyments or by anticipated enjoyment of future pleasures. Such enjoyments, as extra releases, then lead to equal restrictions or difficulty.

Further, a person living through a very happy period may be able for some time to be positively minded. This is so because the necessary restrictions are more easily accepted by the person while he enjoys a plenty of pleasure releases—which have to be paid for later.

All kinds of similar *compensations and shifts within the motivational or pleasure "economy"* are to be expected. Life situations are always complex. But the causal principle governing them is simple: it is the law of value reactions. The equality of the value opposites is inexorable within the organic limitedness. If you overenjoyed a past event, say, a love affair, you suffer, and even hate to recall it, though it was a pleasure.

On the other hand, if you suffered during an event more than was necessary, you can enjoy it in retrospect, even if it was a tormenting experience, that otherwise would not be willingly recalled. That is why people like to tell of past troubles which turned out less unpleasant than expected. Again, all kinds of involved combinations are possible—under the simple rule.

Also, a negative, *rebellious reaction upon restriction* is often to be expected. Restricted children may react by being spiteful, smearing walls, or rioting later as students. This is a natural opposite reaction. But if the educational restrictions are constant enough to establish a new moral normalcy, for the child, he will react by eagerly returning to it after any transgression, rather than by rebelling against it. The key is the really hard, extended conditioning; anything of value is difficult. Those arguing that restriction in education is counter-productive are missing this point.

In all behavior unwanted, irrational *reactions of hate are so frequent* because people are urged, by experts, and attempt, to live with great self-denying love without conditioning themselves, by hard effort, to accumulate the difficult restrictions that this requires. Any positive reaction that is exaggerated, not sufficiently "paid" for, reverses into its opposite. Similarly on the social level, a nation may react with divisiveness, hate and external or internal strife after attempting to bear too much self-sacrifice or love and being unable to do it without such exaggeration.

In sum, the precious, all-determining force in behavior is the conditioned satisfactions or pleasure releases, which constitute our positive motivations and capacities. Pleasure as the release of the life force itself moves and activates everything in the organism. Practically, we know that *we could achieve anything if we had satisfaction or pleasure* for what, we know, perfectly, are the right things to do. But this precious force, the pleasure and satisfaction potential can be gained only through their hard opposites—equal restrictions or conditioned nonsatisfactions.

In behavior, as elsewhere, nothing is gratuitous. Yet the present behavioral theories proceed by the virtually alchemistic logic that the satisfactions or pleasures are to be increased directly—evidently, by their increased enjoyment. Equally alchemistic are the other, easy and weightless factors viewed as decisive: ideas, reasons, perceptions, self-discovery, identity, techniques, mechanisms, roles, awareness, meditation, or consciousness exercises.

The modern scientist cannot deal with the *relevant and weighty, nonalchemic, opposite causation* because his very logic of thinking is contrary to it.

Social Sciences: More "Alchemy" and Confusion

Social sciences are not very important for coping with our present practical problems. This may be so because presently these sciences, "with the most methods and least results,"[17] have no really scientific, causally understood explanations to offer. The ultimate reason is the irreality or practical weightlessness of the ideational causes these sciences deal with, as well as the "scientific," practically alchemistic, like-from-like causal logic used. The general fallacies of the modern human sciences are repeated here.

But in social sciences *the alchemistic confusion is more pervasive* than in other fields. For here the belief in ideas as causes and the direct increased-satisfaction logic govern thoroughly. In individual psychology or behavior, at least the common sense shows that ideas or reasons are *powerless* and that best conditions can have *negative* effects. Such insights are missing in social sciences, dealing with more involved, less analyzable phenomena and ruled by opinions or "philosophies."

Social sciences are virtually dominated by concepts of *ideologies, ideas, doctrines, symbols, myths, philosophies, perceptions* and other ideational phenomena.[17] Books on government or social theories often read much like compilations of philosophies. Experimental observation seems to show that socially or politically people act, as they always assert, on basis of their ideological convictions, reasons and perceptions. These are, of course, determined by what the people feel, and are mere rationalizations or slogans. But every citizen wanting to improve the world or to blame the system, as everybody does, has a political or social philosophy or theory viewed by him and others as the source of his social motivations.

Even when social sciences deal with *values,* these are accepted in their delusory humanistic terms. It is not recognized that the prevalence and strength of a value rather reveals, and depends on, actual scarcity or absence of what is valued. Value feelings, and reactions to factual conditions are misinterpreted, as the actual, opposite or relative causation is not taken into account. Values as social goals and determinants have been accepted with this humanistic logic by theorists of most varied approaches—by C. Wright Mills, Robert S. Lynd, David Riesman, Arthur Schlesinger or Gunnar Myrdal.[17,21]

Social behavior is explained by *intents or intended attitudes,* as in the various voluntaristic, functional, or "game" theories. Best social theories can serve here as examples. The extensively discussed "theory of action" of Talcott Parsons is a voluntaristic theory based on assumptions of intended choices.[17] The functional theories, supposedly best expounded by Bronislaw Malinowski and Alfred Radcliffe-Brown, or the game theory, of John von Neumann, are important pieces of modern social sciences.[17]

In reality, the main social problems are caused by various *negative reactions least wanted or intended, and in no way useful or functional,* resulting from the opposite causation. Here, as in all disorders, the negative reactions are compulsive and unpleasant. Neither the people nor their leaders want them. Nobody wants the irrational hate, aggression, fear, suspicion or any of the negative reactions that cause all our social difficulties.

Social sciences are founded on concepts of *social and cultural causality*.[17] Certainly, it seems that societies often behave in ways which the individuals in it never intended. The reason is the unwanted, "ingenious," opposite reactions man brings on himself. It is the individuals, not the societies or cultures, that feel, act or have a will—in our nonmetaphysical world.

Each individual, in society, is guided by his feelings or pleasure so concrete, strong and precious to him that he would never permit some Society or Culture above him to interfere with it.

Still the social scientists are dealing only with social units and phenomena, not with individuals. The theory that society or culture is the causal unit has, assumedly, been the starting point in social sciences since Durkheim.[17] The social philosophy—one is referred here mostly to Plato, Hegel, Spencer, Comte, Marx, Weber, or Spengler[17]—has stressed the cultural essence or "spirit" of social entities as the causal source.[17] The Superorganic, invoked by Sorokin, Kroeber, or Ogburn,[17] is the modern equivalent of the spiritual essence of societies. Considering that only individuals can act or will, and that they are governed by the pleasure goals they would not surrender to any Society, social sciences are losing themselves in irreality.

The most important fact about the social sciences is that there can be no coherent science of strictly social or cultural phenomena because *no causal laws for them can ever be established*.

Such laws exist for individuals, ruled by the never-changing, natural principle of the organic sameness. But societies and cultures are created and controlled by men, with their always changing, unpredictable ideas, inventions and "improvements"—however futile or disastrous. The incessant *inventiveness and free choice* here exclude the possibility of causal laws.

Social sciences, simply, cannot predict or plan anything, nor even understand causally, that is, scientifically the social phenomena, because there are no causal laws—no rules of what follows or results from what.

Understandably, sociologists have tried to establish "systems" which, much like organisms, would follow causal laws. *System theories* have been proposed by Easton, Lipset, Shils, Apter and

Merton.[17,21] But because of the same ever-changing inventiveness and free choice by men, systems that would obey causal laws, and therefore could be scientifically dealt with, do not exist. The system theories, which should have turned social fields into exact sciences, have not brought any such revolution. Only more complexity has been added. Other theories trying to establish social causal laws have to fail for the same reason.

Behavior of societies is determined by the totals or rough *averages of the value reactions of individuals,* which are governed by the opposite causation. Consequently, social reactions are, in comparison, very slow, of average value, and only generally articulate, as can be seen in economic booms and recessions.

A society may be aroused by some *leader or idea,* but after it goes through long reactions and counterreactions the end result is a small progress that the society would have attained, at a constant rate, without the exciting leader. One may, individually, often get aroused by some idea and start a great program, which ends in little change after the opposite reactions are lived through. When individuals get socially, generally aroused, the process merely takes more time, and is more confusing, due to the multiplicity of interactions.

But however complex the forms of social interaction, the determining substance is the reactions of the individuals in the society. Thus the opposite causality—ultimately due to the organic limitedness—rules here, as it does in psychological disorders or functional diseases. But its logic is the last thing social scientists could accept.

Social "disorder" may be a good example. Hate leading to war or persecutions is usually found to follow strong nationalism as effusion of love for own people or "us," who have no value meaning without opposite "others." In the Nazi Germany such love, trust, hope, or the sense of belonging, identity, success and security were enjoyed to ecstasy. The opposite, excessively negative hates, fears and feelings of humiliation caused the persecutions and war.

Nationalism is a necessity in the perennial struggle by men for more positive social capacities, as satisfactions of selfless social reactions. Particularly a developing nation has to intensify the feelings of social readiness of sacrifice or love. The opposite, negative feelings then have to follow. As Gunnar Myrdal explains, "these strivings in the individual countries, in themselves good and rational, result in international disintegration."[21] He logically argues that the highly positive nationalistic emotions are turned into hate by a "masochistic and perverse" tendency of the people to "revolt against their own innermost ideals."[21] Everybody becomes "perverse" under the opposite causation.

The hard *effort to have more of social love, and the resulting "irrational" hate* are the causes of most of international, and internal, strife—that nobody wants. Logically it may seem that shortsightedness of governments and politicians is the cause, as was famously argued by the Nobel Peace laureate Sir Norman Angell.[21] Lack of "political imagination" has been blamed, by Hans Morgenthau, for international dissent. Arnold Toynbee thought that the "fashionable Western liking for political disunity and dislike for political unity" could be easily changed as all customs can.[21]

But the *strife is never liked by anybody,* least of all by politicians, who are not shortsighted or unimaginative either. They merely represent the people, who cannot help the hates or negative feelings, that they don't want. Customs can be changed with disastrous ease when that offers more satisfactions or freedoms. The modern trends of liberalism and license show this. But no amount of good intentions or "liking" can change the negative feelings, incurred as a result of excessive positive strivings.

The same paradox of opposites governs internal strife. The love for "us" here generates the hate for "others" inside the country. Typically, witch-hunts were fiercest when people aspired, unrealistically, to highest Christian virtues that are exact opposites of the hates and fears in witch-hunting. In any zealous positive social movement an *exaggerated* emotional enjoyment brings unwanted opposite reactions. The movement then may be later condemned, though its efforts and overall influence were highly positive. The movements that brought Puritanism or Inquisition are examples. So is the modern nationalism or patriotism.

Another important causal truth is *the paradox of improvements and hardships.* Satisfactions are hailed by a people as sources of its successes, though they lead to immobility or motivational impoverishment. Hardships, "challenges" or difficulties create motivations and capacities, but are deplored by the people as obstacles.

Yet scientists accept the peoples' views—the "spirit" of each era—and perpetuate the disastrous improvement logic here as everywhere else. Even the theories on "challenge," including that of Toynbee, hold satisfactions or a satisfactory meeting of the challenge as creative. Actually, nonsatisfactions or hardships are what make the difficult benefits from a challenge appear worthwhile. They also endow people with capacities to exploit the challenge.

It has been always known that *peoples from harsher conditions are more capable.* Nordic conquerors, in three continents, are examples. But it has been argued that great cultures rose in southern, fertile river valleys.[21] The point is that peoples have to be switched, by events, from harsher conditions where they have developed the capacities, to favorable environments, where such capacities can create surpluses and progress. Europeans coming to America exploited exuberantly its plenty of land and resources by using capacities and motivations evolved under conditions of scarcity of land or resources.

Peoples living undisturbed or in unchanging environments, as in jungles, mountains, or Arctic regions, find as normal any, even harsh conditions and have little motivation to change or progress. All human reactions are relative. In our "temperate" zone, the perennial change from the highly favorable summer to the deadly winter has induced people to create reserves and to build or manufacture, in fighting the elements and nature.

Satisfactions, material riches or security, that a society has sought and been organized for, when finally attained, bring loss of motivations and of progress in capacities. The society may then concentrate on enjoyments and exhibit flourish in forms of life and "culture." This is seen as progress, particularly by modern men living with similar, enjoyment convictions. But decay follows such progress.

The cyclic theories of history, perhaps the only ones that offer a comprehensive general law of history, confirm this. The expounders of the cyclic theories, from Vico to Spengler and Toynbee, have demonstrated that doom follows highest flourish of civilizations.

The causal explanation would have been simple for all, even irregular cases,[21] if the paradoxical effect of satisfactions were understood. Instead, the cyclic theories have postulated intricate, purposive, humanly interesting and meaningful laws, as can be seen in the exalted theories of Spengler and Toynbee.[17;21] This is metaphysics, because natural causal laws can be only prosaically simple. But the cyclic theories do prove the factual decay of civilizations after they have reached their fullest satisfactions.

Also *social movements* rise as struggles for more satisfactions or freedoms but become conservative or reverse when they have to face practical problems and responsibilities. The parties of liberals, democrats, socialists and now communists have done so. This creates confusion, particularly when the initial, liberal slogans of the movement are retained; or if the later, creative restrictiveness of a movement is imputed to its early, revolutionary stage, as in the case of Christianity.

The more liberal forms of government, like *democracy,* are also established under the pursuit of more satisfactions and freedoms. It is well recognized that democracy is the "worst form of government" except that is is deemed better than the others. Winston Churchill is often quoted to this effect. It would not have to be that way. During the two World Wars democratic governments were permitted to act dictatorially and accomplished awesome feats.

If we realized how tremendously important a progress is awaiting us, we would permit our democratic governments to become equally authoritarian. The most efficient organizations, like the big companies, are run by one man. But because of our liberal and hedonistic tendencies, we are diluting the power of our governments—and depriving ourselves of the greatest possible progress.

Of course, *communism* is logically the most democratic form of government. The only real freedom and equality in satisfactions is economic, and communism promises it. That is why the more primitive or less perceptive masses bent on immediate freedoms and satisfactions fight for communism. But the practical life, again, requires imposition of restrictions, the sources of all capacities. Communism becomes in practice the most repressive form of government, contradicting its own theoretical, logical tenets.

The dominant value, attitude or characteristics of an era or society are judged in ways contrary to facts because the opposite causation is not understood. For instance, our era will be judged, from its records, as one of anxiety, insecurity and nonsatisfactions, whereas the cause of these feelings is our overenjoyment of unparalleled security, "pampering" and satisfactions.

Similarly the period of the beginning of the Industrial Revolution is seen as the most squalid era, because the squalor was being noticed against the rising improvements. As H. J. Muller says, in quoting H. Heaton, "what was revolutionary was not the evils but the discovery that they were evils."[21] To take a different typical era, the Victorian age, it represents in fact the sharpest turn toward loosening of morals. It is unrealistic to assume that the subsequent modern spirit of moral license emerged suddenly from nowhere. The Victorian age produced the greatest amount of record about puritanism and moralism because these started to be noticed as remarkable, special and discussable customs. Curious contradictions of that age are well documented.

Fixation is an extensive source of confusions. As we saw, any accidental value can become incredibly strong, "true" and endlessly elaborate or rich through the vicious circle of fixations. Particularly social and cultural customs become fixational, for reasons we explained. There is no end to which a custom can become sacred as well elaborately rich, through the Fixation.

Then the theorists accept such holy "treasures" as expressions of the very genius of the people. The best anthropologists, Frazer, Boas, Benedict or Mead, have attributed to customs mythical, functional, "scientific" or practical meanings. Most typical are the sociologists like Levi-Strauss seeking ultimate answers through imputed symbolic meanings of customs.

Actually, *to the very extent that customs are particularly sacred and rich they are fixational.* The really decisive customs, like the need of restrictions, are so general, and hard to follow, that they are not noticed as anything particular, and are not exuberantly enriched. The fixations, of course, are as accidentally meaningless as are neurotic patterns. In brief, social scientists are seeking here the highest revelations and wisdoms from "neurotic," causally accidental elaborations.

Finally, we may say a few words about *economics*. This "dismal science" has been more a confusion than a science. The reason is the inherent paradox of economic, as of all human, progress. Though enjoyment or release—the consumption in economy—is always the motivation, the restriction of it, as accumulation and refinement of capacities or means, is the source of progress.

Capital is created by restriction of consumption and is the decisive factor of progress. Labor is always available, more than needed. And managerial skill, adventure or invention depend on capital, particularly in the modern, vast research and advanced management. Even general learning becomes practically rewarding as well as affordable with growth of capital.

Consumption is the natural motivation in economy and can invigorate it immediately. But in the longer run, increased consumption exhausts economic means. Hand-to-mouth economy is a final example. The modern, Western progress was started and built by "practical ascetics."[17] The industrial revolution originated in the Puritan England. The future progress, with machines doing everything for man, is coming through staggering capital accumulation, attainable by restriction of consumption.

If consumption were the source of progress, we would have an instant utopia. For there is nothing easier than consumption.

But to the modern "scientific" economist increase in consumption—the immediately invigorating factor—is the goal. Consumer confidence is his first criterion. Actually, people are ready to consume boundlessly as long as they are sure of employment. But it is the *capital, accumulated by restriction of consumption, that creates employment.* Even Keynesians recognize that employment depends on capital.[18,19] Keynes argued that with continuous increase in the capital even by mere 2% yearly, the world prosperity would multiply seven times in a hundred years, and many times more with a greater increase in the capital.[18]

We saw that recessions, the main obstacle to all progress, are caused by inflationary difficulties, and scarcities, created by excessive consumption. The ensuing psychological reaction is the opposite of the previous boom generated by increasing consumption. Decrease in consumption as well as in production is the result. The "scientific" observation then shows mainly the lack of consumption, or oversaving as the cause of recession. Excess of savings that cannot be invested is seen as the constant danger by most economists, including Samuelson[19] and Galbraith.[20]

But *reactions during recessions are the reverse of normal attitudes,* as in all disorders through opposite causation. The normal tendency in economy is to expand, continuously. That is why lack of capital, for development which actually lies unlimited ahead, is the constant, first problem. Requirement of capital, for investment, will always exceed availability of capital. Of course during a recession everything goes wrong,[19] as the normal reactions are reversed. Almost anything then can be and has been blamed.[19,20]

The simple causal truth is that economy, to expand, as it normally does, requires capital accumulation, which can be created only by savings. This is hard to do and is the opposite of the consumption. That is why economic progress has come through intense continuous effort, not by the totally easy consumption. It has not come through inventive theories or science either. Ninety-five percent of past economic theories have been proven wrong;[19] and no breakthroughs in the "science" of economics have been reached.

Incidentally, the bases of economic theories are *psychological assumptions,* about motivations, profit incentives, expectations, preferences, marginal values or consumer stimulation. But all determining psychological, value reactions follow the paradoxical causal logic, which the modern economists could never accept.

Just as the economic recessions are a scourge of the modern life, a continuous, accelerated economic expansion would be almost utopian. Clearly, such *expansion requires enormous capital accumulation.* If this is not provided, if consumption prevails, the expansion stops. Then the economic optimism built on consumption stimulation reverses into its opposite.

But "scientifically" a positive cause cannot become negative, and the immediate economic motivation, the consumption is, logically, to be stimulated as a positive factor. *The paradox of all progress*, of restriction of a force or resource for its accumulation and refinement, has been as little recognized here as in all sciences of man. Nor is it understood that stimulation leads to opposite aftereffects, if it is not warranted here by equal expansion of capital, created by restriction of consumption.

VI

MODERN IMPROVEMENTS AND CRIME, DRUG ADDICTION, SEXUAL MALADJUSTMENTS . . .

The modern improvements are, in essence, direct increases in satisfactions and freedoms. Those pampered by such improvements are, naturally, ready to seek them in their completest form —immediate satisfactions with total freedom. This is what *crime* is. Whatever theory is applied, the undelayed satisfaction and unrestrained freedom show to be the subjective sources of crime. It should be kept in mind that the *relative* effect of improvements is the only one that matters. And relatively the modern lower, more criminal groups have attained incomparably higher improvements, of satisfactions and freedoms.

Drug addiction is almost inevitable for those who live only for more satisfactions. Such life brings affective impoverishment, boredom and anxiety as great as is the accumulation of the overenjoyments. And drugs are the perfect, immediate relief for it all—with subsequent opposite effects and the vicious-circle of addiction.

The modern *sexual maladjustments* are only one, though the most important example of how overenjoyments create impoverishment, complexes or maladjustments in any overenjoyed feeling or capacity. Sexual maladjustments are becoming a virtual calamity for modern man, as sexual capacities and satisfactions are being lost. Increasing effort, by doctors, popular "experts" and the sufferers themselves, now goes into dealing with this calamity.

At the same time, the improvements in sexual enjoyments and freedoms have been expanded as never before in history. In all complexes and maladjustments the story is the same: calamitous incapacity or impoverishment upon particularly great improvement.

165

Highest Crime Amidst Greatest Improvements

Of the more advanced countries, ours has provided the indisputably greatest improvements, particularly among the lower groups, in recent times. The *relative* improvements for the main minority group, the blacks, have been spectacular, during the last decades. It has meant, for the blacks, a change from threats of starvation and inhuman subjugation to conditions of welfare care for everybody in need and official protection against any kind of discrimination.

Psychologically such a total change has to result in a feeling that there is not a worry in the world. And this reaction—relative as all value reactions—is the determining factor. The middle-class mentality of self-imposed restrictions and worries has not yet reached the majority of the lower groups.

Amidst these greatest improvements in our country, our crime rate is the highest. It is ten times the crime rate in Scandinavia, eight times that in England and Japan, or seven times that in France.[1,2] And our blacks, enjoying the relatively highest improvements, commit ten times as much crime as our whites.[1,2] This does not mean that the blacks are predisposed to crime. There is no racial or genetic criminality.

The *juveniles*, of all races, are committing half of the crimes in this country. They are, of course, the group that has enjoyed the royal share of our new improvements and freedoms. The excessive care as well as unprecedented licence for our children, during the last decades, in this country, has been the phenomenon noted by every social critic, whatever his theory or interpretation. The youth assimilates the new modern spirit of freedoms totally, while the older people become steeped, with years, in the still persisting restrictive old tradition. The increase in our juvenile delinquency is unbelievable. During the twenty prerecession years the juvenile crimes multiplied 1,600% or sixteen times.[2,3]

All crimes have increased, in this country, by 15% yearly during the prerecession decade.[1,6] This increase can match only that of our prosperity, bringing us the satisfactions and freedoms, enjoyed at the same increasing rate during that period. From 1961 to 1974 the rate of robberies, the most typical economic violent crime, increased 255%; of aggravated assault 153%; of forcible rape 143%; and of murder 106%.[14]

For the year 1973, just before the latest economic recession, the yearly increase for all serious crimes jumped to 17%.[16] During the subsequent years, of the recession and inflation, the increase has been less steep—which agrees with the fact that crime grows together with economic and social improvements.

The immediate behavioral cause of crime is the intent of attaining *undelayed satisfactions with the easiest means* available. This simple, primary fact, whatever its final explanations, would be recognized in any theory. The criminal wants the material or physical satisfactions, that are the same we all want. But he is not ready to delay the satisfactions and develop capacities for attaining them in normal ways. That would require long and hard effort, actually, accumulation of restrictions and nonsatisfactions as conditioned needs, that are sources of all capacities and positive motivations. He cannot bear restrictions or delays, and he uses unlimited freedom in attaining his goals.

The explanations or theories of why the criminals behave in this way are as many as there are general theories about behavior.[4,5] In all of them the underlying belief is *the "scientific" logic of negative reactions coming from negative causal backgrounds*. The real, opposite causality of value reactions which determine the criminal as all other behavior is never suspected.

Even while theorists recognize that prosperity and freedoms bring crime, they look for nonsatisfactions and limitations or frustrations as causes of crime. A leading criminologist, Norval Morris, the dean of the University of Chicago Law School, finds that rapid economic and social progress brings crime.[6] But he still stresses frustrations or nonsatisfactions as direct causes. Another noted criminologists, Marvin Wolfgang, recognizes that crimes come together with increased social freedom; but he does not see increasing enjoyment of freedoms as their cause.[6]

Causally right theoretical understanding of crime would be crucial. The present "scientism" has created here our disasters and failures, while real sciences bring virtually miraculous, surprising new solutions.

Various *deprivation theories* are, expectedly, prevailing at the present.[3,5] The best known theorists here, Robert Merton and Seymour Lipset, have argued that deprivation is felt stronger by the poorer groups observing the success of others and feeling that they have failed. Inequality of means and opportunities, supposedly, contributes to this failure.[3,5] Disappointment and bitterness are greater when expectations rise. This would explain why crime rates soar when general prosperity increases. Hopelessness and bitterness can certainly contribute to crime. They are signs of motivational impoverishment, which can become the cause of all behavioral disorders. Crime is always close to such disorders.

The modern *"scientific" and liberal attitudes* here make all the difference. Before our modern, liberal era, poverty was a scarcity of means which created increased motivations to work hard, out of it. Greatest men and most capable groups, in every nation, have been formed by such poverty. The psychological, key factors here are restriction, and overenjoyment.

If expectations mean hard accumulation of conditioned non-satisfactions, as sources of capacities, then success becomes possible. What is more, then lack of opportunity is not a disappointment but a relief that the strenuous requirements do not have to be met and the accumulated motivational enrichment can be enjoyed more freely. Only to the extent the expectations are over-enjoyed, in advance, the bitterness or depression follows. This simple causal truth explains important practical problems.

The modern poor feel the bitter hate and behavioral impoverishment because they have been encouraged to enjoy their expectations. Instead of accepting hard effort or anxious preparations, they are lured by the liberal drives to enjoy their pride or "identity" and to expect that equality and freedom bring them more satisfactions. The sense of deprivation then has to follow, whatever the degree of real opportunity.

The relative overenjoyment, rather than restriction, is evident in all aspects of the modern poverty that breeds crime. In contrast to the old poverty, the present main problems are: use of drugs instead of lack of means, truancy from schools that are free, avoidance of hard work, lowest morals and dissolute family life, as well as splashy spending at the first opportunity.

The demands of gratification and freedom are such that any restriction is felt as violation of one's rights. Crime is felt justified. "It has reached the point where there are no criminals in jails any more. They're all freedom fighters," says Frederick Hacker, professor of psychiatry and law.[6]

Theories of delinquent subcultures may be next in importance, in the modern science on crime.[3,5] It is shown that the juveniles unable to compete in normal ways for prestige or success seek substitute activities through peer groups or gangs, which offer excitement, fun, adventure and other enjoyments. This permits the deprived youth to attain the generally desired values in substitute ways. The groups involved, either as gangs or as youth with similar attitudes, like the hippies, can be viewed in many ways as cultures. Probably the main theorists here are Richard Cloward, Lloyd Ohlin, Clifford Shaw, Henry McKay and Albert Cohen.[3,5]

From all the involved explanations, within the theory, one thing is clear and generally accepted: the delinquents are seeking, through the subcultures, easier gratifications and more freedoms. The substitute ways are sought because they are easier; and escape into a subculture provides freedom from the usual, restrictive culture.

Pursuit of more satisfactions and freedoms is revealed as the core factor in this, or other theories, because criminals merely want to have in an easy way what all men want. This is self-evidently simple. But theories become complex confusions, because under the present "scientific" and liberal views satisfactions and freedoms are positive values. As such they cannot be related to the criminal character or behavior. Only the opposite causation can explain why and how satisfactions and freedoms—the most necessary values—become sources of crime or of impoverishment of capacities and loss of positive motivations. This is decisive for practical understanding of crime and dealing with it.

The *differential association theory,* established by Donald Cressey and Edwin Sutherland, holds that criminal behavior is learned.

[3,4,5] A person does become a criminal when he lives with criminals. But this only proves that the value atmosphere we live in is decisive. Learning, on the other hand, is a motivationally weightless factor. One can learn great, most useful philosophies, from books. But the values of commonplace people he lives with day by day will have more effect on him than the insights of the wisest philosophers.

Various psychological, psychoanalytic and psychiatric theories on crime have been advanced.[3,4,5] They can be only as useful as are the modern psychology and psychiatry. As we saw these disciplines are presently alchemistic systems of confusion, governed by a causal logic that is contrary to the real causality of value reactions, which determine the criminal as any other behavior.

Finally we have to mention *the labelling and social interaction theories*.[3,5] They seem to be widely accepted, particularly by sociologists. The gist of these theories is that they avoid any "moralistic" concepts and rely on objective statistics or recordings of observable data, without value interpretations. This corresponds to the generally accepted approach, of being strictly scientific, in social sciences. Perhaps it is the only way for social scientists, since dealing with values under the "scientific" logic would create nothing but confusion presently. Unfortunately, in behavior, and particularly in the criminal motivations and drives, the value reactions are decisive for what practically happens.

In these theories our social and criminal systems—which "label" criminals as such—are mostly blamed. Only such "objective" correlations and scientifically registrable, external data are used—with the direct experimental logic.

Modern criminologists and social scientists stress the *observed feelings of frustration and restriction shown by the delinquents*.[2,4,5] But such strong reactions rather reveal that the delinquents are living with equally strong, relative, enjoyments of opposite feelings, aspirations of satisfactions and freedoms. In all strong negative reactions or disorders overenjoyment of positively felt experiences is their background cause. Living in their "subcultures" the delinquents, indeed, seek to enjoy unlimited satisfactions and freedoms.

Absence of restrictions is typical in the upbringing of delinquents.

"Laxness, which is more frequent among mothers than among fathers, is more prevalent in the most delinquent group than strictness."[7] Families without fathers have more delinquents. In all lower-class families, which have more delinquents, "restraint is often conspicuous by its absence."[7] The frequently invoked theory that overindulgence is hidden hate is typical of the logical explanations here as elsewhere; by saying that white is black an explanation is provided—as we have seen before.

But the *logical, "scientific" beliefs* are strong, and best criminologists accept that negatively felt restrictions and frustrations or nonsatisfactions have negative effect. Even such authorities as Sheldon and Eleanor Glueck have blamed directly negative factors like "unsound discipline" or "unfair punishment"[7]—as if reasons determined what the child feels. Similarly, Gluecks have accepted as favorable factors understanding, affection, stability or moral fibre of parents.[4,7] Actually, these are the common-sense notions of the qualities that characterize traditional, well disciplined families in which the parents impose strong restrictions on the child. They live by such restrictions, and the child is for them a part of themselves.

Of course, strict family discipline is felt little where it is as general as an atmosphere. Conversely, occasional discipline or restriction is felt, and reported, as particularly strong where it is universally lacking, mostly in the lower class families. Juveniles from such families are always complaining, to the unsuspecting researchers, about excessive restrictions and frustrations. Facts are always found to justify feelings.

We agree that moralizing about restrictions does not help, and the usual advocates of stronger discipline can contribute little. *What is needed is a scientific, that is causal, understanding,* in our age of sciences. Then the creative function of restrictions and conditioned nonsatisfactions can be implemented in the surprisingly inventive, limitless ways that modern science is capable of. Presently criminologists themselves admit that little has been achieved because no real science about crime yet exists.[3,5,8] The multitude of controversial theories about criminals and crime confirms this.[4,5]

Everything that is considered best for satisfactory adjustment in the present theory is enjoyed by delinquents more than by non-delinquents. Delinquents are more sociable and spend more time in play, are physically stronger and suffer less from fears, inferiority, insecurity, conflicts or turmoils.[7] The great prophet of counterculture, the late Paul Goodman, concluded from best research, like that of Gluecks, that the delinquents were "vivacious, extroverted, less self-controlled, more manly inclined, more aggressive, less fearful of failure and defeat, more independent, more initiating and less submissive."[7] These qualities can, certainly, ensure more satisfactions and freedoms, enjoyed by the delinquents.

It can also be proved that by providing more improvements and freedoms delinquency can be avoided.[1,2,8,9] Delinquents, as all people, live by direct value beliefs, never suspecting the negatively felt causal backgrounds as the sources of their positive reactions. In fact, they will always report, and their behavior will show, that whenever they have done something positive it has been because of some satisfactory inducement or increased freedom.

Men always act by seeking satisfactions or pleasure releases; we do not need to repeat the paradox involved. In all education, satisfactions have to be used as inducements to obtain more restrictions. Delinquents, as well, have to be helped by the same method—not by mere punishment.

This cannot be easy or simple. But sciences—once established, through causal understanding—are stupendously successful in finding effective means. The present efforts fail because of the "logical" beliefs in the benefit of more satisfactions and freedoms, which seems to be confirmed by "scientifically" experimental observations.

Particularly, prison reformers have repeatedly demonstrated how criminals improve in their behavior when more satisfying conditions or freedoms are provided.[1,8,9] Various experiments have been perennially tried; and their first effects have been described, every time, as truly wondrous.

But the end result is always a complete failure.[8,9] The reformatories in this country are one example.[8] Particularly in the Scandinavian countries the reforms have been extensive. At the 1965 United Nations Congress for Prevention of Crime, the representatives of those countries admitted that no progress has resulted from the improvements.[8] The recidivism rate has increased back to the previous 70%, and escape attempts have not diminished.[8] Actually, the results are found not only self-defeating, in the long run, but also demoralizing.[9]

The problem here is the same as in all modern "scientism." Experimentally clear improvements turn into worsening. Scientists argue, convincingly, that poverty and frustrations breed crime. But crime rates go up as prosperity increases. This has been confirmed by crime waves during periods of sudden prosperity, in the middle and late 19th century,[6] as well as during our latest pre-recession years.[1,6] Again, the *relative* increase in prosperity, or in satisfactions and freedoms, is decisive. Such increase is greater also for the second generations of immigrants; and they show higher rate of delinquency.

Crime is high during periods of social or cultural upheavals, wars, revolutions or sudden cultural changes. The reason is simple. Man uses the first opportunity to get rid of the restrictions or conditioning imposed on him by education and culture. Hardly any further explanation is needed. Enjoyment of full, unrestricted freedom, obviously, leads to crime.

The delinquent lacks positive motivations and capacities, which are, indeed, satisfactions and freedoms or releases. But the only usable source of satisfactions and releases, within the organic limitedness, is nonsatisfactions and restrictions. The normal, non-delinquent youth feels *satisfaction* of his needs while he follows what his loving parents and educators want him to do; and those needs are conditioned nonsatisfactions, mostly of his need for security. Similarly he gains the feeling of *freedom,* from conditioned inner restrictions, anxiety or guilt, when he pursues the desired behavior and interests. Thus positive motivations as well as capacities are created.

It all sounds old-fashioned, because it cannot be done differently in any culture. Enrichment of value reactions through their opposites is the only way, under the organic limitedness. And values are the determinants of behavior in its every form or aspect.

In conclusion, we may repeat, for emphasis, that the key to

solutions here, as in all sciences of man, would be a causal understanding, which would make *a true science about crime* possible.
It should be recalled how tremendously efficient a true science can
be in finding the right, detailed, inventive means and devices.
Solutions will never be easy here, because the nonsatisfactions and
restrictions are the hardest things to bear.

But the difference will be that of going in the right instead of
the wrong direction. Nothing of value for man is easy, in the first
place. That is why the present "scientism" seeking solutions in
the easy, direct satisfactions and freedoms is so obviously failing.

Drug Addiction: Typical Improvement Disorder

The modern improvements, the rich life, make it possible for
us to enjoy whatever we want. And the "scientism" encourages us
to pursue satisfactions. Evidently, overenjoyments become customary. The vicious-circle aftereffects, boredom, anxiety, depression and immobility follow inevitably. Drugs are a perfect, immediate remedy for these unbearable reactions. Modern men, used
to all kinds of pills,[15] know this, and are bound to start drug use
at the first opportunity. Our youth grow up with drugs and other
"improvement" means all around them.

Particularly the groups that are free of the traditional, middle-
class restrictions become easy victims.[14] Here belong the lower
class youth; the delinquents, pursuing their excessive satisfactions
and freedoms; groups like the students exposed to liberal education; and people who do not belong to, or manage to escape from,
traditional settings, like the nouveaux riches, stardom people, and
the newly arrived, or culturally liberated groups.[14,15]

We saw that the *relative,* sudden improvements are decisive.
They have made some minority groups like the blacks enjoy, or
aspire to, particular satisfactions and sense of careless freedom.
(Of course, disappointments and complaints are part of it. Men
always want more when they get more.) Under such sudden, relative improvements any group would react with a similar careless
freedom. Racial differences are less important.

Our *youth become the easiest victims,*[10,14] because they are the main beneficiaries of our prosperity. Children in this country have the best of everything. The youth have also more of the modern education with its liberal, "scientific" logic of direct improvements of feelings. Moreover, they lack the practical intuitive wisdom— gained with age—that bitter aftermath follows excessive enjoyments.

Drug addiction will increase with the continued modern improvements in the pursuit of greater satisfactions. Above all, no help is possible while the modern *science is unable to explain addiction causally* or scientifically. Everybody, from the Congressional committees to educators and scientists themselves, recognizes that the problem is unsolvable as long as the causal explanation of addiction is missing.[10,11] It is found "surprising that there is so little understanding of drugs, used by men for thousands of years."[13] Research on the addiction has been enormous. Description of the research on marijuana alone fills four big official volumes.[12] Still no accepted explanation has been reached.[12,13,14]

The confusion of modern scientists about addiction is unbelievable. We saw that addiction is a universal phenomenon. It accompanies the use of all pleasure inducing means, from coffee or tobacco to drugs and alcohol. As a general *uniform* natural reaction it can be governed only by a necessarily simple causal law or principle. This law derives from the fact that excess increase in pleasure releases is followed by their equally excessive restriction.

Of course, the underlying physiologic processes in addiction are ungraspably complex. Also, a drug withdrawal may seem irregular: it is exacerbated at its beginning if the organism had reinforced its countermechanisms, like the Nissl's granules, which cannot be reduced at once. But everything is causally simple on the general, most comprehensive level of reactions, miraculously integrated by the pleasure mechanism.

Addiction is a clear example of the vicious-circle worsening through overenjoyments or increased improvements. As the overenjoyment is followed by deeper worsening or restriction in the pleasure releases, the person seeks to overcome this unbearable, "sickening" reaction by more use of the drug. The opposite causation is the key here. And its logic is contrary to the modern "scientism."

The present incredible confusion about addiction is fully *reflected in the theories about addiction.* Everybody can see that addiction is a problem of enjoyments and aftereffects, of deep, organic pleasures and displeasures. But the leading scientists have used any other concept except pleasure in their explanations.[10;13;15] They have accepted as causes the organically weightless learning, conditioning, cognitive factors, perceptions or social interactions[11;14;15]—everything but what really, concretely matters in addiction and makes the addict seek the drug as well as suffer.

The theories of *conditioning and learning* dominate the present explanations of addiction. Leading authorities, Alfred Lindesmith, Lawrence Kolb and Abraham Wikler, among others, have expounded such theories.[13,14] The conditioning is seen as resulting from associations and learning. Cognitive factors are stressed.

To become addicted the person, allegedly, has to recognize his dependence on the drug and to reorganize his self-concept, incorporating in it this recognition.[10,11] Cognitive, or linguistic association is seen as decisive: if the drug user has not conceptually or linguistically associated his reactions with the drug, he cannot become addicted.[11,13]

These theories are accepted as scientific because they permit the use of the generally recognized concepts of conditioning and learning. They are also "logical," since the opposite causation, of pleasure turning into displeasure, does not have to be dealt with. It is argued that the pleasure or euphoria is not the goal of the drug user, because the addict suffers miserably and there is no directly logical reason why he could not drop the drug.[13,14] Rather, the involvement in the drug culture is seen as the goal. Becoming hooked, supposedly, provides the addict with reinforcement from his peers, or with clearly attainable goals, and prevents boredom. [13,15] The hustling and seeking for drugs is seen as the main attraction.[10,11]

There is no need to explain how practically incongruous such conclusions are. But "scientific" and "logical" approaches do not permit the acceptance of the concepts of pleasure, or of the opposite causation which explains the vicious-circle worsening through improvement.

The *deviance theories* seem to be next in importance.[11,13] The main authority here is Robert Merton. Other scientists accepting the theories of deviance and anomie are Theodore D. Graves, Robert C. Hanson, Richard Jessor, and David P. Ausubel.[13] Here again the factors of learning, understanding, perception, identification and cognitive goal-setting are seen as decisive.

It is assumed that the addict chooses the group culture of deviance and anomie because he recognizes that his initial, high goals are unattainable. He seeks identification with new models or roles in the group, and finds sense of belonging, self-esteem, rewards and a conforming, regulated behavior in the new group culture.[13,15]

These theories are supported by extensive research on *cognitive or perceptual* capacities of addicts. Thus it is shown that addicts are "less capable of conceptualizing the step-by-step means of reaching goals in real-life interpersonal problem situations."[13] We have to repeat that cognitive insights, perceptions, reasons and ideational factors are weightless in competition with pleasure drives.

Such theories are preferred, again, because they offer accepted concepts, like those of learning, perception, identification or role playing, and help to avoid the paradoxical logic of opposite causation of aftereffects. Other theories, about symbolism, unconscious causes, substitutions and conflicts[13,14] can equally remain within the limits of the "scientific" direct logic. The addict, assumedly, suffers from deep-seated depression, boredom and resentfulness growing from unconscious, early conflicts—as has been argued by Anthony F. Philip, and Sidney Cohen of the NIMH.

The "impossible" fact that negative reactions are incurred by the very enjoyment of their positive opposites is thus avoided. There is a "pletora of theories,"[13] consistent with the same logical scientism; but the addictive compulsion has remained "puzzling and intriguing in spite of a century of study," leaving it "all still obscure."[13,14]

The central underlying reason of the failure of modern scientism here is that in each experimentally defined aspect or detail the addictive *drugs show to be clearly beneficial or benign*. They provide relief from anxiety, from self-criticism, conflicts, sexuality, aggressiveness and hostility.[11,13] An effective drug like heroin makes the maladjusted addict feel "normal" in every way.[13] It can always be shown that drugs actually improve our functioning, make us feel more at ease or free to do what we intend to, thus increasing our ability for useful work, according to Robert W. Rasor.[10]

To the extent the drug user is given enough of the drug to avoid withdrawal pain, he remains a normal, positively minded and productive individual, as Louis C. Lasagna has demonstrated.[11] Many prominent people are shown, by Kolb, to have led productive lives while using drugs.[10] Stimulants, like amphetamines in particular, have been used in some jobs regularly, to increase productivity.[13,14] Other drugs are also found to improve creativity and self-understanding, as well as provide relaxation.[11,14] In fact, the first effects of a strong drug, like LSD, are such that they could make people "immensely successful human beings."[15]

Our drug *rehabilitation programs* are enacted under the same general logic of improvements. The best known such program is the methadone treatment. According to its leading theorists, Vincent P. Dole and Marie Nyswander, methadone is to make the addict feel normal[10,13]—though he feels so with his usual supply of heroin. In practice, methadone is more addictive than heroin, even causes as many deaths as heroin.[12,14] The treatment is an "illusion of a solution."[13] But, logically, what more can you want than the restoration of normal reactions or capacities? Less scientifically logical, harsher methods were used in Japan, and its heroin epidemic was eliminated. Suffering the drug aftereffects without expectation of relief is the only way to break the vicious circle.

According to some theories addiction is comparable to illness.[10,14] Actually, drug habits are started through association with other drug addicts, as repeated studies have shown and the "subculture" theories confirm.[7,15] Why should this illness afflict New Yorkers fifty times more often than others? New York City had, at one time, 380,000 addicts, two thirds of all addicts in this country, because it is the easiest place to bring in drugs and organize their traffic.

Generally, environmental difficulties are blamed for addiction.

Environment and background conditioning are also to be blamed for crime. Yet we cannot treat criminals as victims of illness. And material difficulties are not causes of addiction, or of crime.

Amidst the endless theoretical confusion, the *scientists and experts are bound to do more harm than good with their direct improvement logic.* Experimentally, drugs always show to provide direct, initial improvement. The extensive research on marijuana, for instance, has offered ample proof that it is affectively more beneficial than harmful[10,15]—as it indeed is in its experimentally registrable direct effects. Scientists have viewed as nonaddictive a good half of the ordinary addictive means, including cocaine and alcohol, as well as the marijuana.[14,15] But the practical addiction to such means becomes flagrantly apparent. Increasingly, the "nonaddictive" drugs have had to be listed as addictive by the NIMH and FDA.[12,14]

In truth, the practical educators, and the Congress, should not wait for the scientific findings, which only add more confusion. They could decide from merely observing the amount of traffic in marijuana, LSD, pep pills, tranquilizers or other means of emotional "improvement." To the extent anything is that eagerly sought for the enjoyment, it inevitably leads to equal aftereffects and addiction.

The heated *arguments about marijuana* are typical. The more "scientific" theorists find that marijuana is nonaddictive but provides relaxation, freedom from stress, increase in creativity and self-understanding.[12,15] It is also argued that marijuana does not lead to the use of hard drugs. However, it is admitted that marijuana users become part of the drug subculture—and that this does lead to the use of other drugs.[13,14,15]

The very fact that marijuana provides particular enjoyment, as the intense traffic in it proves, is decisive. Apparently, it is a means of overenjoyment, therefore has to create opposite aftereffects and the vicious-circle worsening, to be overcome by use of stronger and stronger drugs. This is a practical, concrete addiction, whether it is called "psychological" dependence, habit formation or anything else.

It is also argued that marijuana is not worse than alcohol or tobacco, therefore should be equally legal. The universality of drinking and smoking only proves that the addictive improvements are generally attractive in their direct effects. Consequently, once an addictive means becomes part of our culture it cannot be got rid of. Legalizing the marijuana, or some other addictive means, would amount to permitting another addiction to become a perpetual, increasing source of new ills.

To the extent we permit *more freedom in use of drugs* we opt for a society of more addicts or malignantly ill, prematurely dying people. Our present addictions, smoking and alcohol, are clear causes of most of our premature deaths, particularly from cancer and heart disease.

In view of the enormous efficiency of drugs they would be used much more "effectively" than tobacco or alcohol. According to NIMH statistics narcotic drugs can shorten life by 15 to 20 years. Freer use of drugs for treatment of drug addicts would have similar malignant consequences. Strong narcotics have to be used to provide the relief. Methadone, for instance, is worse to get rid of than heroin and has to be taken for years.[13,14]

Whatever aspect of drug addiction is looked at, the admitted present *confusion is due to the very logic of the "scientism"* underlying the thinking about addiction. The paradox of worsening through improvement is self-evidently clear in addiction. But it is contrary to *every method, procedure, concept* or way of thinking of the present experimental scientism. It is not realized that all improvements turn into worsening, whether it is the emotions that drugs are sought to sustain or any "positive" effect obtained in dealing with the addiction.

Causally understood science could provide solutions in scientifically inventive, new ways, just as now the "scientific" attitudes have contributed to the increase and confusion in the addiction problems. The scientism of direct improvements in satisfactions has brought the era of pursuit of enjoyments that inevitably lead to addiction. The same improvement logic prevents effective methods for the treatment of addictions, which requires imposition of seemingly diseased restrictions.

Scientific understanding *that all overenjoyments are malignantly self-defeating* could reverse the present disastrous trend. Presently, youth believe in emotional gain through drugs and do not trust what older people say.[5,15] They would, though, accept what science shows as true.

In our scientific age, *science can influence general attitudes*. The way it has created the present trends proves this. Mere explanations, of course, have no power. But general attitudes are decisive. If science established—with a certainty as absolute as, say, that of the movement of the earth—that overenjoyments are malignantly self-defeating, this could change the general atmosphere.

Then everybody, particularly the young, following new, scientific trends, would view an addict as a moron, or a jerk unable to control himself. Such emotionally strong, general attitudes, seen as revolutionary and progressive or "modern," could turn around the youth, now increasingly succumbing to drug addiction.

Sexual Maladjustments, and Behavioral Complexes

Sexual gratifications are "scientifically" the most positive, healthy, emotionally and motivationally enriching experiences. Yet they have always been restricted or sublimated in all cultures. In their sublimated form they are the sources of satisfactions in art, music, literature, much of our ethics rooted in family, and many cultural values growing from the sense of beauty or love of nature. The rule of enrichment of satisfactions through their restriction is illustrated here. It applies to all organic value reactions. Sex is part of organic capacities or energy. When pressing work requires more effort, sexual desires decrease, as all energy is directed into the work.

If sex were not restricted or if its satisfactions were logically, directly maximized, the above values and energy would be lost. The refined sublimated cultural values could not compete with the strong natural sex drive. The crude sex would then appear as the only genuine interest. The other values would be clearly seen as pretentious, stuffy hypocrisies sustained by moralistic lies.

Such hypocrisies or distortions have been easily exposed by the radicals and hippies, even by their noted theoretical leaders, from

Paul Goodman to Herbert Marcuse. The practical results, of the counterculture and hippie movements have, however, proved that the logically real, genuine freedom in sexual enjoyments is rather disastrous. The earliest precursors of our liberated-sex movement were, perhaps, the Brethren of Free Spirit, of the fourteenth century. Their culture equally ended in degeneration. The practical social selection enforces the wisdom of restrictions.

Our general modern attitudes about sex have brought *every possible improvement* in sexual satisfactions. The progress here has been greater than any in cultural history. But the result is a virtual *disappearance of true enjoyment of sex.*[16,17,19] As Erich Fromm has pointed out, sex has become a mere fun. The progress and improvements have turned into a calamity. It seems that we have to relearn how to enjoy the "erotic exuberance" or how to "love simply, dumbly, clumsily and without reproach," as Jacques Barzun writes.[19]

Expectedly, *cultural and social restrictions are blamed* for the calamity, however flagrantly contorted such arguments have to be in view of the unprecedented modern sexual freedoms. Norman O. Brown has built a vast theory on arguments and proofs of the prevalence of sexual restrictions in our culture. Inner reaction of restrictions is certainly strong, actually excessive, after every over-enjoyment. That is part of all functional disorders. In the deeply enjoyed sexual function such restrictions, somatic and psychological, are bound to be debilitating and concrete.

They are "rationally" as well as emotionally attributed to all kinds of outside factors. Men always find reasons for their reactions that they do not causally understand. The restrictive cultural and moral tradition readily appears as the main villain. That is why authorities like Freud, Krafft-Ebing, Marie Stokes or Havelock Ellis can become prophetic leaders enthusiastically followed by the modern men.[18]

Disorders or negatively felt restrictions through sexual impoverishment are strong and "rich," because sexual overenjoyments can be equally intense due to the high pleasure value of sexual gratifications. The above authorities, particularly Freud, deserve recognition for their discovery of the sexual causes of many disorders. But the causal logic used in explaining the disorders is contrary to the actual causation. The *restrictive impoverishment is due not to restriction but to excessive pleasure release,* here as in all disorders.

The directly logical or "scientific" views are here in particular obviously wrong as well as practically harmful. The common-sense practical observation shows that people living with strict sexual morals have least of disorders. The Hutterites have been often shown as an example. It is the people with loosest sex habits that have most disorders. As Hobart Mowrer writes, if Freud were right the psychopaths would be people living in saintliness, whereas the reverse is true. Statistics, notably from the Cattell-Sheier survey, have shown that priests and prisoners suffer least from anxiety disorders. The licentious beat generation has, perhaps, proved best what happens in practice.

The most important fact about sexual life is that *its pleasures or satisfactions cannot exist without equal need as accumulated non-satisfactions or restrictions.* It is amazing how this simple fact, evident from every natural need and satisfaction, is overlooked, by doctors and psychiatrists, as well as by the more popular "experts" writing the perennial best-sellers on sex.

Demand for expert help in matters of sex is constantly increasing, as the virtual modern calamity of loss of sexual enjoyments and capacities is afflicting progressively more people. The foremost medical experts, William H. Masters and Virginia E. Johnson, have offered authoritative help in various forms—lately with quite traditional moral interpretations.[16] Still the underlying assumption is that sexual pleasures are not limited in themselves and can be increased or enriched by added skill and effort.[16] Similar views were expressed before by another great authority, Karl Menninger, who even found praise for better lovemaking techniques.

In any event, the simple, all-important causal dependence of sexual satisfaction on its opposite, the need as nonsatisfaction or restriction, has not yet been recognized.

Particularly the "expert" advice that people are getting most extensively is perpetuating *the blunder about limitless sexual pleasures.* Every few months we have some best-seller in the field, as the jaundiced readers are seeking for relief. The very gist of the expertise here is that sexual pleasures are a limitless bonanza. You only have to learn the techniques, tricks and methods of how to increase the pleasures. This is the way to intense sexual overenjoyments, with equally acute functional impoverishment as inevitable aftereffects.

The normal sexual life, in all cultures, has been one of restrictions. The sexual, as other restrictions are not felt while they remain constant. Moreover, in difference from animals ruled by sexual seasons, man has merely to keep the sex potential available, without the need to exercise it. Minimal amount of restrictions makes this possible. Even animals living in sexual isolation, in zoos, fare better and live longer, if otherwise suited to such life.

Also, the extensive sublimation of sexual interests into cultural values becomes richer, more satisfactory under continuous restrictions. Particularly in the early years of life sexual releases have to be restricted, to provide such sublimation as well as later sex pleasures. Early exercise of sex life makes the individual intellectually less curious and culturally obtuse.[17]

These wisdoms still persist in our culture. But the *"scientific" liberalism is prevailing.* Justifications for the moral restrictions are now sought in logical, liberal terms. It is argued, for instance, that premarital intercourse should not be condemned if the lovers are really, truly in love.[17,18] But any emotion seems completely real and true under a strong, permitted need, as the sexual drive is when it is felt as right and is let free.

Further, the defenders of tradition have to yield to the "scientific" arguments that the positive gratifications of sex are to be made free and fully satisfactory, particularly through sex education. Apparently, the restricting sexual hangovers are felt by many and are attributed to lack of enlightened freedoms. *Sex education in schools* becomes an acute issue. This is witnessed by the activity of wide organizations—SOS, CHIDE, POSSE, PAUSE, SIECUS and related groups—fighting for and against sex education. It is always argued that the negative, restricting feelings, shame or guilt, should be removed, by the education.[18]

Actually, strong negative feelings can arise only through overenjoyments. Guilt and shame come from overenjoyed feelings of merit and pride. This can serve the purposes of restriction in traditional morals. But if sex education really succeeded, to improve a wide range of enjoyments—which here would easily turn into overenjoyments—then equally extensive negative feelings would emerge. Fortunately, sex education never achieves what it intends.

Teachers, as all of us, are dominated by taboos on sex, because cultural conditioning has to be and is an emotional reality, independent from ideas entertained by the person. It is these feelings, the taboos, that are further conveyed to the pupils in class, whatever the ideas taught. This is constantly found to be so, as a great obstacle, by the reformers themselves.[18]

The usual arguments about children lacking the necessary information, getting it from the street, and so on, are superficial. Information or ideas can always be easily acquired and are motivationally unimportant. Children, getting curious about these matters, could learn everything they need to know from a two-page explanation.

The general attitudes of unlimited sexual hedonism may even contribute to *sexual deviations*. Sexual mechanisms can always be radically "improved," by circumventing their restrictive natural requirements of having a highly select partner of opposite sex and a special refined natural or cultural stimulation. If partners of opposite sex are not available, masturbation or homosexual intercourse may be resorted to; and once a way of release is found it strengthens by itself. Or when the normal, refined and restrictive mechanisms become exhausted, more primitive, excessive, direct stimulations may be sought, as in sadism, pederasty or other sexual deviations.

The "improvements" in the sexual as in any function can only lead to exhaustion through overenjoyment. Sexual deviations are due to some exhaustion or impoverishment in the sexual function, however involved the effects. Even the deviations that are genetic, as some of them seem to be, may be due to overenjoyment—in the previous generation. The way one generation lives has an effect on the next, as common sense tells, and as we shall see in discussing genetics.

The point is that "improvements" are eagerly sought and easily attained in sex enjoyments. But overenjoyments are the ways how man brings on himself functional disorders. Yet modern scientists and "experts" always help us to reach the most effective direct improvements—starting with the approval of masturbation as an easy relief.

A more general effect of our liberal and hedonistic attitudes about sex is the *disintegration of the modern family*. The changes here have been "revolutionary," as is being written about and discussed every day.[17,18] Modern marriages are founded on sexual attraction or on love that is mostly sexual. To the extent that anything is started as enjoyment it has to end in lassitude and hangover. Practical common-sense observation shows that this is so. Inevitability of exhaustion upon overenjoyment is the simple causal, scientific explanation.

The *"sexual compatibility,"* thought as decisively important, may serve as illustration. Practically, enjoyment of sex in the most "compatible," fullest way is comparable to overeating because of availability of voluptuous, spicy foods. The result is satiation and disorder. That is why "the better a marriage is, the worse its partners will sometimes feel," as Richard Farson writes.

Particularly because marriage is many more things than sex, the overenjoyments and overvaluations between spouses coming from their sexual relations lead to weariness and undervaluation between them in the wider whole of their marital life. The "beautiful people," movie stars and millionaires, who can choose the sexually most "compatible" partners, have least of happy marital life, though they want it as much as everybody else.

Family has been the basis of our culture and social health. It is disintegrating, and new forms of marriage are sought, because the traditional married life is found unsatisfactory. *This is inevitable as long as constant improvements in sexual enjoyments are viewed as goals of life.* Everybody can see that heightened sexual enjoyments are not attainable within marriage. They have to be sought outside it.

What is generally not understood is that sexual enjoyments as satisfactions or releases are strictly limited to equal needs as nonsatisfactions or restrictions. If the enjoyments are improved, in varied, ingenious ways, then as "ingenious" disorders and incapacities follow, in equally varied, strangely unrecognizable, opposite ways.

Sexual maladjustments are only one, though important, example of how any, seemingly free enjoyment can bring strange opposite feelings, disorders, or *complexes*. These reactions presently remain causal mysteries, because as the opposites of the enjoyment they seem least related to it. Here belong various complexes, like those of inferiority, shyness or guilt, that are constant practical problems for many people. Behavioral scientists and experts here are least helpful. They always accept the logic of direct emotional improvements, which are the very cause of these complexes and reactions.

Inferiority complex is a frequent behavioral affliction of modern men. The person suffering from it is usually one having superior qualities. He may know very well that he is superior and still suffer from the complex. In truth, exactly the person who enjoys his superiority is the one affected.

This is confirmed by the best known work on inferiority complex, namely, by Alfred Adler. He observed, as his case studies show, that the patients suffered from inferiority feelings, sense of failure, dissatisfactions and avoidances exactly where they had particularly tried to enjoy the feelings of superiority and success. To explain how a person reaches the opposite of what he wants and enjoys most, Adler developed his theory that the person unconsciously wants to fail because of conflicts between his aspirations of superiority and sense of inferiority forced on him by social conditions, culture and education.

In our modern life the inferiority complex is frequent, because overenjoyment of superiority has become almost a necessity. In competition for position or prestige between modern urban "strangers," success depends on how superior one can make himself appear to be. The way to play this role successfully is to feel genuinely and aggressively one's own superiority. Such an exaggeration in feelings is inevitably followed by equally strong, unwanted, totally dissimilar, therefore causally unrecognized opposite feelings.

Guilt complex can become a disturbing, unproductive reaction, though the normal sense of guilt, as conditioned nonsatisfaction, is the source of positive motivations. We are strongly, concretely motivated by pride as we avoid conditioned guilt or shame. Irrational, incapacitating feeling of guilt arises upon exaggerated or unwarranted enjoyment of pride. If one fails in his business because of bad luck he can start anew with rational confidence. But if he overenjoyed the success of his business even where it was not due to his merit or was due to luck, he is bound to suffer irrational, depressing guilt even if the failure was not his fault.

You cannot cherish or be proud of something, for a long time, then, rationally, forget about it when it becomes unattainable or disappointing.

The opposite feelings, of guilt and merit, or of shame and pride are interdependent. Everybody can see this, by simple commonsense insight. If one falls while dancing he feels shame, to the extent he enjoyed the pride or showmanship. Less shame would be felt if he danced reluctantly or recognizing his clumsiness. But the causation through opposites can never be accepted by scientists and experts. They always try to help us remedy our complexes by explaining and urging, logically, that we should improve or increase our positive feelings, though this can only deepen the complex.

Excessive shyness may be another good example of complexes that seem to have no apparent causes. The person suffering from it has least reason to feel shy. He is the one who aspires most to have, and has to a high degree, the qualities of social grace or refinement that should make one feel least shy. Moreover, shy persons are individuals living in a rich inner world where they enjoy at will the feelings of these desired qualities. Thus they have more than others of accumulated feelings or inner experiences ensuring them against shyness.

But here, as in all overenjoyments, the result is an opposite reaction. The boy secretly in love with a girl dreams of her and enjoys feeling himself attractive, intelligent or suave in the imagined situations with her. Then upon meeting the girl in reality he feels much like a man having lived in warmth and being exposed to outside air.

The decisive factor is the exaggerated, prolonged enjoyment of a feeling. A return to reality or normal conditions from a long excessive experience becomes an equally strong change in the opposite direction. Milk tastes bitter after you have drunk very sweet coffee. The point is that *normal conditions become here causes of abnormality* which thus seems to arise without cause—or for some mysterious reason. Also, the person does not know that he lives with exaggerated feelings. They have become for him a general inner atmosphere. Only when transition from it to the outside world becomes necessary, the complex emerges.

There are as many complexes as the values we overenjoy. In fact, everybody has some complex, to the extent he has tended to overvaluate himself in some quality. Conversely, "positive complexes" are possible. They are not strong or frequent, because nobody indulges in genuinely depreciating himself.

Complexes as minor disorders and disabilities we constantly live with are rarely recognized, except for the stronger ones, like those of inferiority or guilt. People merely reckon that men are often unreasonable or react irrationally. Scientists and experts, finding in such reactions all kinds of negative feelings as the immediate causes, try to help us overcome such feelings.

This is a nuisance. Overcoming or avoidance of the feeling of inferiority is what creates the inferiority complex. Here, as everywhere, the *improvement of a value reaction above normalcy— above values warranted by the reality—leads to the opposite reaction.*

VII

HUMANISTIC VALUE DELUSIONS AND
THE MODERN ILLS

In the past the humanistic learning supported the restrictive moral and cultural traditions. But the modern humanistic attitudes are becoming logical and "scientific," which practically amounts to turning against restrictions. For logically and "scientifically" values, as satisfactions and freedoms or releases, are expected to grow from backgrounds of a like nature, of satisfactions and freedoms.

Restrictions are condemned by the most vocal modern humanists exposing the traditional superstitions, seeming backwardness and hypocrisy. The moral and cultural tradition had to be superstitious and contradictory. The humanistic thought has always extolled the belief that values derive from positive value sources. Since the opposite is causally true, the practical need for the restrictions or conditioned nonsatisfactions had to be explained by superstitious and contradictory inventions.

Superstition and hypocrisy had to become part of the continuous, deceptive tradition. Above all, the modern "science" has proved the old restrictions to be sources of stress and disorders. We saw how restrictions appear, experimentally, as causes of disease— while they restore the release reserves.

The modern humanists are succeeding in their liberalist rejection of restrictions. The modern, rich life and the permissive, "scientific" attitudes provide and encourage unlimited enjoyments or improvements in our feelings of well-being. The end result is an increase in the vicious-circle overenjoyments and functional diseases, as well as in the other modern, self-inflicted ills.

In addition, all humanistic thought promotes the self-enslavement by men to their own, "neurotic," value fixations. This thought stresses the verity of our deepest values. And nothing is felt more deeply or richly than the endlessly elaborate fixational values. Fixations are dominating the cultural or social customs and values that matter most. Further, fixations as well as the diametrically wrong humanistic causal logic are perpetuating the value delusions, contradictions and self-defeat in esthetics, art or literature, and particularly in philosophy.

Humanistic Truths Become Practical Fallacies

Important, concretely decisive attitudes result from the humanistic causal delusions about our practical everyday values. Love, freedom, beauty or positive interests are pleasurable satisfactions. Under the nonrelative, "logical" humanistic thought these values are to be increased directly, by creating more possibilities for their enjoyment. This promotes the trend of more satisfactions and freedoms, hedonism and permissiveness, in our culture and education. The result is a *total change in our cultural tradition.* Of course, most, people still have a good intuition for what is right. But unless the true causality of our common values is explained scientifically, that intuition cannot be sustained in our scientific age and is to wane.

Love has been hailed as the greatest value on earth, in every kind of theory, by Empedocles and Plato, or Buber and Tillich.[3] Is has also been shown to be the deepest satisfaction and fulfillment, sometimes compared to the highest sexual gratifications. One can refer here to the greatest authorities, old and new—from saints and prophets to modernists like Sorokin, Unamuno or Sir Julian Huxley.[1]

Love is seen as a panacea not only in education but also in medicine and psychiatry, as has been notably explained by Menninger or Reik. In a collection of articles, *Love Today,*[3] the powers of love are expounded as solutions for nearly every human problem.

We fully agree that love can be the panacea for all our main ills. This only proves that satisfactions or pleasure releases are the sources of all human capacities and well-being. For love is merely a wealth of satisfactions and releases, or of motivations for their attainment. In any language "love" expresses some high enjoyment or motivation, of virtue as well as sin. One can love his fellow men, or his drink. Particularly, people "love" to hurt each other —when they need compensations for their overenjoyment after-effects.

In brief, love is an organic satisfaction. *It can derive only from an equal need as nonsatisfaction.* The need here is mainly the first, most powerful of all needs—that of survival. The child knows, instinctively, that he cannot survive if he does not follow his parents. He does whatever they want him to do, to conserve their favor. This conditioning of course goes on every minute of the child's life. That is why it is so powerful; and as little noticed as the atmosphere we live in. The parents only want the child to be like they are. They simply treat him, instinctively, as part of themselves—which is the highest love. The greater the security they offer, the more threatening appears to the child any loss in it.

Thus love and refined perfection of security are the means of conditioning. But the underlying force is the threat to survival, the most infernal of all threats. The heavenly love, the satisfaction, is as strong as is this threat, the conditionally nonsatisfied need.

The need-satisfaction equality is evident in every kind of love. Trained animals really love their master. But this love is created by conditioning the animals' fears, deprivations and needs. If the trainer applied real love, satisfying what the animals really want, they would remain wild beasts.

Men love God to the extent they suffer threats or needs. Disasters and afflictions are the surest things to make people turn to their "loving" gods, with feelings of love and gratitude. Peoples have gods where they have dire needs, threats, dangers, fears, or values growing from needs. Of course, such love of God is deeply genuine—because the needs are distressingly real.

The point is that love is a gratifying, easy, warm, heavenly and positively felt satisfaction to the same extent that its causal source is a hard, threatening, infernal, negatively felt need. Here, as in any value experience, the positive capacity, satisfaction or release has to be "paid" for by equal opposite hardship, nonsatisfaction or restriction. If love came "logically," as a gratifying capacity to be increased by addition, by its more intense enjoyment, *people would just be paragons of endless love.* For who does not want gratifications, that also become the most positive capacities?

Yet every theorist or expert on love has only extolled the deeply gratifying, freely available satisfactions of love providing us with enriching, positive motivations and interests. Any idea about the ugly value opposites would be rejected as a horrible fallacy. The classic expert on love, Pitirim Sorokin, has stressed it as a freely flowing gratification and enrichment, to be attained by insight, explanation, identification, acceptance, catharsis, transfiguration, and similar gratifying, near-ecstatic experiences.[2;16]

Of course, a thinker like Sorokin had to notice that love is often too clearly born from suffering, frustration or calamity. But he has explained this as a process of clarification of insights, through "polarization" of values.[16] Another authority, Rollo May, sees love as a "sharing of pleasure and delight" with others, or as ecstatic acceptance of the universe, that men miss because of philosophical misunderstandings about the "daimonic" principle, lack of "intentionality," misunderstood nature of love, or failure to expand consciousness.[6]

The fallacies about love as gratification to be freely enjoyed have led to practical misunderstandings and failures. The worst aspects of the "free" education originate from such misunderstandings. If the love is a free, natural enjoyment, then strenuous effort or discipline should be avoided. In the simplest case, the result is a spoilt child. In our schools, the damages of "free" education are repaired, from time to time, by return to conventional methods after repeated disastrous experiments.

The "alienation" of our youth, that has particularly shown in the generation gap, or in the student riots, is another inevitable result. If love is expected to be received as a free, generously, unconditionally given feeling, then parents and educators are hypocrites imposing, in practice, unnecessary, evil repressions, and telling lies.

Love is only one, though the most important, of the practical values that humanists have completely misinterpreted causally. We may look at *beauty* as, probably, the second most glorified human value. The esthetic values are often hailed as the highest goals of human culture, and as deeply revealing sources for knowledge.[1;6;7] They are accepted as solutions for the difficulties of modern life.[1;9] Even our moral, altruistic growth is, assumedly, nurtured by esthetic experiences.[1;11] Beauty is the very prototype of sublime, spiritual value, in philosophy and literature.

But beauty is a satisfaction growing from base, harassing non-satisfactions or disturbances. There is hardly a difference between esthetic enjoyment of the beauty of nature and finding satisfaction in sexual admiration, soothing rest, drinking cool water after thirst, or eating after hunger. Evidently, the enjoyments of rest, food or water result from hardships of exertion, hunger and thirst. Sexual satisfactions come from base, harassing instinctive drives. Our strongest values, earthly or sublime, derive from our needs of survival or security, from infernal threats to our existence.

A feeling of beauty of any exalted intensity could be created by previous imposition of equally strong deprivation, need or threat. Think of the beauty of the world sublime beyond words for the man doomed to death permitted to live. Deprivations or threats cannot be imposed experimentally. But "experiments" in which the positive opposite is induced first and the negative follows next are being performed by the thousands of drug users every day. The feelings created by drugs can be as sublime and genuine as the most spiritual experiences. This has been confirmed by scientists, philosophers and writers—William James, Henri Bergson, Aldous Huxley or Somerset Maugham.[16]

The causal interdependence of the value opposites is equally clear whether the negative, or the positive experience takes place first. The evidence is striking. A highly effective drug, like the LSD, creates an experience of supreme beauty or religious exaltation, stronger than the person has ever known. But the aftereffects are a virtual inferno, so horrifying or impoverishing that the person may commit suicide or kill somebody in bestial rage.

The advocates of deep esthetic enjoyments should remember that every enjoyment or pleasure release brings an equal opposite

value experience—that efforts to increase or deepen any enjoyment are simply self-defeating.

Of course, the role of esthetics in our culture is as complex as
all human adjustments are. Art serves the conditioning and refinement of interests in our "spiritual," traditionally restrictive cultural
life. In all conditioning, pleasure releases have to be used, as
inducements, to attain restriction of pleasures, in the end.

Feelings of beauty are *mysteriously confusing* also because, in
human thinking, beauty includes all the generally integrated value
reactions that go beyond separate concrete satisfactions like eating
or enjoying rest. Such generally integrated feelings may include
all kinds of satisfactions—of security, growth, or physiologic comfort—in all their *myriad complexity* of natural purposes evolved
through millions of years. The feeling of beauty is experienced by
us as a pleasure integrated through "every cell" in us.

The main source of mystery is, of course, the never suspected
causal relation of beauty to its value opposites. In your enjoyment
of the quietude and fresh air of the country, the causal source is
the past background of noise and smoke of the city. But value
opposites are so totally different from each other that in a complex
feeling like beauty nobody sees them as related.

In our strongest experiences of beauty their causal backgrounds
are our equal most disturbing needs, of survival, security or growth
—the accumulated nonsatisfactions in such needs, the past harassments or threats. But when the deep involved feeling of beauty
as the mysterious *integrated strong satisfaction* of the equal needs
arises, it is accepted in its totality, of nature and origin, as a
supreme value in itself. You may feel as if every disturbing question has been answered and every mystery solved.

Strong experience of beauty has been sometimes described as
leading to a sense of discovery of God.[11] This is ironic, considering the real causal sources of such experiences. But the deception
is neither strange nor rare. A simple drug, triggering organic releases, and causing infernal aftereffects, can bring a sublime sense
of religious "revelations."[7] Any value, a heavenly exaltation or
an ordinary satisfaction, derives from its opposites. You may read
a novel or watch a movie for its happy ending; but such ending

would be nonsensical without the anxieties and difficulties preceding it.

What is true of love or beauty applies to other values. For instance, our sense of *order or harmony* in the universe grows from our desperate need to find it amidst the chaos that governs the universe. As men painstakingly work for and constantly center on the rare, desperately wanted order, they value it above everything else and finally see it as the very essence of their world.

Similarly, we concentrate on, and view as the essences of our lives, the *"purposes" and "truths"* that we badly need because of their factual lack or rarity.[16] *Morals* is a primary value because it is wanting. Natural appetites, like sex, may be as important as morals for normal life. But they are not valued, because they are never lacking.

Happiness is the main value in practical life. And as we saw, it clearly comes from its value opposites. The surest way to lose it is to try to attain or enjoy it in the strongest, direct way. Those who have written about happiness have found it paradoxical.[5,16] Interestingly the writers often fail to connect experience of happiness with the opposite backgrounds they themselves describe.[16] Usually, a moment of bliss is described, as occurring after or during a period of great stress which is mentioned only incidentally or as a curious coincidence.[16]

Inducement of feelings of bliss through painful torment or exhaustion has been always practically known. It has been practiced by shamans, flagellants, penitents, ascetics, yoga, practitioners of Zen, or savages performing exhaustive dance rituals.

One can easily see how life could be more productive, rational or farsighted, and free of disorders, if the old restrictive wisdoms about happiness could be sustained, against the modern hedonistic drives. And no loss—or gain—in happiness would result.

We have to mention *Freedom,* the highest social value, extolled everywhere and by everybody. In itself, without restrictions as its opposites, freedom has no meaning. Freedom has become the highest value—repeated in constitutions, revolutionary movements, and everyday aspirations—as people have met with tightening social restrictions. Since the more advanced people have established more of the necessary social restrictions, they also have richer theories, monuments and ideas about the value of freedom. Moreover, a highly advanced people living in the atmosphere of continuous social restrictions do not notice them particularly, and rather praise the few freedoms they enjoy or aspire to.

It then may look as if the more advanced peoples have progressed because of their pursuit of the value of freedom. This is what humanistic theorists are teaching as scientific truths. These then are brought to the less advanced emerging nations, by their educated leaders, though their people need social restrictions more than anything else. The civilized nations have become possible because their people have built the tradition of hard restrictions through hundreds of years.

In conclusion, we have to explain that by exposing the negatively felt, causal sources of value reactions *we are not rejecting values.* On the contrary, we are explaining them causally, and that is the only, scientific way of how to promote them. The humanistic value beliefs, contrary to causal truths, rather exacerbate the modern fallacies. Logical emphasis on direct value enjoyments and freedoms leads to hedonism and permissiveness. Values are lost, not advanced by attitudes contrary to causal facts.

Values as the positive reactions, satisfactions or releases, constitute our capacities. However, they can be increased not directly or "logically, by their greater enjoyment, but by the hard accumulation of their negatively felt, opposite causal sources, the conditioned nonsatisfactions as needs, or restrictions.

Culture Dominated by Value Fixations

The humanistic belief in the *verity of our deepest values* has a particularly insidious impact, in practice, through the cultural *fixations,* which determine our ways of life. For our fixations have the deepest or truest value for us, while they actually may be as irrational and useless as neuroses. We explained the vicious-circle growth of fixations through merely accidental or meaninglessly recurring, initially insignificant value experiences.

You may recognize the fixational nature of irrational customs, taboos or "culture" of primitives who may spend all their surplus means and efforts on elaborate, often disfiguring fashions or endless rituals. But we are not different. *We equally have no understanding of our self-enslavement to fixations.* In effect, our beliefs in values, which sustain our fixations and are deepened by them, are worse than primitive. They are exactly contrary to causal facts. And value beliefs or feelings determine here what seems right or true. We may not accept cults or taboos incompatible with scientific knowledge; but no such knowledge exists in regard to fixations and values.

It is important to note that *fixations are strongest where people use their surpluses* of means or free time, and that surpluses are the factor that makes progress possible. If a people have little of surplus, they merely satisfy their primary, natural needs, while struggling with natural difficulties, in the rationally most efficient, nonfixational ways. Nature, in difference from the men-created culture, does not favor fixations, which are harmful to survival.

Animals, in experiments, did at first fixate on some one food. But their natural needs soon forced them to seek other foods. This shows that fixational tendencies are inherent in organic value experiences but that natural selection counteracts them. Also, restrictions on enjoyments, in general, counteract fixations, which are outgrowths of tendencies to deepen satisfactions.

Thus fixations are bound to be strongest in the enjoyment of *cultural or social values,* beyond natural needs, and in the use of surpluses by peoples who are *not restricting* themselves nor are engaged in strenuous practical efforts of survival or of aspired progress. Our latest culture is fraught with such conditions, conducive to fixations. Our own-created cultural or social values, in relation to natural needs, are becoming dominant. The argument that men seek variety becomes untrue. In experiments, men do prefer variety, in colors or forms. But such natural, primordial, "childish" preferences are of no consequence amidst our *cultural or social* elaborations as tremendously vast as is the modern efficiency.

It cannot be overemphasized that *surpluses,* whether in capital, time or other means, are what *make all progress possible.* There is no progress if people merely get even in their bare survival. But in our present culture most of the surpluses—everything above the primary necessities—is wasted on fixations.

We spend all our surplus resources and efforts on what fashions or customs say is "in," right, beautiful, enjoyable or new, though it may be less beautiful, less worthwhile and even less enjoyable than what we have already. The proverbial competition with Joneses that governs most of our lives consists of such efforts. For instance, in the garment industry, more effort is spent on fashion, attraction, "beauty," or frills than on real usefulness, comfort or beauty. The expensive fashions of today will look ridiculously ugly a couple of years from now. Whether it is the women's contorted gowns or men's ties, we are compelled by the fixational fashion or custom. Without it we could have simple, comfortable, really beautiful clothes; for beautiful is what is naturally simple.

The fashions in clothes are only a more visible example. All other *surplus spending by modern man*—on cars, homes, furnishings, or social "musts"—is similar. Billions of dollars are spent on advertising and selling, as well as producing, what is merely fashionable. To take only the yearly change of cars because of new models, it has cost us hundreds of billions of dollars over the years—enough to bring progress to underdeveloped countries of the world.

The extensive use of the car, in general, is mostly due to a value fixation, that grows from the natural pleasure of riding. In all times carriages or coaches have been fashionable in similar ways. Our "car culture" is not rational.[10]

We never see the irrationality of our fixations, because they are part of the atmosphere we live in. Only by looking at some customs in other cultures we can see how costly and irrational they are. The social or *cultural musts and status competition* may consume the whole life effort of those people who have most of surpluses to spend. The latest modern fixations on social musts and "status" are particularly costly, because of the mass following and competition. The Christmas season alone determines the course of commerce and great part of industry for months, while billions of dollars are wasted.

All kinds of observances, or of competition with the Joneses have been constantly increasing. Most everybody now participates in the expanding "social" or seasonal events and celebrations, from yearly vacations to lavish weddings. Merely because we "must" or something is "in" we waste on appearances, fashionable living, social observances, "cultural" interest of the moment, conspicuous consumption, or pursuit of habits set by stardom people.

Our whole material culture consists of such efforts. Marxists and radicals can easily prove how every one of our cultural values amounts to a useless "bourgeois" aberration, though they themselves evolve even stronger fixational cults.

Fixations become sacred institutions or *intensely enjoyed interests,* even if there is no rational basis for it. Our sports, like baseball or football, are an example. People from some different culture would find our games hardly of interest and our often hysteric enthusiasm about them ridiculous for adult people. But from within our culture it is foolish even to question the value of the games, though objectively their influence is appalling. Such sports make our youth, even that capable of direct intellectual interests, imitate as their heroes men excelling merely through superior muscles and reflexes of animals.

Even more serious than our fashions and everyday customs are our *cultural value fixations.* Our sacred values of liberty, individuality, human nature, basic rights, or constitutionality, are actually fixations about our *ways of life.* Any one of them can mean, and has meant, different things at different times with their peculiar fixational ways and *"truths."* But such values are invoked as sacred, unquestionable verities. They become the greatest obstacles to progress.

Stagnation and fixational self-enslavement become sacredly strong, while progress requires "impossible" new changes and rationally planned effort. We shall see how social integration is progressing while the humanists are decrying the horrors of "anthill" society and "brainwashing"; or how the human race is being abominably degraded because of sacred protection of our primitive reproduction habits. Eugenic control could save millions of individuals from shameful suffering. But fixations are strongest in such most important areas, governed by the ways of life that have been always there.

Fixation is strong in formation of our *"higher" culture,* arts, literature, contemporary thought and social conformity. The very notions of what is culture, learning, or treasures of our civilization are determined by fixations or tradition. We are as limited as the Medieval scholars were in clinging to their learning or sacred treasures; only names have changed, and proliferated. The humanistic belief in the deepest, "truest" value feelings still dominates our higher culture, though the source of such feelings is mostly the "rich" but meaningless, accidental fixations.

Conformity of behavior and opinion grows, much like fashions, through the vicious circle of fixations. People know intuitively, from experience, that once a value starts becoming somewhat general it can acquire strength beyond all reason. Everybody fears to be left out of what others value, therefore rushes into the new fashion—which further reinforces it. Thus an accidental preponderance of a value, at one moment, can start its continuous vicious-circle dominance.

The self-enforcing irrationality of *fixations can cripple behavior.* Cults of cattle, bulls or cows, for instance, emerged among various peoples, Egyptians, Greeks or Hindus. The reason was the continuance of the appreciation of the animals. Repeated valuation of an object starts a fixation. As the object is valued, the capacity to appreciate it increases, and it is valued even more. The vicious circle then can create peculiar excesses. The cow has become so sacred to the Hindus that its use is now limited, though initially it was the wide use of the cow that started the fixation.

Also a less usual event or coincidence can start a fixation if, at the time, valuations around it become somewhat general, as in the fashions. Observances of foods, like those of kosher, may start with accidental associations having, evidently, no valid justification. But by continued fixation an observance can acquire a value so deep that nobody dares to question the crippling enslavement to it.

In our fixations we avoid beliefs that are superstitious in the light of our sciences. But there is no science yet about values or about the fixation itself. When we oppose construction of a dam or atomic plant to protect a hill, or a river bend painted by a school of painters, we are not very different from the Indians who were awed by their sacred caves or mountain tops. Any place or object can become truly sacred, in every way, once the value fixation around it has started, accidentally. Any other river bend could have served equally well to start that painting fashion or the later fixation about the place.

We admit that *fixations can, often, serve moral and creatively cultural goals,* by strengthening the tradition, of restrictive conditioning. Cultural and moral customs are easier followed or expanded when we have pre-established pathways and backgrounds for doing so. Moral commands and beliefs acquire force of taboos and of fixational compulsions. The customary becomes unquestionable.

Still, fixations always tend to deepen what is gratifying, easy, selfish, wasteful and emotional or irrational. In contrast, difficult restrictions, or hard rational values, like the love that brings utopian benefits for all in the end, is required in creative morals. That is why *some richest, most elaborate morals lack real, creative morality.* The humanistic attitudes here are least helpful. They favor the emotional, positively felt, gratifying, divinely rich cults and values.

However, cultures and morals are always complex, and interference with them can be destructive. Pleasures are often used as inducements in restrictive conditioning. A custom may be irrationally fixational, but if it is discredited, as a superstition, the people who followed it may lose their moral discipline, that was conditioned under the custom.

In sum, our culture is dominated by value fixations, particularly in our use of surplus means and of surplus time or capacities. Fixations are insidious because they turn our *accidental* or essentially *meaningless* customs and fashions into *unquestionable* values. We are not different here from savages spending all their efforts, above primary needs, on silly ornamentations or rituals without stopping to think how they could make their lives completely different. For as regards the "rich" fixational values, we are equally ignorant about our enslavement to our own-created fixational ghosts.

And as we saw, it is the *surplus* that makes all progress possible but is now wasted. A hundred years from now it will seem strange how we could waste our surpluses on silly fashions and other fixational musts while capital accumulation was badly needed to bring about a different future miraculous by our standards.

Humanistic Delusions in Art, Literature and Philosophy

The humanistic world is best represented in art, literature and philosophy. The typical humanistic fallacies are also best revealed here.

Art turns into a mockery under fixations and causal confusion about esthetic experience. Literary appreciation is also distorted by fixations. Moreover, literary fiction, in general, is causally incongruous, because writers have least of the wholesome, practical intuition of what is causally true. Such intuition is embodied in the practical, "contradictory," seemingly superstitious and hypocritical restrictive tradition, which the authors oppose most. Finally, philosophy has perpetuated every humanistic causal delusion about values, knowledge, mind and the universe. This has led to the admission, in philosophy itself, that it is an impossible, futile task, in its usual, normal form.

ART AND ESTHETICS have become a religion for the most civilized modern men. Would anybody aspiring to be a cultural person dare to reject the admiration of art? The cult here has come by value fixations, as all cults have. It has an aura of higher culture because it has come from the higher, more educated, leisurely classes. Christianity similarly came with the higher, Roman civilization, and at the period of its peak fluorish nobody dared to reject it, for fear of being viewed as uncouth barbarian.

The point is that presently the adoration of esthetics is a *superstitious cult*. It may be good for cultural conditioning—for refined restriction of cruder natural drives—as many cults are.

But art admirers view it as a higher, even metaphysically spiritual value without knowing what it is or does.[11,12] This is superstition. Even the best authorities in the field do not know for sure what art is, and can offer only endless, controversial theories,[11,12] as we shall see in a moment. The cultic nature of art is particularly evident from the requirement that the admired work be an original, not an imitation.

The old masters, even the most original modern painters—Picasso, Matisse, Modigliani, Braque, Klee, Miro or Chagal—have been imitated to perfection. Objectively, the works of all of them, particularly of the old masters could be improved in their every curious aspect. Forgers, like David Stein or Elmyr de Hory, have imitated series of masters, and have done it so well that not even experienced art collectors can discover the fake. Experts have to use special techniques, analyses and X-rays to distinguish originals; and only half a dozen specialists for each master or period can safely tell an imitation.

Thus as regards everybody, except the rare experts, museums should offer us enjoyment from widest choices of imitated, and improved, masterpieces. *Such an idea is a sacrilege, because modern esthetics is a religion.* Only the original work, much like the true bone of a saint or the hair of the prophet, is a proper object for the adoration. We do not doubt the genuiness of the esthetic experience of most art admirers. It may be deep, rich and true in every respect. But so are all fixational values; we explained why.

Art is a perfect medium for fixations. The value object here yields enough pleasure and a wealth of enrichment of background for further appreciation, to make the vicious circle deepen with automatic inevitability. Esthetics will grow as a perfect modern cult, as long as the self-enslavement through fixations is not understood—whatever its incidental merits.

The esthetic cult can have aspects of a religion also because of *the mysterious value of experiences of beauty.* Here we have to expose the prosaic, rather ugly causation of such experiences. It is regrettable to turn against esthetics, which plays important role in cultural conditioning. But perhaps the understanding of what is true—simply, causally or scientifically true—has a priority for man as intelligent being.

Anyway, the real source of our feelings of beauty is not any higher spiritual reality but *the causal opposites of the value of beauty*. Among these opposites are our disturbing natural needs, harrowing drives, nonsatisfactions, wants and oppressive threats. Particularly the needs of survival and sex are involved. We used as illustration the man condemned to death permitted to live, who sees the world sublimely beautiful. We also saw the causal dependence between paradisiac beauty induced by a drug, like LSD, and the infernal aftereffects.

Everything that is negative, and general, in our existence, serves as the causal source for the general positive reaction—by "every cell" in our body—that we designate as beauty. Because of the myriad complexity of nature, the process is bound to appear a mystery. It is not difficult, though, to see that ultimately the esthetic values are of organic origin. For instance, feelings about perfection of the human body or of nature correspond to organic values.

Art can *intensify such values* with endless inventiveness, that can become equally mysterious because the underlying value causation is not recognized. For instance, contrast by underemphasis or imperfection[11] may be used to bring out emphasis or perfection, though the artist may not understand the exact causation. In a more direct way, a natural stimulus can be artificially intensified. In painting, the colors and forms can be manipulated, contrasted, purified, refined, exagerated and enriched endlessly.[12] In music, its standard value, of human voice, can be amplified or refined hundredfold by instruments and orchestra.

But however manipulated, the values of beauty or esthetics are, ultimately, *organic therefore subject to the opposite value causation*. The negative causal opposites, though, are never suspected. The experience of beauty—already unfathomable in its natural myriad complexity—becomes even more mysterious in esthetics.[12]

Under this sense of mystery fixation rules supreme. It is fixation that determines whether an artist is worshipped as a genius or remains unknown. As a work of an artist is noticed and evaluated, the background for its enjoyment expands, which leads to still more evaluation of it. All that is needed to start this vicious-circle fixation is to attract attention.

Here the phenomenon of *contrast* helps. A style or a work of art appears more striking when it is presented as a contrast against previous background. *Originality* in art has this effect, therefore is so important. The highest "originality" is reached in the modern art as it replaces the previous artistic refinement with abstract smears, or beauty with ugliness.

Thus the modern artist can legitimately attract greatest attention by *absurdity*, as did Picasso by painting disjointed noses and limbs, or eyes in the stomach. Once the fixation is started, by the attention, the value feeling for the work or style deepens, into a genuine, rich appreciation. Also, the artist may, indeed, feel reaching greater originality by extreme contrasting. But art critics and their followers are fixation victims of mere sensationalism through absurdity.

This is reflected in the endless *absurdities of modern art*. Think of the abstract art, pop art, op art, sop art, plop-plop art, or other constantly added, very "original" forms of art. A bed mattress streaked with paint is a famous work of art. So is a six-by-six-by-six-foot cube that the artist ordered by phone. The notorious Brillo boxes are made to look exactly like Brillo boxes. Identical squares of white canvas representing nothing except pencilled-in words River, Mountain and Spring are accepted as works of art. The "portrait of Marcia Tucker" is a four-inch square piece of unpainted wood on empty canvas.

Any smear on canvas, by ape's fingers or donkey's tail, could be foisted on critics as a work of art if enough effort was made to conceal the deception. Prizes have been awarded to such "paintings," in exhibitions, by unsuspecting art critics.[16] The art of Paul Klee or Joan Miro is earnestly compared to "paintings" by four-year-olds.[16] Many artists, including Picasso, have been viewed as continuators of primitive art.

Actually, the *primitive artifacts* are queer or distorted due to lack of skill and to the intent of making them extraordinarily strange for greater impact in rituals. They certainly resemble modern art, that opposes previous, artistic skill and strives for sensationalism.

Originality as contrast or opposition to previous values and styles in art is important. Contrast enriches experience. All styles of art have arisen by such opposition. The prototype of all styles, the impressionism, was seen as an outrageous insult to artistic sense. The very name Impressionism "was given by a journalist in a spirit of derision."[11]

But in truth, the richest surprising originality or contrast could be attained by being brought out against fullest reality, with rich, concrete points of reference. *We should demand such originality. It would reveal the real artist,* much like rich, detailed originality distinguishes a gifted comedian from a slapstick clown. That would help change art from smears and absurdities to rich, detailed works of talent.

We should also understand how we have become enslaved by fixations to the cult of present styles and geniuses. The cultic appreciation here is as rich as in all cults. It cannot be changed, even if it were important to do so. But with a causal insight, intelligent people should at least stop adoring as revelations of spiritual mystery mere smears of paint, inflated plastic hamburgers, or heaps of broken car parts, just because of names and styles.

The main insight should be that values and enjoyments in esthetics derive from very prosaic, even distressingly ugly, opposite causal backgrounds—not from exalted mysteries of heavens. A feeling of beauty is as intense as was its opposite, harsh and base causal source.

The *causal confusion in esthetics* is evident from the multitude of controversial theories about art.[11,12] Even great supporters of modern art find it confusing. Sir Herbert Read found that degeneration of art or distortion of its very purposes, of beauty and order, is inherent in the progress of modern art.[16] Etiene Gilson has accepted the violation of beauty in modern art as a prerogative of genius.[16] Confusion about art and its ambivalent, paradoxical nature is recognized by sober critics. We may refer here to books by Virgil Aldrich, George Dickie, Albert Elsen, E. H. Gombrich, or Morris Philipson. Typically, Jacques Barzun argues that modern artists are confused "unwilling enemies" of true esthetics, "doing the work of dehumanizing they abhor."[4]

Generally, the naive, cultic acceptance of esthetics as source of lofty values and truths dominates most theories. Art is viewed as revelation of God, manifestation of the secret laws of nature, "inkling of God's beneficent creation" or expression of inner transcendental knowledge, allegedly, postulated by Plato, Kant, Schelling, Hegel, Nietzsche, Goethe, Coleridge, Croce, Dewey, or Heidegger.[11,16] Even the abstract smears of modern art are to be accepted as expressions of hidden revelation of God, according to Jacques Maritain.[16] In fact man's strongest sense of values, as satisfaction, is always born from his direst needs as nonsatisfactions, in religion or any "higher" system of beliefs. The esthetic cult only confirms the irony of sacred values originating from harshest disvalues.

Esthetics would not have to be a nonsensical superstitious cult. It can serve as an excellent medium of cultural conditioning. Music and art in churches did so. But the modern art is degenerating into a confused fixation, permitting travesty and licence. No wonder that modern artists and the truly absorbed, total followers of modern art are often cultural decadents, living in moral degeneration, alcoholism, drug culture or sexual licence.

There is no virtue in esthetics themselves. The Nazis were great lovers of art at its best. They even could find justification of genocide in genuine admiration of Wagnerian music. Esthetics as the modern fixational cult can exacerbate our unwholesome enjoyment tendencies and aberrations, as all fixations do. This has to be weighed against the advantages of esthetics as an excellent medium for cultural conditioning.

LITERATURE is, obviously, very important in our intellectual life, culture and education. Unfortunately, the modern literature would teach us about practical life the opposite of what is causally true. It expresses in the most "logical," liberated way the humanistic value beliefs. Writers are, generally, the sensitive enjoyers of values and believers in deep feelings. They are embittered by the seemingly unnecessary restrictions, irrational superstitions and hypocritical contradictions of life. This passionate sense of the truth of values and of their denial by the world is what makes writers create their vocal, most recognized works.

Since the real value causation is exactly contrary to such sense of values, the fictional creation in literature is never true to life causally.

In literary fiction the author creates his own characters and their behavior. Evidently, without a correct causal understanding he is bound to *create a virtual freak world of causally mismatched behavior and events.* It is true that all men, similarly, lack causal understanding of their behavior. But in practical life the ubiquitous contradictory and illogical, selectively evolved ways lead men to the right behavior. In literary creation no such "absurd" limitations hinder the author. He creates a world that complies with the directly logical human value convictions—which are contrary to the real causality.

In fact, every causal fallacy of psychology or humanistic thought, that we have explained, is compounded in literary fiction. We find everywhere, in literature, the belief in positive reactions from positive enjoyments and in negative effects from restrictions or frustrations; as well as the alchemy of weightiest capacities, or ills, arising from mere ideas, insights, thoughts, reasons, intents, coincidences or unconscious causes. In typical modern writing, by Sartre or Beckett, a person may be suffering a never ceasing anguish or despair, while in reality a background of such experiences would create a reaction of joy and optimism.

In our era of admitted total confusion in the sciences of man, what guides people is their healthy intuition, evolved from the day-by-day practical experience, and providing a causally congruous behavior. But writers, generally, have least of such healthy, practical intuition—and most of the "logical" value convictions. That is why authors are mostly maladjusted people, leading disordered lives.

They are overenjoyers, and do very well in expressing, passionately, a host of emotionally deep and rich experiences. As Leslie Fiedler says, all great writers need a charismatic weakness, a psychological flaw, which drives them to alcoholism, drugs or psychic disturbances. Our greatest masters, Fitzgerald, Lewis, Wolfe, O'Neill, Faulkner or Hemmingway, would fit this description, as would most of the famous writers of genius of the world literature.[13] According to Gore Vidal, it is difficult to think of a single contemporary American writer of any note who is not either an alcoholic or on the way to becoming one.

The great authors may be interesting and convincing in expressing, richly and deeply, the "logical" passionate thought about human experiences, feelings and values. But to expect true causal insights about practical life from them is like asking business advice from bankrupt spendthrifts. *Literature deepens the universal value delusions* which have kept men from discovering the causal truths in all fields of human sciences.

Fixation, in literature, rules our feelings particularly about the value of classical works—of Homer, Cervantes or Shakespeare. *The Odyssey* is a kind of ancient exaggerated miracle Western, without the slightest psychological rendering of true characters or genuine real-life interests. *Don Quixote* was intended as a hilarious story, but is a series of practical jokes so sad that it now serves as an example of the tragic sense of life. Even Shakespeare is for us a genius mostly because of our fixations.

Anybody presently starting to write as Shakespeare did could not expect many readers, or any response. Such work would be found artificial, contorted, exaggerated, lacking in subtle characterization, imputing childishly stupid thinking, relying on blood or miracles for drama, and not rising above impossible plots or unnatural, distorted language. But the style of Shakespeare has become for us, through agelong fixations, as sacred as are similarly contorted passages from scriptures.

The classics are significant as literary monuments. But who could read them with a real-life interest? A writer intending to sell today a similarly written work would not even be thought funny. His work would be simply below every standard of interesting, talented writing. The only source of interest or of talented creation is the real life. Lacking the real-life interests, the *classics are works of poor talent.* The argument that interests were different in the old times is not true. People in all times have the same, sensible interests, for what is real or true. But the authors then did not deign to go below highly learned or unusually remarkable matters; or to abandon the traditional, fixationally valued forms of writing.

PHILOSOPHY is not practically important, but it is the main embodiment of the humanistic theoretical thought. Revealingly, the progress of philosophy is marked by a self-defeat, amidst incredible complexity.

Philosophy as the system of universal truths should be the simplicity itself. All great discoveries show that universal truths are simplest. But the only concrete attainment of philosophy is its staggering complexity. No modern philosopher is so naive as to expect coherent answers from philosophy. And a logical system-building would be considered anachronistic, in modern philosophy, though the very essence of a credible philosophy should be a full logical system.

The reason for *its own defeat of philosophy* is its aim of attaining complete, true-in-itself, final knowledge and ultimate meanings of values. This is unattainable, because values are relative and knowledge, as we saw, is a value process. Everything is valued, differentiated or known by comparison with something different, ultimately opposite. The very act of knowing requires not-knowing or need to know. As Pragmatists say, an all-knowing God would have nothing to know or think about.[15]

Knowledge, or value, has to be always imperfect or relative, to include the opposite. And nothing can be "truly" known, in itself or with finality, because everything depends on something different, further and further on. Philosophy is on the cognitive level what neurosis is on the emotional. In both, the satisfaction, the final value, seems just at the reach of the hand. But as it is reached it disappears, because it requires its opposite to exist. Thus the delusory search goes on and on, as a more and more involved elaboration—in neurosis and philosophy. The cognitive "neurosis," though, is acceptable culturally, as it intensifies preoccupation with intelectual interests.

The relativity of knowledge, and philosophy exclude each other. *If knowledge is relative, philosophy is impossible.* This dichotomy is general, and we do not have to go into analyzing separate systems of philosophies to refute them. Recognition of the relativity amounts here to a different world view. You do not have to refute the pre-Copernican systems in their terms after you have the understanding of the simple, though seemingly impossible fact that the earth spins and orbits. Those systems were so complex that you, probably, would not even succeed in refuting them in their terms.

The dichotomy between the relativity of knowledge and philosophy is evident from the general goals of all philosophies. The main such goal is to attain the *knowledge of everything in itself.* Philosophers have tried to explain the world, or the reality, by some one essence like Substance, or by concepts like Forms or Monads that are mere multiplications of one essence.[14;15] This is true of systems ancient and modern, with the Being of Eleatics, the one God of Medieval philosophers, the Idea of Hegel, or the Space-Time of Alexander.[14,15]

But because knowledge is a relative value process, such explanations are delusory. If everything is explained by, say, Idea, this leads to a further problem of explaining the Idea; and if it is explained by, say, Spirit, then this has to be explained in its turn. Nothing can be known in itself or with finality as the very gist of philosophizing requires.

Already the first truly modern, critical movement, the empiricism, notably represented by Locke or Hume, led to the insight that we know things not in their own but through our ideas or sense perceptions of qualities or values of things, their "colour or form, heat or shade."[14] Thus even a concrete thing, like the book before you, consists only of your various sense perceptions or values, which in their turn depend on other values, and so on.

Finality of knowledge is required under the philosophical goal of a cognitive satisfaction. There is no satisfaction if you have to go on differentiating endlessly. But endlessness is inevitable exactly when you try to known anything philosophically or completely, whether it is the book or the immense universe. You cannot stop, in the quest for final knowledge. For you can know something only against something else. Philosophers have speculated about the endlessness of remarkable phenomena, like movement, extension, creation or causality; one can think here of the paradoxes of Zeno, the antinomies of Kant, or the arguments on the illusion of causality of Hume.[15;16] But the endlessness is true of everything, even of the tiniest or dullest thing or event.

Thus philosophers, while arguing about the great aspects and causes of the universe, have not deigned to think of the endless smaller and smaller universes inside every atom. Objectively, the smallness is as valid as the greatness. And if we could go down into the atom toward smaller and smaller differences we would, necessarily, find them at some infinitesimal level. Thus infinitely small universes inside the atom, with their own atoms, and so on, are a reality as true as the universe we know.

The *world of values* is, of course, the most important, underlying concern of all philosophies. Each philosopher has accepted and defended the higher value notions of his time; our present nonconformity or negativism is only another contemporary value outlook or fashion. The ancient defense of virtues as absolutes of happiness or of the golden mean was transparently naive. Obvious cultural differences or relativity of virtues and value standards was not recognized; even slavery was seen as the only possibility. The Medieval philosophers extolled the Christian values, coping as best they could with the problem of the necessity of evil.

Above all, the modern philosophy has turned to values as sources of truths, while realizing the impossibility of a philosophy of reason.

The turning point is, probably, the monumental work of Kant. He proved that the philosophical truths cannot be attained by reason.[14] This should have meant the end of philosophy which is always an endeavor of thought. The practical reason,[14] actually the world of moral values, was accepted by Kant as substitute for reason. After him pure reason has been hardly resorted to as the exclusive source of truths; and value notions have become the main criteria.

The next great philosophers, Fichte and Schelling, saw the ultimate truths in the feeling of ethical self and sense of beauty.

The rising romanticism and idealism turned to similar emotional and value concepts. Post-Kantian philosophies of Eucken, Lotze, Windelband or Rickert stressed ethical, religious and other pure value experiences.[14,15] Schopenhauer's Will, Nietzsche's Will to Power, Bergson's Elan Vital, or Croce's Spirit are emotionally or intuitively discovered realities. Intuition, "direct" knowledge, immediacy of feeling, even "animal faith" have been chosen as substitutes for reason.[16] Actually, these ways of knowledge are closest to pure value experiences, to satisfactions dependent on their unsuspected value opposites—therefore are the most deceptive.

The value approaches have also been misleading in the philosophical ideas about the *Mind*. Under the value outlook, any evolutionary, selective or adaptive *adjustment looks purposeful, in its final form*. The disturbing, past, difficult development by which the selective adjustment is reached is disregarded because it is contrary to the final value aspects of the smooth, purposive adaptation. This outlook delayed the insight into the simple natural selection in biology. It still dominates in the fields of mind and values. The Mind is seen as a purposeful, spiritual reality in itself.[14] The evolutionary, biologic bases of the mind, like the mechanisms of pleasure, are overlooked.

This implies the incongruous parallelism as an unnoticed part of almost all philosophies, since they all recognize the Mind.[14,15] As an immaterial reality the Mind cannot move or affect causally the material world. Therefore your mental feelings and the corresponding physical, organic reactions are causally unrelated happenings miraculously arranged to coincide, by Somebody.

Probably the most usual argument for philosophizing is that the world we know may be a mere appearance fabricated by our mind.[15] But if thinking is recognized as a biologic process, then the mind is of the same reality as all existence. And if all existence is unreal, everything is equally real. Nobody would doubt that our pleasure reactions are as real as the world they derive from. And they are the prototype of the sources of all thinking, as a value process.

The capacity of our mind to grasp the world is invoked or

implied in the subtlest modern philosophies. Since the mind knows the world, both are assumed to be of the same nature, governed by a unifying principle. The world is thus seen as an emanation of a Mind. This has been the main proposition of Neo-Idealists, Green, Bradley or Royce, and the underlying certainty in the systems of some best known modern philosophers—Croce, Gentile, Renouvier, Russell or Whitehead—as well as of all Idealists, from Plato to Hegel.[14;15]

Thus man first has struggled to grasp the world, through *age-long efforts* of language, concepts, ideas, or methods of thinking, then turns around as a philosopher and *wonders how everything is so miraculously grasped by his mind.* The illusion of purposefulness of the last phase of adjustments still dominates here, in various ways, as it did in biology before Darwin.

The most modern philosophical movements have turned, in their search for truths, to all kinds of sources: practical success, common logic, science, literature, aesthetics, emotion, intuition, instinct, or any experience.[15] We can refer here to pragmatism, empiricism, phenomenology or existentialism, and the eclectic systems of philosophers like Dewey, Santayana, Russell, Whitehead or Hocking. Apparently, strict reasoning is replaced by value experiences—which are most delusory. Generally, two main approaches, positivism and existentialism, have been prevailing.

The *positivism* dominates in the analytic philosophy, logical positivism, language philosophy, conventionalism, fictionalism, instrumentalism or operationism. Philosophy as it has always been known is rejected and knowledge limited to that of empirically verifiable facts and to tautological statements or conventional fictions.[15] The way the logical positivists want it, "there would be no books written on philosophy, but all books would be philosophically written." Similarly, the leader of the language philosophy, Wittgenstein, stated that the aim of philosophy is "not a body of propositions, but to make propositions clear."[15]

But, apparently, the problem is deeper. The perpetual evasiveness of simple truths—due to the universal relativity of knowledge—is not overcome. If the problem was merely that of logic or language, then agreements would be soon reached, particularly

on the simplest, most fundamental truths. Yet the new efforts
have only revealed more difficulties and failure, but not solutions.[14,15]

The *existentialism* is generally recognized as the leading movement in modern philosophy and thought. It is typical of the
general abandonment of reasoning in favor of value experiences.
The final truths in existentialism are the deepest negative feelings: anxiety, dread, despair, isolation, futility, or senselessness.[15]
Such excessive negative sense of the world cannot arise without
equally excessive opposite emotional backgrounds or expectations.
The unprecedented "pampering" of modern man is clearly the
cause of the existential, uniquely negative modern attitudes—
comparable to the fears and anxieties of overprotected children.

The existentialism is thus a misunderstood phenomenon of
psychological pathology rather than a system of ultimate truths.
Perhaps it is only fitting that this becomes the final achievement
of philosophy.

The Value Delusions and Our Self-Inflicted Ills

It is true that the loftily expounded humanistic satisfactions,
the "higher" or "spiritual" values, are different from crude overenjoyments. Still, such satisfactions require organic releases, that
are not gratuitously given. In the simplest terms, the "higher"
enjoyments serve to overcome general feelings of anxiety, depression, boredom or inadequacy. This amounts to overenjoyments of the positively felt opposites of these feelings. *The aftereffects are therefore an increased anxiety or depression* in general,
undefinable forms. Use of some drugs provides similar general
sublime experiences. And the more exalted the enjoyment, the
uglier the aftereffect.

It is not the immediate effects of the "spiritual" enjoyments
but their *unsuspected secondary influence* that brings the concrete
disorders. As the general, undefinable anxiety or depression increases, through the added enjoyments, stronger means of relief
become necessary, and the impoverishment or disorders follow.
Continued, general "higher" enjoyments seem always beneficial

and are not strongly noticed. But their richly accumulated influence becomes source of equally "rich" deepened aftereffects requiring the stronger means. The "flower children" started with general, "higher" enjoyments. But the end result was use of drugs, mental exhaustion and need for thrills, as in the Manson murders.

An important fact is that the "higher" value enjoyments are satisfactions of one's *most general needs,* of survival, growth or superiority. These needs control, in a general way, all other, secondary experiences. As one enjoys the sense of assurance or self-fulfillment, through the "higher" enjoyments, other gratifications are felt as permissible or flow more freely—with the vicious-circle effects of overenjoyment as a result.

On the wider, cultural scale the "higher" or "spiritual" value enjoyments and beliefs play a similar role. Affirming the verity of value feelings, they favor a freer, more genuine pursuit of positively felt values or happiness in our culture. The result is the modern humanistic *attitudes of more satisfactions and freedoms.* They have created the atmosphere of hedonism and liberalism or permissiveness of our era. Enjoyment of the positively felt values or satisfactions and freedoms has been a logical goal in all modern humanistic thought.[5] The "pursuit of happiness," as well as the assertions of freedom, became part of our Constitution in the spirit of humanistic enlightenment.[5]

At that time, though, these were rather "glittering generalities," as Howard M. Jones writes in his book *The Pursuit of Happiness.*[5] Deep enjoyments as fulfillment of life, hailed by Emerson, became practical concerns in a new era, enounced in the thought of William James.[5] The preoccupation with satisfactions has become since a serious business, exploited by advertising, vast industries and mass media.

As Jones describes in the book, numerous authorities have been dealing with the problem of how to increase the enjoyment of satisfactions in their various forms of happiness, joy of life, interest, enthusiasm, peace of mind, relaxation, freedom of gratifications and avoidance of "conflicts" or restrictions.[5] The most recent best-sellers on the positive enjoyments are offering the final logical solutions. Total, selfish satisfactions and freedom, in disregard of the traditional, moralistic restrictions, are advocated.

Mildred Newman and Bernard Berkowitz, writing on *How to Be Your Own Best Friend,* urge more freedoms in our enjoyments without concern for others or for the old restrictive rules. Wayne W. Dyer, in *Your Erroneous Zones,* advises us to "outlaw self-denial unless it is absolutely necessary—and it rarely is." We are not to be concerned about approval by others and not to deny ourselves anything. Similarly, in *You Can Cope,* Bernard Poduska urges us to care only for our own feelings and not to worry about the rest. Love of self, in our satisfactions, is seen as the goal by Bob Hoffman in his *Getting Divorced from Mother & Dad;* or by Richard G. Abell in his *Own Your Own Life.* Social or cultural restrictions, as the causes of our unhappiness, are condemned by Fitzhugh Dodson in *The You That Could Be.*

But even our leading authorities, such as Mumford, Fromm, Dubos or Huxley, see salvation in deeper, more intense enjoyments of our value feelings—though in the more traditional cultural spirit.[1,9] The enjoyment of positively felt satisfactions and freedoms, that values ultimately are, is simply part of the humanistic value beliefs. Even critics and writers like Herbert Marcuse, Paul Goodman, Norman O. Brown or Charles Reich who see all, including sexual restrictions as causes of evil, have been taken seriously within the humanistic theory.[9]

The results of our "sensuous" culture, which is now expanding over the world, are disastrous and paradoxical.[9] The people enjoying more of the happiness, satisfactions and freedoms, are least happy and are tormented by anxiety, stress, behavioral impoverishment or disorders. Of course, explanations are sought in the materialistic, technological or "nonhuman" nature of our culture.[9] But as we saw, men know perfectly what their most satisfactory "inner," fulfilling experiences are; exactly because they overenjoy them, they suffer the ugly opposite reactions, of the impoverishment and disorders.

The most typical example here is the young generation that grew up before the latest recession, under unique conditions of satisfactions and freedoms, in the liberal humanistic atmosphere. We have to think of the *"alienated youth,"* and the *student unrest,* of the late sixties, as well as of the continuous *generation gap.*

Perhaps the best survey here is the noted work of Kenneth Keniston, *The Uncommitted Alienated Youth.*[16] The opinions and attitudes by the youth showed that they wanted increased "awareness, passion, pleasure, immediacy of feelings . . . zest, and exuberance," that would give life immediacy of experience, spontaneity, wholeness and fulfillment. This corresponds to what the humanistic experts have always expounded.[4,8] It is a clear, logical proposition *to have the enriching positive emotions or capacities directly and fully,* without the seemingly unnecessary, enslaving restrictions. The practical limitations are blamed, as usual, on technology, with its cool efficiency, control, materialism, competitiveness, "upwardly mobile strivings" and insensitivity.

The central belief here is not different from that of the great critics of our technological civilization, Jacques Ellul, Erich Fromm, Herbert Marcuse or Lewis Mumford.[9] It implies the absurdity that man does not know how to enjoy the pleasant enriching feelings; that he serves the nonsatisfying and impoverishing cold technology because of some such miscalculation.

Understandably, when the *"counterculture" youth movements* first appeared they were seen as bringing a welcome change. The "flower children" or hippies were compared to the early Christians. Even sober humanists, like Jacques Barzun, Abraham Maslow or Arthur Koestler,[16] hailed the new spirit. Yet hardly any movement has been so clearly degenerative and culturally disruptive as that of the counterculture, beatniks or hippies. It has left behind mental disorders, crime, spiritual as well as material poverty and cultural desolation.

The humanistic, logical ideals of value enrichment and freedom can lead to ugly disorders. Typically, in the notorious murder trial of Charles Manson and his hippie gang, its members, former college students, testified that he was the only person who showed in life what they had been taught about values.

The *field of learning about values* is, if possible, even more confused than the other fields of human sciences. Hundreds of theories are offered but no accepted explanations have been reached. Most frequently it is even said that no science of values is ever possible, though values are accepted as the bases of behavior and thought.[14,15] At the same time, values as *general natural* phenomena, governed by an evidently *uniform organic* principle, can only be simple causally or scientifically. The laws of the relative causation show how simple the explanations could be. All this points to a prevalent confusion about values in the world of modern learning.

This may explain the regrettable fact that usually *our centers of learning become the nests of culturally disturbing and degenerative movements,* like those of the student unrest. The educators cannot help the disturbances, because they are themselves equally deluded or do not understand how the human value reactions work. Less learned men proceed by their practically evolved, sound intuition. Anyway, instead of providing healthy leadership, our highly educated groups are culturally more disruptive than helpful.

Here we have to emphasize that *the humanistic value delusions have prevented development of real science about man* in all fields. As we have repeatedly explained, the direct, logical value beliefs show as true the exact opposite of what is causally true. But humanists want to view under the value aspect all, even physical, sciences. Presumably "Eddington or Einstein arrived at the truths in the same way as did Shakespeare or Rembrandt," according to Jacob Bronowski.[7]

The famous dictum "Beauty is truth, truth beauty" is repeated by best authorities. Jacques Barzun argues that "the Romantic doctrine is as tenable as that of latest physics."[4] One supposedly gains by leaving a lecture on astronomy and by going outside to look at the stars. Humanists want to invest literature, art and philosophy with authority of sciences; and such works as the *Golden Bough* by Frazer or writings by Freud are invoked in support.[1,7]

The result can be only a further delay in development of sciences of man. Beliefs in the *verity of values* dominate the humanistic thought. And they are, as we saw, *totally misleading causally.* Since the first requirement for a science is causal understanding, the humanistic thought is worse than useless in any science. No wonder that humanists feel like the Luddites, in their confrontation with science, as C. P. Snow explains in his noted discussion on the schism between humanities and sciences.[16]

The delay in the development of the sciences of man becomes practically disastrous. In our age of sciences the old, intuitive, necessarily superstitious beliefs cannot be well upheld. The restrictive cultural tradition is being discredited. More enjoyments and licence are favored, under our "logical" beliefs in values and freedoms. *The result is more disorders, psychological impoverishment, and functional diseases.*

We do not doubt the noble intentions of the humanistic believers in values. But the totally wrong causal logic, that such beliefs embody, prevents rather than helps promotion of human values, as capacities or positive satisfactions and releases.

VIII

THE UNSEEN HALF OF
THE UNIVERSE

Even in the fields of the most certain sciences, like physics and biology, modern man has remained virtually blind to the causal, "negative" side of their phenomena. Hence the universally admitted mystery in the theory of modern physics, and clear, unwarranted confusion in the fundamental biologic concepts, of the living process and genetics. This mystery and confusion should be the scientifically clearest evidence of the humanly natural, one-sided blindness still prevailing in all fields of modern science.

The cause of this blindness is *the nonrelative view which prevents man from seeing the opposite, "negative," causal sources* of his values, that constitute his reality. Of course this, causal side of the reality is its more important half, since it determines the rest—as we have seen already in the fields of human sciences and values.

Man tends to see or know only the positive values, which he seeks, never their negative, causal opposites, which he avoids. In ordinary cases man, generally, knows the negative causes, like thirst or need, though in his own experience he may not connect a value, such as a feeling of beauty with its causal opposite, a background of harrowing needs. But in those cases where the negative, causal opposite is universal, he loses even such ordinary insight into the "negative" cause. To the extent anything is universal it is not perceived or "known," because man knows only by differentiation. We do not experience or know the atmospheric pressure, that is universally there.

In any event, a *fully universal* causal source of our values, as

222

their "negative" opposite, would never be recognized or known by man. It would, rather, remain a meaningless nothingness.

Now, the most universal and most "negative" causal source must be that of our universal most positive, most concrete values —of our *physical or material reality we exist in.* Consequently, the general causal source of our positive, material world is an absolute, universal, therefore unrecognizable negativity or nothingness. The material world derives its reality for us, certainly, through the "nothingness." If everything were matter, without the nothingness, we could not know what matter is. It would not exist for us.

The Universal Causal Source of the Effects in Matter

Evidently, *matter and the "nothingness" are two equal opposites,* each deriving its effects from the other. Let us give the name of Field to this "nothingness" as the causal source of all effects in matter. The compression of atoms, and the wave nature, transmission and uniformity of matter effects in the universe are sufficient to reveal the Field as an ever active or pressure-exerting universal, homogeneous and fluid immensely strong or dense force or medium. Once we have learned these properties of the Field, we can explain the endless other, admitted causal mysteries in modern physics, and astronomy.

It should be emphasized that we are *not proposing here any hypotheses or assumptions.* We are merely looking at matter and its effects in the two-sided, objective way—free of the natural human prejudice of accepting the positive values while rejecting their "negative" causal opposites. Under the unprejudiced, relative view, the Field is as self-evident from the effects in matter as light is from presence of shadows, or as sand is from footprints in it.

The Field is, surely, a "nothingness," if only because it is the opposite of matter. But as the causal source of effects in matter it is the more important, dominant, half of the universe, and as real as matter. Of course *the values of the Field* as the opposites of the values of our reality are absolutely unacceptable or "atrocious" to man (ultimately, we know everything through values or value processes). The values of the Field are "oppression," absolute compulsion, dominance, and denial of freedom.

That is why the Field is inherently unthinkable to man, though without its negative values man's ultimate values of freedom or of force of self-realization would have no meaning. Force without opposition would be a formless dissipation, and freedom without limitation a pointless void.

The *common-sense objections* against the concept of the Field as a universal dense medium are untenable. Einstein said that fish cannot know water they live in. Equally, men cannot recognize the far more universal causal medium of their world. The objection that we could not see or move through the dense medium is unscientific. Exactly seeing requires the light waves that only such an enormously dense medium can transmit. And not even a molecule moves in you, or anywhere, unless moved by force—the invisible something characterized by requirement of opposition—which, evidently, inheres in the Field. Then, *if the Field itself is what moves every molecule, there can never be a different effect, like hindrance to the movement,* in the Field.

Every great physicist who has made discoveries or offered causal explanations has done so by recognizing a medium, an Ether, forces in space, fields, or curvature of space—which are only different names for the same medium[2] performing the same functions.[4] This is true of the work and theories of Boyle, Huygens, Newton, Faraday, Maxwell, Fresnel, Kelvin, Lorentz, Hertz, Lodge, Einstein, and other more modern physicists, as we shall see later. Einstein sought final explanations in his unfinished Unified Field Theory.

But, curiously, the physicists remained bound by the human prejudice. Thus even Newton and Einstein argued that a medium would interfere with movement of bodies.[1,2] In fact, as the concept of the Ether still persisted, experiments on Ether interference or drag were performed, by Fizeau, Fresnel, Hertz, Stokes, Lodge, Miller, Kennedy, and Michelson and Morley.[2]

The humanly "prejudiced" thinking of physicists shows here clearly. They were ready to recognize a universal causal medium but did not realize that *such a medium could be millions of times denser or stronger than any substance yet would still remain unregistrable,* by any instrument. Objects moved by a water stream cannot experience friction by it, or any particular, different effect, from being moved by it. And all effects of matter result from Field moving it, or rather its particles. Since instruments consist of matter, and act on matter, everything, again, is "moved" by the Field, which therefore remains unregistrable, except through the ordinary effects of matter.

The atmospheric pressure is far less universal than the Field, yet remained unknown for ages, even to scientists using all kinds of machines. In the Field you cannot create vacuums or differences, necessary to know or differentiate it. You would have to use force to do so, but that is inherent in the Field itself, with its cosmic pressure. And "vacuums" in the Field—actually, slight, self-created distentions or waves in it—are automatically quanta of matter as its opposite.

Of course, the *Ether or any medium conceived in the traditional, nonrelative way is an incongruity.* Such Ether would, indeed, interfere with movement, or be registrable in some way. So would any "field."

Einstein stressed the concrete reality of the field. He found that "we have two realities: matter and field"; that the "field became more and more real," though "we have not yet succeeded in formulating a pure field physics"; or that the "field is, for the modern physicist, as real as the chair on which he sits."[1] Einstein used the field equations of Maxwell, whose concepts of the field or Ether were very concrete. They were quantitative representations of Faraday's Ether with all its "lines" and "tubes" of force as "states of stress in an elastic body."[2] Equally concrete were the models of Ether in other theories, of Lord Kelvin or Sir George Stokes.[14]

Evidently, such field or Ether, in its various forms, would be like another kind of substance, incongruously, exerting the resistance or showing registrable shapes and qualities. It is important to stress that only an absolutely *universal, uniform medium as the causal source or opposite of all effects in matter* can be as unregistrable as nothingness while being millions of times stronger or denser than any substance.

The modern physics, understandably, has remained here ambiguous. As G. R. Harrison says, "ether has been junked and physicists talk about warped space, the fourth dimension and relativity . . . so they feel happier."[14] But "when we endow space itself with properties such as curvature, we are making it play the part of an ether," in the words of Sir Edmund Whittaker.[2] Typical are the arguments of P. W. Bridgman, a Nobel laureate in physics. He argues for the existence of a medium that can never be discovered by instruments because these themselves are part of the conditions affected by the medium.[4] But he finds it "a bit shocking to realize that the concept of empty space can have no guarantee that it is anything more than an artifact of our thinking."[4]

The most interesting recent theory on the forces in "empty" space is, probably, that of John A. Wheeler, "one of the architects of modern physics." He sees the whole space filled with infinitesimal electromagnetic fluctuations of "stupendous" energy. This is close to a concept of a universal medium of immense force, unregistrable because of its universality. The idea that a universal medium would be nonexistent for man in the way water is for fish was expressed already by Sir Oliver Lodge.[14]

The evidence of the universal causal medium is often so general that it is not even thought of. The forms and effects of matter are uniform throughout the universe. But only the "nothingness," the Field, is there everywhere, to create it all in the same and, as we shall see, simple way. Without the Field we would have to assume that a miraculous intelligence, myriads of angels, are manufacturing and repairing everywhere precisely in the same way each one of the intricately uniform particles and effects.

Moreover, all effects in the universe, of gravitation, electromagnetism or radiation, are *connected or "bonded together,"*[4] with something between them. Also, most of the effects are in the form of *waves*. The "nothingness' around us is crowded with waves— from cosmic rays to TV transmissions. But waves can exist only in a medium and have no meaning without it. As Einstein pointed out a wave must be *in* something.[1] The modern, quantum physics founds its explanations on "wave mechanics," under which all physical effects are waves in motion and matter itself consists of waves.[3,5]

The endlessly discussed *particle-wave dilemma* is another evidence for the existence of the Field. All the fundamental units of matter—atoms, nucleons, or electrons—have been discovered to be systems of waves, as well as particles.[2,3,5] This has been established by the greatest physicists, Schroedinger, de Broglie, Born or Heisenberg. But how could a "corpuscule have anything to do with a wave," in the words of Einstein.[1] The explanation is automatic if the Field-matter opposition is recognized.

A wave in any medium is a continuing effect of a loosening or state of emptiness in the medium. But an emptiness in the Field is automatically a quantum of matter as its opposite. In its static state, a particle is compressed by the Field on all sides equally, therefore acts as a spherical wave system, because both matter and the Field are fluid pressure opposites.

The *enormous force that compresses atoms* is the great mystery of physics. It is self-evident if we consider that the Field as the cosmically immense force opposed to matter surrounds it and acts against it on all sides. (All cosmic magnitudes are immense in human terms.)

Because the pressure of the fluid Field is, necessarily, uniform, all matter particles are equal. The standard, initial particle, the hydrogen atom is an inevitable product of the Field pressure. Any larger piece of matter is automatically broken up and reduced to the limits of hydrogen atom, at which it can resist further breaking up. Conversely, smaller pieces of matter, like photons, can accumulate to the same limit, the hydrogen atom. Hydrogen, supposedly, constitutes 98 percent of interstellar matter; it is the newly created material for the eternal rebirths of stars.

The other, larger atoms are created by the same Field pressure, under the special conditions of enormous concentration of matter and counteraction by the Field during creation of stars and planets. The Field compresses two primary atoms because that permits a gain by the Field as the dominant opposite. Each atom as an elastic spherical wave system within an elastic compressing medium has a margin of compression by which it exerts its normal counter-pressure or balance against the Field. If two such full atoms are compressed into one, they can maintain the same balance with only one margin of compression, abandoning the other to the compressing Field. The two multi-unit atoms can be further compressed in the same way—rendering the well known "packing loss."

An important fact here is that the spherical waves constituting a "particle" are the *standing or stationary waves.* For they travel in opposite ways within the fixed sphere. And stationary waves are always equal within their system. Thus the waves within the atom are like concentric layers that are of the same thickness. They are also of equal mass. For the inner layers are denser or more compressed exactly to the extent they are smaller, because the lines of the concentric pressure become denser, more crowded, as they converge toward the center. (Mass is only a function of Field-matter pressures and counter-pressures.)

The modern, quantum physics, indeed, reveals that particles act as "standing waves, represented mathematically by the surface harmonics of a hypersphere."[2] Einstein praised de Broglie's explanation of "particles" as standing waves, which measure only in integral numbers and can change only by jumps. But he pointed out that such a system cannot exist without a medium.

The usual explanations of matter as consisting of particles do not correspond to reality, according to the founder of the modern, quantum physics, Max Planck.[3] "The particle as imagined in the classical picture *does not exist,"* in the words of Sir Edmund Whittaker.[2] Typically, the Nobel Prize for work on the structure of the atom has been awarded to E. P. Wigner, J. H. Jensen and M. G. Mayer, who established its "shell model," with protons and neutrons arranged like onion shells and nothing in the center.

The peculiar, *dual nature of the electron* is particularly revealing. Electron has been clearly observed and measured as a particle, in various experiments, notably by Thomson and Millikan. But equally conclusive experiments, beginning with those of Davisson and Germer, as well as comprehensive theories, particularly by de Broglie, Schroedinger and Heisenberg, have shown the electron to be a wave.[6,8] Electron even passes through two pinholes at once as only a wave can do, and forms typical wave patterns, showing in the electron interference experiments.[6] Apparently, electron as a matter quantum is a wave when it is inside the atom or in transmission; but it becomes a particle when, in an isolated static state, it is compressed from all sides by the Field.

The other peculiarities of the electron are due to its origin. When the nucleons—actually spherical layers or waves—are compressed and lose a margin of expansion, which constitutes the electron, for each compression, they can be viewed, "with certain difficulties,"[2] as protons and neutrons joined together. A nucleon minus an electron then is calculated in as the proton. Any such combination tends to regain the electron, therefore is "positively" charged. If energy or quanta of matter are poured into atoms, the compressed nucleons tend to regain the lost margins of expansion: all electrons appear. But the Field is always there to recompress them, instantly, when definite limits are reached, or when normal conditions return.

Such appearance and disappearance of the electron explain its ghost nature: *the electron is a mere potential of expansion of a spherical wave.*

The ghost-like, even "spiritual" or ideal nature of the electron has been extensively discussed, by famous physicists, notably by Sir James Jean and Sir Arthur Eddington. In the formulation by de Broglie, electron as any "particle cannot be observed so long as it forms part of the system, and the system is impaired once the particle has been identified."[5] Actually, all "particles" or nucleons can appear as true, round, particles only outside their normal, spherical-wave systems.[6] But the confusion has led to the sophistry of the famous *uncertainty theory* of Heisenberg.

If electrons were particles inside the atom they would, necessarily, be all uniform and behave in the same way. But as has been established, under the *exclusion principle of Pauli*, there can not be in an atom two electrons having the same set of quantum numbers or the same behavior status. This is what has to happen with spherical waves or layers in the atom, since there can be only one of them at each distance.

In all properties of elements the compression of nucleons is revealed. Two neutron-proton compressions can be further compressed, within an atom, by the Field, leaving only one margin of expansion for all four; and such a four-nucleon formation can be doubled with another. Atoms having numbers of nucleons that do not double up evenly have therefore more actual electrons and are chemically more active, while an even doubling, and further doubling, confers particular stability. This explains the properties of elements, as indicated by the *periodic table,* governed by doubled-number patterns, particularly the octets of electrons.

Physicists have construed an admitted fiction about electrons combining in virtually miraculous shells that accomodate only certain numbers of electrons. In reality, all the electrons are not actually present, because an electron is a mere potential. This is why an element having 18 or 54 electrons is as inactive as one having only 2, though the "sharing" of electrons would make elements with more electrons exceedingly active. Other facts explained by the "shells" are due to the combining of nucleon waves into superwaves.[14]

The *"sharing" of electrons,* as the mechanism of chemical bonds, is due to the same, simple principle under which elements are formed. By compressing two or more particles the Field can squeeze off looser electrons and still leave the molecules with sufficient, balanced margins of expansion. No sophistry about miraculously discriminating shells is necessary.

The old theories about ball-like electrons and nucleons are hardly tenable. The famous experiments by Rutherford, or Compton, would have shown equally good agreements, about "particle" interaction and angles of collision, if wave systems had been assumed as the interacting units.[14] The quantum physics shows that all movement is an effect of waves.[3] Compton saw photons and X-rays as well interact in the same particle pattern, but they are clearly waves. Rutherford, sending alpha particles through metal foil, found it was like shooting bullets at tissue paper and then seeing some of the bullets shoot back.[2] Apparently, the process was that of absorption and re-emission of wave systems. The "particles" shot back sometimes with delays a billion times longer than a collision of particles would permit.[14]

Absorption and re-emission is the way photons, electrons or even rapidly moving nucleons travel.[6] It is incongruous to assume that a photon runs as a particle from the sun, or that electrons run all the way through the wire, though the amount of electrons supplied at one end of the wire does appear at the other. Yet even Einstein wanted to deal with photons and electrons only as with particles.[6] Local oscillations, that is, absorptions and re-emissions of matter quanta, agree with all facts.[2,3] Even in the Wilson chamber, particles passing as mere physical balls could never create the tracks. A process similar to ionization, to absorption and re-emission, produces the straight tracks in the uniform bubble chamber, as ionization produces the path of lightning.

But the confusion, started by interpretations of experiments like those of Rutherford, has left us with "explanations" as specious as the Ptolemaic astronomy. The *atom is pictured as an emptiness* with electrons as small as bees in a football field, or nucleons as small as softballs in it. The argument that the electrons circle so fast as to form a shield does not help, because the electrons of other atoms would be moving equally fast, therefore would penetrate the "shield" and enmesh the atoms instantly.

There is "no real existence for either Bohr's or Rutherford's atom model," says Schroedinger.[5] And the two are the physicists offering the best defense of the particle theory. In Bohr's theory the electron is, miraculously, held in orbits having only the radiuses of square integrals 1, 4, 9, 16, 25; and all its effects are products of its jumps from one orbit to another. There is no causal or even physically comprehensible[6] relation of such jumps with real emission and absorption of energy or matter quanta.

The point is that only the concept of *atom as a spherical wave system* corresponds to reality, but such atom cannot exist without the compressing Field as the causal medium. The absorptions and emissions by spherical stationary waves can explain the above miracle of square integrals[6] as well as of the other quantum effects, governed by wave mechanics.[3] Thus "all frequencies emitted and absorbed by atoms correspond to transition from one quantum state to another . . . represented by mathematics of hyperspheres."[2]

Modern physicists are ready to recognize that the only comprehensive explanation is the spherical stationary wave system of the particle. But *without the Field as the compressing medium such system and its action are utterly inconceivable.*

Causal Explanations of Admitted Mysteries in Physics

The most discussed mystery in physics is, probably, that of the *nature of light.* How can light be waves at one instant and matter quanta or particles at another?[8] It is like having the box full and empty.[6] We showed how a wave in the Field has also to be a quantum of matter. Thus the explanation of the dual nature of light is automatic—as we saw in discussing the particle-wave dilemma.

Another mystery is how can light wave travel without dispersion or loss. The reason is the absolute density of the Field. If you hit a metal rod or a column of mercury at one end, you get an equal, almost instantaneous thrust at the other end of it. The Field, of course, is much more compact than any matter. Light is created when the Field squeezes off surplus matter quantum from an atom or "thrusts" into it, to the same extent. As it does so, it leaves a loosening behind, which is then filled by further Field thrust-in, creating further loosening, and so on, *as in all waves.* We saw that such loosening is, automatically, a quantum of matter. The immense pressure of the Field holds the quantum together; and as the opposite of the Field, matter can never be absorbed by it.

Enormous pressure, of billions of pounds per square inch,[3] is required to propagate the transverse waves of light, at its enormous speed.[6] Such "enormous" scale here merely means that the measurements man uses are enormously tiny in cosmic terms—which scientists know already.

Further, *an "elastic solid" would be required* to transmit the perfect transverse waves of light. Solids may have also longitudinal waves, but these decrease as the solid gets softer and more elastic.[6]

The Field can have all the properties of solidity while being perfectly fluid, because there are never any particles or divisions in it to interrupt its solidity. As has been noted by Asimov, the usual properties of molecular matter make "no sense whatsoever when applied to an absolutely continuous substance such as that which light ether is considered to be."[8]

All forms of radiation—as well as the mechanism of all movement—are similarly explainable by the action of the Field.[14] Even the mysteries of the humanly fascinating story of the expanding universe or the "big bang" can have a simple mechanistic explanation,[14] since in any medium waves lengthen as they travel long distances.

The strange phenomena observed in *quantum mechanics* are due to the Field-matter interaction and to the stationary-wave systems of particles. Any such system can change only by becoming another stationary-wave system, measuring again in integral numbers, of a different set. Evidently, the change can be only by jumps or discontinuous transformations. Discontinuity amounting to oscillations or reversals results from interaction between the Field and matter as two elastic opposing or counteracting media. They can act only by oscillations between extreme limits for the same reason that an elastic ball, musical cord or surface of a drum oscillates between opposite extremes. The comparison of atom radiation with vibrations of a drum was used by Einstein.[1]

The elasticity of the two opposites is the clue. The spherical wave of matter, when it starts gaining matter enrichment, expands to the extreme at which it cannot further resist the pressure of the Field. At that point the opposite, similar action by the Field starts. Each wave or quantum resulting from such oscillations is the universal "quantum of action" known as the Planck's constant, which is the last, indivisible quantum of all radiation and energy, or the ultimate grain of the universe.[2]

Another universal quantum phenomenon is the inverse relationship between the length of a light wave and its energy level.[6] This is so because each spherical wave inside an atom has, as we saw, the same mass but the total volume of a more external wave is larger. Absorption of a more external wave by the Field therefore yields the same mass or quantum of energy but takes longer time and thus creates a longer radiation wave.

Further, the spherical-wave structure of the atom explains the relationships of *squared integrals in radiation frequencies,* as revealed in spectra series. Because the atom consists and acts as *spherical* waves, the squared relationships are automatic. And since these spherical waves are "stationary," they can measure only in whole integrals.

The reverse process of radiation is the absorption of radiated quanta, by atoms they encounter. Evidently, the same relationships must apply here, since the absorption process, as generally accepted, is that of resonance between similar harmonic systems.[2] It is the absolutely dense Field that makes the resonance between systems at enormous distances perform as effectively as if there was no distance at all between them.

A uniquely significant explanation results, from the Field concept, for *the uniform speed of light.* Only a transmitting medium can make light travel always at the same speed. Otherwise the speed of light emitted from an approaching system would be increased, and from a receding system decreased, by the movement of the system. When physicists had to abandon the incongruous Ether as medium, they eagerly espoused Einstein's theory of relative speeds for different systems.[14]

Einstein as a mathematical genius could work out his predictions without naming the "impossible" reality he was dealing with; mathematicians do not have to visualize the things their formulas apply to. His theory derives from a simple basic principle, as all great discoveries do. This principle is the uniform speed of light—possible only with a transmitting medium.

Naturally, physicists wanted to add a visualized reality to the mathematical formulas. The curious Lorentz-Fitzgerald contraction of moving systems was suggested. On a fast moving system everything, including clocks and measuring sticks, was assumed to shorten and time to slow down. This theory—always considered as a mere assumption[3,14]—is not helpful.

Two, opposite changes would be required to explain how the approaching as well as retreating systems compensate for the assumed changes in the speed of light. Both contraction and lengthening of distances, or both slowing down and speeding up of time, on moving systems, thus would be required.

Of course, a mathematical formula can give both plus and minus at the same time, with a factor like the square root, used in the equations of the speed of light. In the world of reality, however, the same factor or cause cannot be bigger and smaller or have positive and negative effect. Nor can a system at one moment be assumed to be standing still, at the next to be moving. Such assumptions have been used to obtain the same relative time effect with both approching and receding "contracting" systems.[1]

It is argued that in the world of the Relativity Theory you can assume that system A is standing still and system B is moving; or that the former is moving and the latter standing still. Then, in the case of approach under the first assumption the time will be slower on system B; but in the case of retreat under the second assumption the time will be slower on the system A. Since the times and speeds derive their values from relative comparison, the result can be shown to come out the same in both cases. But in reality, again, it cannot be that the same system is either standing still or moving.

Yet the contraction assumption and particularly the slowing down of processes on moving systems have been widely discussed. It makes the theory appear mysteriously wondrous; and men love mystery. Thus science writers have speculated, expansively, about astronauts becoming younger when traveling at speeds of light.

Certainly, such astronauts could catch a ray of light that passed us a time ago, and thus recapture a tiny past effect. Fliers of supersonic planes can do the same with sounds, which are a bit more substantial. Yet they do not regress in time. Rays of light or sounds are only tiny facets of reality, while the whole universe, with every atom in it, would have to be changed back, to attain regression into the past. Time is merely the relationship of changes which are infinitely many.

The point is that with a medium the uniform speed of light, as everything else, is automatically explainable. Sound moves

uniformly through the air and no contraction or slowing down of
time on moving systems, say airplanes, has to be assumed. The
frequency of sound changes with an approaching or retreating
airplane. So does the radiation frequency from moving stars or
galaxies, as is well known in modern astronomy.

Further, the compressing Field accounts for the effects of the
"curvature" of space. As we shall see in explaining gravitation,
the Field pressure uniformly decreases or becomes one-sided
around bodies of matter. Such uniform gradations in the Field
pressures are identical with the "curvature." Light, propagated
by the Field pressures, has to bend toward a gravitational body
because from that side the pressure is less. Concrete structural
properties of gravitational curvature were used to explain phenomena like the abnormal revolutions of the perihelion of Mercury.
Such properties are the same as those of the gravitational gradations in the Field. The concrete properties of the "curvature" *must
be of or in something equally real.*

But science writers cannot resist the fascination of mystery,
and speculate about a *curved universe* with a different geometry,
and about universe travelers always returning to their starting
point. This is a mystification. A *geometric* straight line does not
curve, and you can travel by it, however the sphere of the universe around you may—or may not—curve. There is a perfect
curvature within the gravitational space around our earth, but we
still can travel away from it instead of returning back within this
curvature.

Also the *"fourth dimension"* has been turned into a mystery,
though Einstein was careful to point out that the application of
the fourth-dimension time coordinate is similar to the method
used in making timetables of trains or graphs of weather reports.[1]

Gravitation. The most puzzling, generally avowed mystery in
physics is the gravitation. Newton himself recognized that attraction of bodies without anything between them "is to me so great
an absurdity . . . that no man can fall into it."[2] He speculated
about particles of Ether being finer in the vicinity of bodies.[2] But
he finally admitted the mystery by attributing the cause of the
force of gravitation to God. Einstein's curvature of space—iden-

tical with the gradations in the Field—is an equal mystery if there is nothing to be, or act, curved.[8]

The explanation of gravitation is self-evident if the Field is thought of. As the Field pressures push in, let us say, on one side of a body of matter they are shielded off so that on the other side the universal pressures are onesided. The overall result is a sphere of one-sided pressures around the body.

Since all particles and matter quanta are activated by the Field pressures, they automatically move toward the gravitational body because from that side the pressures are less. A very large and dense body of matter is required to produce any noticeable gravitational effect, because the Field is all around the body and inside it, therefore makes the shielding only slightly effective. That is why gravitation is such a weak, shadowy force, in comparison with the pressures that compress atoms or propagate radiation.

The "shielding" also explains why gravitation quickly decreases with distance from the body. Physicists have calculated that rays or fast-moving particles shooting at a body uniformly from all sides would create around it a shadow or shielding similar to gravitation.[2] The strength of such shielding showed, in the calculations, to measure by the inverse square relation to distance, exactly as the force of gravitation does.[2] However, any rays of gravitation or "ultramundane" particles have remained mere assumptions—while the Field pressures, acting necessarily in the same way, are everywhere.

Gravitational areas with their one-sided Field pressures affect all physical phenomena, governed by the Field. Radiation, as a product of the Field pressures, slows down when it goes out, from a heavy star, against the one-sided pressures of the Field, and its waves lengthen. The result is the red spectrum shift. All movement, being created by the Field pressures,[14] is hindered when it goes against gravitation and is accelerated when it goes with it. This is sufficient to explain all centripetal and centrifugal effects without the requirement of the "strings" of attraction.

The difference between the general and gravitational acceleration is a curious problem, raised by Einstein in his Theory of General Relativity. Whereas a big or heavy body requires more force to be accelerated, all bodies big or small, heavy or light, fall with the same acceleration.

Evidently, the force that makes bodies fall is already inside all matter, therefore does not need to be added or accumulated from outside as in general acceleration. This inherent force is the Field pressure which compresses all matter particles exactly equally, therefore makes all matter accelerate uniformly, in the direction of the lesser pressures. Denser matter embodies more of the Field pressures, on its more numerous or massive particles, therefore is heavier.

The explanation of gravitation by the curvature of space brings out the whole problem distinctly. The gravitational curvature or structural gradations of space postulated by Einstein—actually, identical with the gradations of the Field pressures—definitely requires a medium. Einstein found the curvature to be as real as the level gradations on the bowling green. Evidently, the curvature must be in something equally concrete, but experimentally unregistrable—as only the Field can be.

Electromagnetism. The causal source of electromagnetism has never been discovered. Scientists merely know that the "energy of electric charges and currents is not situated in the conductors with which they are most obviously associated, but is diffused throughout the surrounding medium."[2] The causal explanation is automatic if the Field is recognized: all electromagnetic effects result from self-equalization of pressures within the Field as a fluid medium.

The equalization starts when inequalities of enrichment in matter are created. When matter is enriched, by addition of electrons, it is more easily compressible. The Field presses in, thus forcing the electrons along the conductor until the pressures and matter enrichment are equalized throughout the Field, around and in the conductor. The effects are the current and the electromagnetic forces around it. (Converse inequality is created by matter loosing electrons—and the process is merely opposite.)

Further effects result from the Field leaving instantaneous loosenings behind—much like in radiation—as it presses into the conductor. Then, if other matter is passed through this area its atoms expand or accrue because of the loosenings. It becomes enriched, therefore compressible by the Field or capable of creating current. Thus the inductance, as well as the creation of electromagnetic transmissions and fields, is explained. If matter is left free near the space where such loosenings in the Field become saturated, it naturally moves into the area of the loosenings, because the Field pressures from that side are less. This explains the various movements and "gravitation," particularly by metallic and ferromagnetic substances, within fields around electric currents.

The central, evident fact in electromagnetism is that the unit or "grain" of action here is the electron. Only the kinds of matter that can respond to this grain, like metals and ferromagnetic substances, produce the electromagnetic effects. They readily absorb and transmit electrons and their "pulses." Other substances may not respond at all to this grain, or may break down electrons, thus creating heat and light.

The attraction of opposite charges, or repulsion of charges of the same pole, is an automatic result of the self-equalization of the Field pressures. When direct equalization of differences in electron enrichment is impossible because the bodies with the different enrichment or charge are apart, the Field automatically tends to bring them together to equalize the differences. Conversely, by pushing apart equally charged bodies the Field diffuses the pressure inequality in that area.

It has to be remembered that all matter and charges in the bodies are ultimately causal products of the Field, and that the omnipresent Field controls all effects as if everything were in contact, except that the electron equalization or the current is delayed as long as the bodies are apart.

It is interesting to note that electromagnetic phenomena can be shown to resemble those of fluid mechanics. Thus bodies with cavities through which liquid can flow, and bodies pulsating in unison, when immersed in a liquid, exert mutual forces on each other similar to electromagnetic attraction.[2]

Naturally, if the Field cannot move the bodies to attain equalization in charges, it dislocates, at least, the charges within the bodies. One effect is that a neutral body acquires, in its parts facing a charged body, a charge that is opposite to that of the charged body. As one side of the body thus gathers all the positive charges, the other side is left negatively charged, or vice versa. This can explain the various phenomena of electrostatic induction.[14]

Interesting is the fact that no electric effects arise in hollow spaces inside conductors. Scientists, though, know that space, not conductors, creates electric effects.[2] Evidently, it is the immense Field pressures accumulating through the vast space that determine, overwhelmingly, all effects. The Field pressures from the smaller space inside the conductor cannot prevail in any way against those immense outside pressures.

Magnets are easily understandable as products of the Field pressures around a current. These pressures deform the matter they meet on their way and go through. Some metals retain this deformation or erosion after the current stops, and thus become permanent magnets. Such erosion may be visualized as a directional asymmetry. Since a better balance is attained if this asymmetry is matched with opposite asymmetry, or at least with a nondistorted metal, the magnetic attraction is the result. The Field as the medium connecting everything makes the attraction effective at distance.

Magnets, in nature or in machines, when put in the path of the Field pressures around a current, become aligned in the same direction they were eroded, since this offers the easiest way for the Field pressures to go, again, through them. All observed properties and action by magnets are explainable by these principles, if the actual directions of such effects by the Field are considered.[14] Thus in electric motors the Field pressures are more effective depending on such directions of the magnetic "erosions." This creates tendencies that move current-bearing conductors. As the "erosion" is increased, by electrically sustained magnetization, the movement gains force.

Our explanations of electricity and magnetism agree with the more detailed descriptions of complex lines of forces and with numerous other effects physicists have observed.[14] The greatest authorities, Faraday, Maxwell, or Lord Kelvin, had to assume very complex lines, vortex filaments, tubes, whirls, spheres or wheels of Ether to have some explanation.[2] It is even worse not to see any causal source for the effects. Then skillful and intelligent creation and maintenance—by angels—for each one of the complex and varied phenomena everywhere would have to be assumed.

Scientists have not even started to think of the one simple cause behind the complex phenomena, because the universal strong or dense yet unregistrable medium is inconceivable under the non-relative view. Physicists could explain incomparably better what we have indicated only in principle, if they recognized the clearly existing forces in the space as deriving from the absolutely omnipresent therefore unnoticeable medium.

We may mention, very briefly, the *creation of stars and planets*. Masses of matter starting, accidentally, to accumulate create a stronger gravitation and accumulate even more matter. Since such chain reaction creates an abnormal condition sustained only by further increase in the process, the first accidental stop in it starts a reverse chain reaction. As the Field pressures start dispelling the accumulation this increases their effectiveness which dispels matter even more.

Such *opposite chain reactions* can explain the pulsars, the pulsing action of quasars or galaxies, and the novae, as well as less spectacular, slower reversals in the lives of stars. One result of the extreme, opposite chain reactions, in the formation of suns or planets, is the creation of heavier elements. Above-normal impact of the Field pressures during the counter chain reactions compresses the simpler atoms with added strength,[14] squeezing off the "packing loss."

In the formation of *planets* the determining fact is that in any fluid medium, as the Field is, a movement always creates secondary countermovements. The simplest example is a falling drop causing splashes upward. The "splashes" from the forming sun become an outward radiation of mass of enormous dimensions, in uniform, even stationary-wave patterns that can explain the regularities of our planetary system, indicated in the laws of Kepler. The existing theories imply that our planets were created by some extremely rare event. But six out of nine planets in our system have moons or planets of their own—formed by the same process of mass concentration and secondary countermovements.[14]

Everything in the universe *rotates, spins, whirls, or spirals* in space, because this is what happens in any compressing medium. In water or air, similar whirls, twists and cyclic movements appear in streams, winds, storms, tornadoes or cyclones—wherever pressures have built up. A pressure that tries to dispel a formation while at the same time confining it from all sides, has to create the whirls, spins and spirals.

Finally, we have to emphasize the symmetry in the universe, of *negative and positive* opposites matching each other everywhere. This points to a universe governed by two opposites. We may mention here the negative particles and negative radiation.

Actually, the *negative "particles"* are only the necessary opposite effects, in the Field, of positive effects of matter. If physicists see most effects in matter as particles, they have to find their opposites, in the Field, also to be particles. For most of the two hundred new, esoteric particles,[14] physicists have indeed discovered and listed their negative counterparts.

In thinking of the *negative radiation* we may recall that the Field, while being absolutely fluid, is also perfectly "solid." Therefore, any counterthrusts from atoms into the Field are carried by it, a little like vibrations from hits would be by a metal. Such counterthrusts may result from new atoms springing into existence, by absorption of matter quanta. Physicists have connected negative rays with creation of new atoms.[6] Further, matter may carry negative rays somewhat like the Field carries the usual, positive rays. A molecule yields to the thrust of the negative ray, momentarily loses a matter quantum and compensates for it by absorbing a matter quantum from the next molecule.

In the end we have to emphasize that physicists themselves find the theory of *physics to be in a state of complete confusion and mystery.* As Planck states "not a single instance of causal connection" is found, in modern physics,[3] and "it is impossible to demonstrate the existence of the real world by rational means."[3] Uncertainty, indeterminacy, mere probability, acausality and the double-truth complementarity are accepted as the fundamental principles.[6,8]

Of course, if there is no causality, if it is not clear what comes from what, there can be only incoherence. No wonder that the greatest theorists—Eddington, Jeans or Schroedinger—have accepted "spiritual" and metaphysical concepts of physical phenomena.[2,8] The principle of complementarity, enounced by Bohr, permits a double-truth logic—so that even justice can have two complementary, different meanings, according to Bridgman.[4]

Instead of causal laws, only statistical aggregate probability is discovered, in modern physics. Apparently, there is one, simple cause behind the statistically *uniform* effects. But because the physicist does not see what it is or how it works, he can only register the statistical uniformity.

The theory of modern physics is so confused that the greatest modern physicists, Einstein or Planck, have found themselves before a hard dilemma.[3,8] Einstein's remark, that God could not be playing dice with the world, has been often quoted. The mystery is spilling over to other fields. If the physics, the most exact of sciences, has to be so ambiguously metaphysical, then every humanistic mystification—from philosophy of free will to a theory of ESP—seems justified.

Actually physics should be the simplest of sciences. The fact that mathematics can be used throughout physics reveals the absolute uniformity or inherent simplicity of its phenomena. Only something that coincides with the way all men exist, therefore corresponds to the simple, universal, mathematical forms of men's thinking, can have such mathematical uniformity.[14]

It is not the first time that a field of science has sunk into complex, mystifying confusion, because some simple causal truth had remained unthinkable. The Field, certainly, seems impossible. But even a great discovery, the Copernican system, was rejected as contrary to common sense, by the very founder of experimental scientism Francis Bacon. We better take the advice of John A.

Wheeler that "only when we recognize how strange the universe is will we understand how simple it is." The unthinkable Field concept permits simple, almost self-evident explanations everywhere, even under our pioneering discussion; a physicist could improve the explanations beyond comparison.

The Field is what physicists always have, or should have, sought: *the missing causal source with cosmic strength and universality yet as invisible or unregistrable as nothingness.* And all that is required is the removal of the natural human prejudice against the "negative," causal sources of the positive values; and the realization that absolutely universal causal backgrounds are as *"nonexistent" as water is to fish.* The properties of the Field then become clear from the ordinary effects of matter. No assumptions or hypotheses are required.

Causal Insights for the Theory of Life and Genetics

The *living process* becomes plainly understandable if the Field-matter interaction is recognized. Life is a particularly general and uniform natural phenomenon. As such it is, necessarily, determined by one natural causal principle, which can be only simple. It would be fundamentally clear to everyone if the action of the Field was perceived. In the opposition between the Field and matter, the living process is the reverse of the predominant processes like fire created by the dominant Field: life can be viewed as "negative fire." It is a chain reaction by matter against the Field, just as ordinary fire is a chain reaction by the Field against matter.

Scientists have compared life to fire. As Philip Handler says, "flames not only reproduce by means of sparks, but also show metabolism and growth."[9] At the same time scientists find that life proceeds by "negative entropy," which is the exact opposite of what fire does.[14]

In fire the Field, as the dominant opposite, destroys matter enrichment with explosive suddenness and simple ease. But the living matter, as the dominated, "oppressed" opposite, can proceed with its chain reaction only by circumventing the Field, in "surreptitious," involved, endlessly delayed and extended ways. This is what makes life enormously complex, penetratively flexible, long-lasting, extensive in all its forms, and endlessly "inventive."

The causal source of the chain reaction of life is the *giant size of living molecules,* which is the most evident, universal and striking property of living matter. While nonliving molecules may have only dozens of atoms, with a couple of electrons to be shared in forming bonds, the living molecules may have millions of atoms. Proteins, the determining forms of living matter, can have molecular weight of tens of millions.[14] The DNA and RNA polymers are even more gigantic, in comparison.[14] Moreover, the molecular enrichment or the number of electrons to be shared in living bonds is correspondingly large.[10,11]

A giant molecule, arising like a negative spark—under conditions we shall explain later—offers protection against the pressures of the Field so that in its "shadow" other matter and energy can accumulate. *This increases its power, which in turn attracts more matter and energy, in a chain-reaction way.* Absorbable matter, and energy mostly coming from the sun, is required to sustain such reaction and keep it from collapsing. Atoms always absorb energy or matter enrichment, but under the Field pressure they immediately give up the enrichment. They can keep and accumulate the enrichment in the protective "shadow" of the giant molecule.

Such enormous accumulation of enriched atoms then can evolve all kinds of bonds and grow into rich formations of endless combinations. Scientists know that "the large numbers of electric charges" as well as the great size of the living molecules enable them to form *"liquid crystals," that living forms are.*[11] According to A. I. Oparin, a leading international authority on the theory of life, "energy rich bonds" form the "aperiodic crystals" or protein crystals of living matter.[10]

All crystals are formed by attraction of molecules under "gravitational," protective action of crystal cores, amidst *invisible pressures.* The molecules fall in "predetermined" positions where they find the best balance or protection against the pressures. Evidently, the pressures are those of the Field. That is why scientists have difficulties understanding the dynamics of crystallization.[8]

The "gravitational," protective action in living processes is particularly evident from the way the emergence of living compounds requires the proximity of the giant, living molecules. *Enzyme action is typical:* presence of living molecules makes formation of living compounds possible. As stated by Asimov, the enzyme "merely offers a surface upon which a reaction can take place."[14] We would call it protective area instead of "surface." Enzymes, in their turn, are formed in the same way by proteins, which are likewise determined by the RNA and DNA polymers.

Similarities of living processes with *crystallization* have been often noted. Crystals are found to be "self-propagating" much like living matter.[9] Action similar to crystallization—resulting from specific protective attraction amidst pressures—explains how living matter can grow in strict order, by selectively assimilating food from the environment.

Everything is predetermined and selective here because the universal pressures by the Field do not permit any deviations in the way molecules find their best protection or balance under the given composition of the "crystal" cores and of the elements in the environment. The possible combinations here are astronomic, because of the endless numbers of bonds and molecules of the living "crystals." And the innumerable facets of each such "crystal" determine, further and further, the tiniest details of the whole organism.

The decisive factor is the strict universal presence of the Field pressures. These pressures determine with cosmic force that each "crystal" and molecule find its exact form or position in its one and only, best way. That is why living forms are so rigorously *"predetermined," as if governed by innumerable laws*—or as if predestined for definite purposes. Of course, selection leaves only those, "purposeful" forms which are fit to survive best and exactly reproduce themselves.

Biologists have, hopefully, turned to concepts like tropism[11] to explain how, for instance, roots turn downward under gravitation. But such forces or laws attributable to them are only few, while the laws governing living phenomena are endless. The control by the Field of the living matter at every point is the simple unseen source of such endless laws or "purposes" for every minutest thing in the living world, which otherwise has to appear a metaphysical miracle.

The above processes, comparable to crystallization, can explain the predetermined *growth* and search for specific material or *food* by living forms. The final function of life, namely, *reproduction* is equally an automatic outcome of the pressures of the Field acting on the accumulation of living matter.

Scientists know that "a growing colloid particle may reach a point at which it becomes unstable and breaks down into smaller particles, each of which grows and reproduces."[10] In reproduction, the unseen pressures and tendencies of the Field and living matter are the underlying causes. The Field tries to break down any matter accumulation, but matter accumulating within the protective fields of the giant molecules tends to hold together.

Under such two opposing tendencies a living formation starts breaking up at one point of its growth but does so by keeping as much mass together as possible. The result is division into *only two units*, that hover within each other's field forces until each grows to its full size.

During such growth the two units become exactly equal, for if one is smaller it attracts more matter from the other with which it is joined. Any other dissimilarity is equallized in the same way, between two competing yet joint units, under the same pressures and forces. The double helix construct offers an atomistic explanation of the reproduction by joined units.

Life, despite its universal uniformity and therefore necessary simplicity, is the great mystery in science. The *present theories* of life are not less conjectural than our explanations, but are hardly maintainable. They have never even enounced *one universal and uniform principle,* which is, evidently, the very essence of life. Like fire, life is everywhere the same and an exclusively singular phenomenon. As some scientists have pointed out it is a unique process contrary to the general laws of entropy;[10] it remains always the same;[11] and it acts like a special kind of a yet undiscovered charge, or a "special form of movement of matter."[10,11]

But all the scientific speculations about life perpetuate the belief that life evolved cumulatively and gradually by complex uniquely rare chance combinations of matter without any special principle. If this were so, every one of the myriads of the miraculous living forms and mechanisms would require a similar uniquely rare combination. Yet living forms evolve and grow under ordinary conditions, all the time and everywhere. They do so under the singular cosmic drive or force of living matter, comparable to fire. Without such universal drive or principle, the accumulation and corresponding complexity of any living form would be impossible in our physical universe governed by destruction and dispersion of all accumulated organization or enrichment of matter.

The principle of selection has been invoked, particularly by Oparin, to prove that gradual accumulation of chance improvements could work in evolving life.[10] But any form of matter increasing in size and multiple complexity would be least fit to survive in the world tending toward entropy and minimal organization—unless a special drive or principle promotes it.

Finally we have to try to explain the *origin of the spark of life, of the giant molecule.* Very peculiar conditions would be required for it, since under ordinary conditions the Field precludes or destroys any essential increase in particles of matter. We can think of the peculiar, ambiguous conditions during the cooling off periods of our planet.

First, such cooling off is still a continuation of intense burning or yielding to the pressures of the Feld. This yielding to the Field also produces in it the momentary loosenings that constitute all radiation. Thus the universal cooling off also creates saturation of loosenings in the Field. In such a saturation it may happen that the loosenings may accidentally concentrate, at one crosspoint, to the extent of creating a spot in which the Feld pressures are momentarily absent and a giant molecule can instantaneously accumulate. Second, the cooling off may offer conditions cool enough for the incipient living formation to survive immediate destruction by burning.

This conjecture is confirmed by experiments that have produced compounds resembling living matter. In the frequently mentioned experiments by Oparin, Urey, and Miller, electric sparks or charges were used. This can, naturally, produce conditions of saturated loosenings in the Field, for periods short enough to prevent burning up of the new compounds. In other famous experiments, by Sidney W. Fox, or Gerhard Schramm, high heat was used, in ways that prevented it from breaking up the compounds.[14] Shock waves, that can create for mere instants temperatures of several thousand degrees, have expectedly been found ideal for creating compounds similar to living matter.[14]

As we have seen, scientists know that *giant molecules acting through their catalytic field forces* are at the root of all living processes, or that life resembles fire. But only the unseen Field-matter interaction can explain life as the negative fire and the giant molecules as the catalytic sparks that sustain it.

The Field-matter interaction in the living process further explains the causality in *genetics,* which is next in importance for the biological sciences. Such explanation offers an alternative to the clearly unsound theory of modern genetics that the destructively chaotic "gene mutations" are the sources of organic adaptation which is a virtual miracle of endless exclusively purposive precision.

According to the modern genetics genes as bearers of characters never change except by the destructive mutations. Surely, experiments always show the unchangeability of characters or traits, first decisively demonstrated by Mendel. *Preservation of sameness* is, indeed, the universal law of organisms, as we have seen everywhere. But we have also seen that this law *does not preclude change by conditioning.* Only, the genetic conditioning can never be discovered by experiments.

First, such conditioning is that of the organism as a whole, with myriads of interdependent processes being imperceptibly gradually affected, while experiments can deal only with isolated, clear-cut elements. Secondly, the conditioning is illogical or "deceitful," as it uses drives for turning them, in the end, against themselves. Third, the direct, initial results—that experiments reveal—are contrary, in conditioning, to the results finally attained. Whether it is educational conditioning or animal feeding, the first reaction to the conditioning is opposition, while compliance results in the end. If one is being conditioned to eat mostly one certain food, say rice, he will reject it in favor of some other food on any single occasion; but he will end by preferring it in general, as his usual food.

All in all, experiments can show only the genetic unchangeability of traits; and a modern scientist would have to be crazy to oppose evidence from experiments. The modern experimental genetics remains a system of half truths. Organic conditioning and the imperceptibly gradual changes are determined by the simple, integrated, pleasure or value reactions of the *organism as a whole*. But experimentally these factors are ungraspably complex, and paradoxical.

The imperceptible changes of traits of living forms as organic wholes can be understood, schematically, if one thinks of the action of the living matter through its fields of forces. As we saw, living forms, comparable to crystals, are determined by the fields of forces of living matter that is the center and source of such fields. Thus there is always the *center-and-field* interaction, even if it is ungraspably complex. Viewed as one whole, the organism is determined by a genetic center of matter acting through its fields. The stronger the center in some facet, the more extensive the corresponding organic function or form organized by the field of forces.

What is more, the center-and-field interaction is *reciprocal*. A greater accumulation of living matter increases its field of forces. But a stronger or wider field permits larger accumulation of matter. Such two-way influences can be observed in any interaction between matter as center and its field forces. In electromagnetism, increased charge in a body strengthens the fields around it; but strengthened fields around a body increase its charge. In burning, a greater initial size of fire at a given spot intensifies the conditions of combustion there; but, also, more intense conditions of combustion, like heat, dry air or burnable material, increase the size of the fire.

For an organism the strengthening or advantages from the field are ultimately those from the *external environment or conditioning*. But they reach the determining center of the organism only through innumerable levels. For each such level the "environment" or conditioning medium is the next more external level. That is how the acquired traits reach the genetic center that determines the whole organism. Because this center is so deeply hidden under the endlessly numerous levels, evolved through millions of years, the changes induced in it by the environment or conditioning can be only imperceptibly slight.

Yet however infinitesimal or humanly imperceptible the changes, absolutely *every one of the endless environmental influences leaves its corresponding effect*. This is how the adaptation to environment can be so gradual as well as purposive to every tiniest, humanly inconceivable detail. It is attained by myrial additions, through ages, of repetitive influences that leave their averagely streamlining infinitesimal effects, like sandstorms polishing the cliffs or water streams forming a river.

The *"backward" action, or reverse transcription*, from the more external levels toward the organizing core, has been confirmed by recent experimental findings. Howard Temin proved, in his famous experiments on the "reverse transcriptase," that RNA can organize DNA. Other researchers have demonstrated similar reverse action for a dozen of viruses.[14] Generally, it is common knowledge that environmental or conditioning influences during the individual's life induce adaptive changes which remain through several renewals of cells and of everything else in the organism.

This means that the mechanisms which shape the organism, and which usually are the "genes," have been adaptively changed by environment or conditioning. In fact, the Darwinian theory, which provides the only, genial explanations for biology, requires the *inheritance of such acquired* adaptive, gradually accumulated changes.[11,12]

Darwin sought to explain the inheritance of the acquired traits by his theory of pangenesis. He reasoned that each cell in the organism releases gemmules which form the reproductive cells. This is a "scientific," atomistic way of seeking an explanation, whereas the organism always acts as a whole with astronomically multiple complexity. Anything that happens in the organism is, indeed, a product of everything else in it. The reproductive cells are thus, undoubtedly, created by the whole organism. They are centers of organization of the future organisms and replicas of the center of organization of the parent organism.

But such center can be, and is, *present in the organism everywhere, dispersed and involved in every mechanism. Yet it can still act as a true, single center* to which every influence flows and from which all organization emanates, including its own reproduction in millions of replicas.

That is how nature works in its myriad complexity, under simplest principles. In this case such principle is the *both-way interaction* between the organizing center of the organism and its fields of forces affected by the environment or conditioning. *Purposiveness* in such interaction is automatic because the influences proceed on exactly the same lines both ways, and strict purposiveness of every line of influence, from center toward environment, is established by selective adaptation. Eyes of crabs, developed for use of light, under its stimulation, atrophy with absence of light during their existence in caves.

Perfect *purposive* adaptation to conditions of environment is the glaring fact of everything known in biology. The whales, porpoises, seals, manatees, various reptiles, and even penguins to a degree, have been shaped into "fishes" by the sea. The wings of birds, bats and butterflies have been shaped by the flying, into best adapted almost uniquely similar shapes in spite of total genetic dissimilarity of the species.

Second, this adaptation is endlessly *gradual.* All evidence of evolution, from every geological finding, confirms this, particularly by revealing the transitional forms, everywhere, from crude, rudimentary beginnings to miraculous final adaptations gradually accumulated through millions of years. Darwin saw that evolution is not determined by "sports" or sudden deviations. Even if sudden changes occur, they require infinite tiny adaptations, to become viable.

Now, this purposive adaptation and gradualness are exactly contrary to the totally *disruptive and sudden* "gene mutations" that modern genetics accepts as the only source of evolutionary change.[11] The mutations are assumed to arise from physical or chemical accidents, like cosmic rays, heat, or atomic shocks. The incongruity here becomes evident.

There are some seven octillion molecules and ten trillion cells in man.[11] Every one of these would require controlling genes, to emerge or perform in its one-and-only purposive way. Since everything in the organism has to agree with everything else, each such gene could change purposively by mere accident only once in billions and billions of times. Thus for every possible *purposive change* there would be *billions of deformations*. And even a single abnormal mutant "sticks out like a sore thumb," in the words of Sir Peter Medawar.[14] Evidently, adaptive gradual evolution would be the last thing achievable by the gene mutations.

In every living form, hand, eye, or heart, all the billions of cells and molecules are arranged and perform with streamlined smoothness, *without any* nonstreamlined or out-of-place formations. The organism, or the beehive, can be so complex yet *so unfathomably purposive because each of its endless million-year elaborations is only an adaptive expansion of some previous purposive mechanism.*

In brief, endlessly gradual additions, through ages, of only adaptive, imperceptibly slight, myriad changes can explain the miracle of the astronomic purposiveness in nature. All this is the very antithesis of the abrupt destructive chaos that the mutations have to bring. Selection, naturally, eliminates any influences by the mutations; it can never be helped by the mutant changes, bringing billions of deformations for any possible improvement.

Moreover, who or what created the billions or octillions of the purposive genes, in the first place? Nature can create astronomic purposive multiplicity, but then it must have a purposive simple principle to work by. Such principle, as we saw, is the "backward" action or "reverse transcription" of the environmental or conditioning influences.

It is true that geneticists can point out, in extensive discussions,[11,13] various phenomena like the chromosome rearrangements or breakages, polyploidy, genetic drifts and other kinds of genetic interactions, which seem to permit some selective evolution in ways explainable by the theory of unchangeable genes.[11,12] But in all these phenomena the adaptive characters are already there and the changes involve their mere recombinations.

The *concept of the gene* itself has been widely argued about, and the more cautious geneticists hardly accept it anymore as a genetic "atom" that the experimental geneticists, in their work, require it to be. As T. Dobzhansky points out: "talking about traits as though they were independent entities is responsible for much confusion."[12] What has been discovered about genes, like the gene maps or enzyme effects of assumed genes, is fully explainable by the natural fact that a major part of genetic material connectable with a trait or process may be, expectedly, located on one spot in the chromosome or in one strand of DNA. This is causally very different from existence of separate genes. In a chromosome, as in an organism, factors for a certain process, like eating, may be centered around one spot, like the mouth. But mouth as an isolated unit cannot organically exist and would be causally incongruous.

Only the *organism as a whole,* of myriad elements, is determining in living processes, but it cannot be dealt with by the modern, experimental genetics.

Modern genetics is a gigantic science that mainly explains the endless possibilities of combinations of permanent traits. Actually, the permanence of traits, or the maintenance of sameness by the organisms, is so clear that it needs no proofs or explanations. When general genetics deals with changes it only "explains" after the fact how the genes must have mutated—which happens always accidentally, therefore is *beyond the control by the geneticist.*

Thus, even the enthusiasts of modern genetics admit that it has remained "a pure rather than applied science."[13]

At the same time, controllable genetic influences on man are of enormous importance. Degenerative diseases, like cancer, have been traced to *inheritable* chromosomal or gene abnormalcies, which can be acquired during lifetime, specially through the excessive or artificial lifelong "improvements." The fate of our future generations genetically depends on how we adjust, overadjust, "sin," condition ourselves or react to environmental adversities. But the modern geneticist can only wait for the accidental—inherently destructive—mutations as the sources of genetic change. The above influences, or overadjustments, can be controlled only through the *reactions, like pleasure, of the organism as a whole.*

Of course, when geneticists deal with practical problems, they ignore the theory and try to obtain new, better, *changed traits* as practical breeders have always done. Or they accept *adaptations to the needs of environment* as the explanations of any observed trait or capacity of a species.

In practical breeding and in evolution, the combination of traits by crossbreeding, as by all sexual reproduction, is the primary, easy way of improving the stock. But mere recombination of never-changing characters cannot create the new, completely different permanent myriad traits, that evolution and practical breeders obtain and use besides the mere combinations of existing characters. Yet according to the modern genetics, even selective breeding can do nothing more than "disentangle a mixture of variations" of existing, unchanging traits.[13]

We have to add the concept of *Inner Selection,* to explain how the purposive adaptation works through every tiniest mechanism inside the organism.

The usual theory of selection implies that at every improvement in a species all its members perish except the one who has the improvement, and his progenes. But as we saw, virtually infinite numbers of tiny changes have to accumulate with such multiplicity that they seem imperceptibly continuous. The infinite improvements can be provided, without the destruction of the whole species at each of them, only by the Inner Selection, in which every tiniest form inside the organism improves automatically, by the simple principle of selection. Schematically, every mechanism or release follows and deepens automatically the channel that offers better, stronger flow.

The only additional principle needed is that of subordination. The lower processes, though they automatically self-increase, must stop doing so whenever this does not increase the higher process they are subordinated to. One can imagine a simple model for such subordination, like lower conductors getting always shut off if the higher conductor fails which it does whenever it is not favored. Anyway, if every mechanism thus automatically self-improves while permitting equally automatic self-improvement of higher mechanism and thus of the whole, then integrated adaptive progress is inevitable.

Nature, working with astronomic multiplicity, can create astronomically complex seemingly miraculous purposiveness if the simple principles by which it works are purposive or adaptive. The "backward" action or *"reverse transcription"* of the environmental influences, and the *Inner Selection* are such principles. They are sufficient to bring about the virtual miracles of nature by way of a mechanistic process and blind selection.

In conclusion we may emphasize that the concept of the Field, as the unseen, "negative" causal side of the physical reality, not only reveals how blindly one-sided the modern scientific views still are even in the most certain sciences; it also shows how simple and self-evident the explanations become once the seemingly impossible relative-value view is accepted.

The nonrelative view is like that of the fish not knowing the water they live in. The relative-value insight offers, as we saw, unsuspected causal explanations for everything man feels, does, knows or experiences, since it all is determined by his value reactions. Even his physical world consists of what he experiences or knows through his organic mental value processes.

IX

THE LIMITEDNESS OF MAN AND HIS DESTINY OF UNLIMITED MIRACLE

The inevitable limitedness of man, as organism, does not preclude increase in his capacities, which are, at bottom, satisfactions or releases. These can be increased unlimitedly because their causal sources, the needs as nonsatisfactions, or restrictions can be so increased. This has already been started by evolution and culture.

The higher animals are more restricted, through their larger brains, which work, as we saw, by way of restrictions. As to culture, all vigorous cultures and morals are systems of restrictions, almost by their very definition. Selection promotes, blindly, the progress, as those species and cultures which embody the restrictions survive better.

Evidently, if instead of the blind selection, progress is finally engineered by plan, the difference will be like that between a beaver dam and an interstate hydroelectric system. The present "sciences" about man, however, are closer to being alchemies than sciences, for reasons we explained. But once real human sciences advance, *men will become self-creators,* engineering and expanding thousandfold their capacities. Real sciences, as presently in the technologic fields, achieve such miracles. The only thing men cannot attain is a gain in value feelings, which is as impossible as mountains without valleys.

Nor can men make themselves immortal. Man will remain a mortal in his physical existence—in everything that is real to him —whatever his soul may be. But when man knows how to engineer his reactions, he will plan his feelings, of equal values and disvalues, to occur so that death is as little catastrophic as he wants. Thus men will free themselves of the problem of immortality, which is practically that of the fear of death.

Man's real *"immortality,"* or redemption, of any meaning, in the world that is real to him, lies with the future of men. That future can be as inconceivably miraculous as is our conscious life in comparison with, say, the existence of primordial trilobites. The very fact that we cannot know or conceive how dazzlingly different that destiny of man will be harbors our redemption. If our present miracle, the consciousness, has evolved by blind selection, what could not men attain in their self-creation by intellect? The future miracle is, evidently, to be such that our every possible aspiration or effort may well be justified or redeemed.

Causally Understood Science the Key

In every field, the science as the way of proceeding with coherent effort, that is, with causal understanding brings, in the end, limitless progress. Presently only the technologic fields are scientific, and the miracles there are greater than the powers of gods people could imagine a few centuries ago. We have to emphasize that in the fields dealing with man the present scientific and humanistic thought can only be unscientific or incoherent, because here its very logic is contrary to what is causally true. Under this logic, of direct increases or "improvements" in satisfactions or releases, modern man has brought on himself all the disasters of disease, abnormality and disorders.

Naturally, these "improvements" are enormously enhanced by the modern technologic resourcefulness that brings us the rich life. The result is that the technologic progress has become a scourge of calamities. One can understand, therefore, that many modern prophets, perhaps the most clamorous and often quite popular ones, have *turned against scientific progress.*[8]

Our learned groups are now frequently seeking their insights rather from mystifications, proferred by authors like Carlos Castaneda or Theodore Roszak, about sorcery, shamanism, drug trips, hallucinations or other irrational experiences. The popularity of esoteric cults, from transcendental meditation to Arica, that we have mentioned before, is typical of the trend.

It is ironic that exactly those people who have most passionately advocated the deepening of enjoyments of our experiences are condemning the progress. For it is the modern trend of enjoyments that has turned our progress, with its opportunities of prodigious improvements, into the source of the calamities. Throughout history, the logical progressists, righteously fighting for more freedoms and satisfactions, have brought revolutions and conflicts that have killed millions, by innocent, unintended confusion.

The reason for such confusions has been the same that is perpetuating the modern mystery about our functional diseases and disorders. It is the lack of insight into the paradox that human value reactions and capacities, as satisfactions or releases, derive from their opposites, the hard restrictions.

This insight is the key, because it amounts to the causal understanding as the only possible basis for the sciences of man, however such sciences are established. There can be no science without causal understanding, without the knowledge of what will cause what. And, particularly, no science is possible with beliefs that are contrary to causal truths. This is presently the case in the human and social sciences. Everybody, however, writes and talks as if these, "soft" sciences have arrived—though endless controversies and confusion in these fields are noted everywhere.

Once a *causally understood science* of man begins, the controversies about the need for more progress are bound to disappear. However sophisticated the criticism of progress,[6,8] we all want to increase our capacities or avoid disorders. Science can provide the understanding of how this can be achieved. Of course, the most difficult thing will be to follow such understanding, to accept the restrictions or conditioned nonsatisfactions. But whatever the difficulties, science will enable men to start doing what they really intend or have to do. Rejection of science amounts to a flight into incoherence—however fashionable it may be.

The opposite or relative causal logic has to be emphasized. Value reactions derive from their opposites, and determine what man feels, wants or is interested in. Also the human capacities, the releases of pleasure or life flow, are made available through their opposites, the restrictions, as we have repeatedly explained. Thus everything men want and are able to achieve is governed by the opposite causal logic. But this logic is contrary to the very way of thinking in the present scientism and humanistic thought.

In brief, we have here virtually *two, contrary world views,* the present one and the one revealing the relative or opposite causality as the basis of sciences of man. We may, therefore, have to say more about the opposition or restriction as the universal source of progress and reality.

Opposition is the mainspring of the universe. Force would be a meaningless dissipation without opposition; and matter could not have any form or effect without the nothingness which is its opposite in every sense, as we saw in discussing the Field. On the next level, of living nature, the opposition or "oppression" by the Field is what creates life, making it endlessly "inventive," penetratingly flexible, expansive, long-lasting, and "purposively" predetermined, as if governed by innumerable laws. On the highest level, the brain and consciousness represent the furthest step of progress through opposition or restriction.

Consciousness amounts to a life within the organic life of the individual, as it delays and stores the lower brain reactions, thus providing memory, and foresight through it. Such life requires its own resources. They are provided by restriction on releases. This is not very different from what higher organisms do in all creation of their reserves and more evolved adjustments.

The restriction that has created consciousness requires action by the organism against itself, as if its own obstruction. This is an extraordinary, unnatural, inherently abnormal procedure. That is why the consciousness has to be an exceedingly rare phenomenon, emerging from some extraordinary upheaval. It may be significant that man as conscious being, with his larger brain, evolved during the ice ages, the hardest period for his species.

All *evolution* of species is a product of opposition or restriction. The selection works by way of opposition or difficulties. As the living forms encounter such opposition, they "seek," selectively, more circuitous and complex adjustments, which are richer, in human terms. It can be said that the higher living forms are results of disasters imposed on the species by the opposition or difficulties. The primitive animal has been subjected to the tortures of living on dry land, suffering the rigors of climate, famishing from lack of its usual foods or avoiding increased dangers, before it has become richly "endowed" to cope with the difficulties.

Darwin's theory of survival of the fittest, under adversities of the chaotic world and cruel competition, amounts to a recognition, in one area of sciences, of the principle of creation through opposition or difficulties. His theory is a marvel of self-evident simplicity, that even a child can understand, as well as of an unparalleled richness of explanations. The mysteries that philosophers and scientists had struggled with for millenia, the very "purposefulness" of the living world, have become clear under the simple concept of the Darwinian selection.

In all fields similar explanations could be reached if their real causal truth, the same principle of opposition, as the spring of the universe, was recognized.

But this causal principle of opposition is the very *antithesis of human beliefs* in value and purpose. That is why the causal explanations for the sciences of man will have to wait—even longer than did the simple truths of the evolution by selection—under the sacred beliefs still dominating modern thought. Let us look at the most certain of such beliefs: the "inviolable" innate human values, the progressive social nature of man, or the sublime sources of human morality. We have to repeat that by exposing the unthinkable, opposite or "negative" causal sources of values we are not rejecting values but are rather offering explanations which could help their scientific, potentially miraculous enrichment, that only a causal understanding can bring.

Social and cultural progress requires *integration* of society into a veritable organism and *transformation* of man's natural, selfish drives into love and interests for the others integrated in such organism. This, practically, means creation of the *"anthill" society* and conditioning by *"brainwashing."* These are the most odious things to every theorist, writer, philosopher, scientist or spiritual leader.[2] The practical progress is moving in this "odious" direction, as is typically foreseen by writers like Orwell or Huxley, who are horrified by the prospect.

Men will progress in spite of the individualistic and liberal ideas of humanists. Organically integrated and totally conditioned people will enjoy a hundredfold increase in efficiency, and the highest practical selfless love for each other. This will render meaningless the selfish individual freedoms, or the humanistic love which is, at bottom, a biologic, sexual, or pleasurably egoistic drive.

Social cooperation is typical of the progress against human nature. This cooperation is almost the only immediate source of our progress. But it has to be imposed on men by death-or-life threat, against their deepest natural "values" extolled in the humanistic individualism and love of freedom. Without society there would be no specialization, industry, morals, organization or anything larger than a family group could build. But social cooperation has emerged only because of the gravest, insuperable danger to man—threat from other men.

In the last few thousand years the human race has approached overpopulation at a progressive rate and the progress has increased at the same rate. The late homo sapiens, like the Cro-Magnon man, had as much brains as we have. But he did not progress at all, for hundreds of thousands of years, because his intelligence made him the ruler of nature, free of critical difficulties. Only other men, with equal powers of intelligence could present a radical threat to him.

This started happening when increasing populations came in contact. Primitive tribes, as extended families, faced destruction at the hands of any larger groups. Thus groups had to become larger and larger in order to survive. For there is only one certainty when strange groups meet: they kill or enslave the strangers of the weaker, smaller group—or eat them, which rare species do. The most closely integrated, great societies, of Western Europe emerged during the Hundred Years' wars.[17]

Of course, after the society has developed and imposed the needs or restrictions on the person, he derives equal satisfactions or sense of values from them. Philosophers then view this as proof of the "social nature" of man. They also find an elaborate set of social adjustments, which are harmonious in their last phase, here as in any selective adaptation. Purposive, higher social principles then are postulated. In truth, if men were social by nature, societies would not need the complex codes, morals, laws, institutions or the whole intricate social culture.

Morals are products of opposition of human natural drives. They are restrictions of the "animal" instincts, by their very definition. Love of neighbor is the core of morals. This love is attained by opposition of the instinctive selfish interests of man which constitute all and only natural drives of the organism. As we saw, one's love of man or God is a satisfaction growing from its equal opposite, the harrowing conditioned needs. Even after a person has acquired the moral virtues, of inhibitions, shame or sense of guilt, he views them as unfortunate afflictions. Particularly the logical and scientific, modern moralists condemn such negative, restrictive reactions.

Sin, in its nature, is revealing. Moralists have branded sins as ugly. This is a joke for the modern, scientific man. Sins are pleasant, invigorating, satisfactory, liberating and positively felt in every way, in their direct effects. Men have always loved intoxication, or forms of Bacchanalia, to get rid of moral restrictions. Modern life has added revolts, rationalistic enlightenment and liberalism, cultivated by the humanistic thought, education, literature and "scientific" theory.

Thus the real nature of sin, as an overenjoyment of releases that necessarily brings impoverishment, is not recognized. The traditional, often harmless sins are still condemned. But the present far more important sins, our main overenjoyments, are overlooked, though they bring us impoverishment and disorders—from heart disease to economic slumps. Such real sins are rather found as desirable goals, because of their directly satisfying and liberating effects.

Progress, in general, is attained by *opposition of human natural drives,* by men being forced into it, against their will, through difficulties they encounter. Looking back in history one may wonder how people were so myopic as not to see the advantages the progress was to bring. Moreover, it is not difficult to see what the future progress requires.

Just more reasonable attitudes, of cooperation or interests beyond narrow selfishness would bring enormous benefits for all. This has been theoretically clear in the various utopian visions implied in most of the leading ideologies. All utopias are logically possible. But people are not "reasonable" or unselfish. *The cooperative love or "reason" can be created only by opposition of the fundamental, selfish drive.*

Finally in the immediate practical fields—of human health, capacities or motivations—the opposition or restrictions, as we have seen repeatedly, are the creative source. Thus the course of advance from primordial life to enrichment of conscious capacities has been the road of opposition or restrictions.

The next phase will be one of far greater progress, through imposition of *restrictions by causally understood science.* We have to stress that this science will have to be completely different— based on the presently unthinkable principles of "negative" value sources. It will therefore bring equally unthinkable changes and progress, of presently inconceivable dimensions and acceleration, as scientific planning will replace blind cultural selection.

What the *future science* will be like we cannot know. But as the guide to the highest phase in evolution it is bound to follow the principle of opposition and restriction, the causal sources of all reality and evolutionary progress. At present, the best we can hope is to make clear that the principle of restriction, embodied in man's cultural and moral, necessarily superstitious tradition, is to be upheld by causally understood efforts rather than being rejected as contrary to science.

The modern humanistic *value attitudes* can only hinder progress. Under the present "scientifically" logical views, enjoyments become desirable goals. For, in fact, science shows all, even highest values to derive from satisfactions. Enjoyment of most varied values has been urged as remedy against the fateful shallowness of modern life, by the most prominent and popular writers, such as Bertrand Russell, Sir Julian Huxley, Lewis Mumford, Erich

Fromm, Karl Jaspers, Paul Tillich, Arnold Toynbee, or Herbert Marcuse.[17]

In a collection of essays, *The Place of Value in the World of Facts,*[13] leading scientists, from all fields, reaffirm the belief in the enjoyment of higher values as the goal of human progress. Another, similar collection, *Values and the Future,* shows that modern critics see values as the established customary value feelings—which are mostly fixational. Deepening of qualitative experiences has been expounded by prominent scientists of varied fields and times, from William James to René Dubos.[5,17]

In truth, increase in the *"qualitative"* values is an effort *as futile as chasing one's own shadow.* There can be no value experience without exactly equal opposite experiences as past backgrounds or later aftereffects. That is how organic reactions work, within the limitedness of the organism; and even the sublimest value feelings derive from the organic reactions. Enjoyment in any form is an expenditure of releases and can have only impoverishing effect—which, to the extent of its intensity, can accumulate to become cause of anxiety, stress or functional disorder.

Of course, the writers and scientists have in mind the feelings of enrichment that accompany positive reactions, like love or interests. Here we may repeat that all positive reactions are most desirable, and pleasant. But they, as satisfactions or releases can be made possible only through their opposites, needs or restrictions—conditioned fears, nonsatisfactions or frustrations.

Indeed, practically, these *negatively felt causal opposites* are the constantly and painfully accumulated sources of the feelings of satisfaction or value. The big problem is to create and conserve these sources, not to exhaust them by enjoyments, which seem so desirable and are so convincingly advocated. The task can become involved.

For instance, enjoying music, going to opera, seeing beautiful things, traveling, or having sublime thoughts—these enjoyments derive from the conditioned *sublimation,* nonsatisfaction or practically frustration of our natural needs, of security, sex or growth. But sublimation is hard, cannot be expanded easily, and it would be perhaps better if we directed it toward the progressively useful satisfactions, of love or interests. For, if we concentrate on the "higher" enjoyments there is less of satisfaction potential for the useful interests; these then, *practically, become less attractive.*

We admit that in practice the whole economy of satisfactions can be as involved and contradictory as are all human adjustments. The "higher" enjoyments can serve as inducements in the system of refinement or restrictions, which can be added unlimitedly. But the rule, rooted in the organic limitedness, is simple.

The "qualitative," sublime enjoyments are *not gratuitously given,* to be increased directly by more intense effort to enjoy them. Who would not love to live in an endless bliss of augmenting his positive enjoyments by the highly pleasurable drive to enjoy them more? Indeed, we all try, every minute of our lives, to increase our happy, most positive reactions, but come out just even. Apparently, the other, opposite half is part of the game.

But the "logical" theorist, ever averse to the fact that values derive from what are felt as disvalues, never notices the real *causal backgrounds* of his value experiences. He may have memorable moments of sense of sublimity or harmony, therefore may urge people to stop in their rush and yield to higher thoughts. He may not notice that the sublimity, much like the delight of rest, is felt only if he had rushed, worried or worked hard. Those who retire to enjoy fullest leisure soon find that its enjoyment has disappeared. But the opposite causation is always unthinkable. Though the sublimest sense of beauty is experienced by, say, a prisoner released from a dungeon, the theorist never considers past ugliness or harassments as the causal background for his experiences of beauty or harmony.

The decisive point is that the deepening or *increase of "qualitative" values is self-defeating,* because exactly equal opposite value experiences are their causal counterpart. Only the increase in "quantitative" values, as conditioned satisfactions, is attainable. And the negatively felt restrictions have to be used in their conditioning. By this hard, "negative" effort the usable progressive interests, or love as cooperative abdication of selfish drives, can be increased, to any extent—sufficient to provide utopian benefits and care for everybody. Not any "deepening" of experiences, but rather making the conditioned satisfactions "shallower" should be the goal, so that more extensive content can be worked into the organically limited potential of reactions.

Yet the qualitative deepening of experiences, in various forms, is urged by the humanist writers and scientists so faithfully that every noted authority could be quoted in reference. The fallacy is, of course, compounded by the fact that positive experiences, as satisfactions, do constitute our capacities—after their potential has been accumulated through opposite backgrounds.

The humanistic advice here, if it was really followed, would bring disasters. Even the most heavenly direct enjoyments lead to exhaustion or disorder, in proportion to their intensity. Drugs that induce truly religious experiences have disastrous aftereffects. And organically the result is the same whether the release is obtained by a drug or by direct psychologic, hormonal stimulation.

A less dangerous article of faith of humanists may be mentioned. Fairly generally it is argued that the ideas of the *exalted human nature* and values, or of his godly image, have to be sustained to conserve progress. To what extent this belief is held can be seen from an authoritative work, *The Difference of Man and the Difference it Makes,* by Mortimer Adler. This belief reflects the more general, practically alchemistic view that ideas can determine behavior. But scientists did not become bestial upon accepting Darwin's theory. And grandiose conflicts of ideas of philosophers, claiming world-shattering upheavals of thought, have no practical impact. They remain interesting as games of argumentative skills.

All present ideas about the future capacities of man are bound by the *virtual alchemy* that modern thought perpetuates everywhere. We explained how the positive, most pleasant, experiences are viewed as sources of capacities, and mere ideas or perceptions are accepted as determining factors. This alchemy is inherently followed not only by humanists. Scientists proceed by the same beliefs; we saw this repeatedly in all fields of human and social sciences.

We may also mention the frequently expressed view that human capacities can be enriched through discovery of new working *methods and techniques.* This approach has been articulately expounded in the books of John R. Platt.[10] It is argued that mere "seed" operations or new devices can change the course of progress, as has been done in the past by inventions of alphabet, coins, stamps, keys, tokens, cards or computers.

According to the synergistic views of R. Buckminster Fuller, the results of technologic progress will be completely different, qualitatively superior to the means used in promoting it.[12] Similar, inherently alchemistic assumptions about easy progress through mere techniques underlie various modern approaches, particularly those relying on cybernetics and system-analyses.

Whatever the methods or means suggested, mere use of technical improvements, machines or systems, without hard conditioning of the organically relevant, pleasure mechanisms, cannot increase human capacities. These can be created only by the difficult acceptance of restrictions, as sources of releases. *No easy shortcuts,* however inventive, can help. Inventions can be horribly or self-destructively misused by confused minds, impoverished by "improvements." The modern man is destroying himself exactly because due to his inventions he can live without restrictions which are practically the sources of all his capacities.

Particularly *communications* have been viewed as means of easy promotion of progress. It seems, indeed, logical that if only people learn how beneficial the progressive ways are, they will accept them. That this simple truth does not work is revealing. Progress does not come by way of people accepting what is good for them. It comes by being forced on them, because it requires hard effort of restrictions. The problems of communication, perhaps, cannot be discussed without mentioning the theories of Marshall McLuhan.

According to McLuhan the form of communication or medium is more important than its contents. Thus the "hot," electric form of the television medium is blamed for the numbness of reactions of modern man. This is another example of trying to explain how the modern men drive themselves into their negativity by mistakes. For in McLuhan's theory, as in other modern explanations, it is accepted that positive, pleasant experiences are the desirable positive sources, but that we miss them because of our wrong pursuits and means used. This amounts to admitting that men do not notice when they are missing pleasures or are hurting themselves. Besides, forms of communication are *weirdly different* for, say, deaf or blind persons, who behave quite *normally*. The deaf and blind Helen Keller, communicating only through pressures on her hand, was as normal as the best of us.

The most important scientific efforts of promoting human capacities are presently those directed at *use of drugs, electric stimulation, hormonal compounds,* "memory molecules," or other means of technology and molecular biology. Drugs have always been viewed as potential means of mental improvement, by as disparate psychologists as Freud and Skinner.[14] Even practical, important men, of science and administration, such as Glenn Seaborg or Julius Axelrod, have predicted revolutionary improvements through use of drugs.[14]

There seems to be no reason why our intelligence could not be improved "after we succeed in stimulating the working of the brain, just as we do with other less exalted vital parts," according to Jean Rostand, an internationally known biologist. Such methods for increasing everybody's intelligence are predicted as coming soon, by psychologist David Krech, psychobiologist James L. McGaugh, biochemist Floyd E. Bloom, or psychiatrist Nathan S. Kline, among others.

Those looking into the future have always viewed drugs as important means of improvement and control. Aldous Huxley saw use of his fictional soma as essential part in lives of future men. Herman Kahn predicts that by the year 2000 men will be wearing pleasure consoles and using drugs for political control as well as mental improvement.[1]

Various artificial means, including hormonal and electric stimulation, will supposedly be used for shaping of personality, improvement of intelligence or cure of disorders.[8,14] Experiments, like those by R. Heath and W. Ross, on control of behavior by electrodes or electric fields, are often referred to.[11] In his well documented book, *Future Shock,* Alvin Toffler predicts that the psychic environment of men will be changed with precipitous speed by the extremely efficient means of our science and technology.[3]

However complex the means used in such direct improvements, *the end result can be only equal opposite aftereffects.*

We may repeat here that no science can construct or change purposefully or organically the living processes, which work with astronomic multiplicity. Therefore the organism has to remain the same and returns to its normalcy or sameness by opposite processes after any "improvement." We have explained that even if some organic change were obtained it would, again, become part of the limited organic normalcy, to be conserved by the opposite reactions.

Unreversing improvements are obtainable only to the extent they remove some abnormalcy or restore normalcy. That is why the usable source of capacities is restriction, nonsatisfaction or need, as conditioned abnormalcy that provides the potential of satisfactions or releases during return to normalcy.

With this in mind, one can understand the "evidence" of artificial improvements often referred to. In the experiments by José Delgado or Carmine Clemente, aggression in bulls or cats was spectacularly stopped by electric impulses in their brains[11]—which returned them to their feeling of normalcy after disturbance or excitation. Similarly, in the operations by Drs. Vernon Mark, and William Sweet, permanent improvements were obtained because some abnormal condition or disturbance in the brain was removed.

In conclusion we may emphasize that the present scientific and humanistic efforts and ideas about promoting future progress have remained uselessly "alchemistic," even potentially harmful. Increase in enjoyments of positive reactions, by direct and artificial means, or by ideational attitudes, is seen as the logical goal—since satisfactions, indeed, constitute our capacities and positive motivations. If such improvements, by the pleasant, or easy ideational and technical means were possible, men would long have acquired, irresistibly, the limitless capacities. Evidently, the "logical," generally accepted beliefs here are causally untrue.

The requirement of the negative opposite in creation of the positive reactions reveals the opposite causality, the exact contrary of the present logical beliefs. The causally understood science, that will turn men into self-creators, will have to proceed by the presently unthinkable logic that opposition, nonsatisfaction or restriction is the source of capacities or releases.

Immortality, Religion and the Unknowable

Immortality is man's ultimate value and belief, as he exists for the sake of continued existence, which is the source of all his values. Even if one rationally knows that immortality is impossible, he could not continue living with a true conviction that it all is to end in nothingness for him. Psychologists and philosophers have argued that even if immortality is only a belief we should sustain it, because it satisfies our deepest need. One can think here of William James' treatise *Will to Believe*.

Unfortunately enjoyment of something that is not true, and thus is "exaggerated," brings opposite reactions. Overenjoyment has to be paid for, whatever the overenjoyed value or the way it is pursued. Enjoying the belief in immortality, when this belief has to collapse, at the time of death, amounts to accumulating the horrors of death to the last moment.

For the fact is that man as organism dies, and that his organic life is the only thing and everything real to him. This is not a proof against existence of *soul*—if we can call it "existence." The belief in soul is degraded if we attach human value meanings to soul. Our values, the sources of our reality, derive causally from nonsatisfactions or imperfections. The eternal soul, perfect in itself, should be above that. Moreover, to the extent a soul were to participate in our value reactions it would be subject to the equivalence of values and disvalues, of organic growth starting from zero and its destruction by death ending at zero.

In value terms *death amounts to equalization* of our values, accumulated during organic growth, with equal disvalues, when that growth is destroyed. All value feelings are elaborations of organic value processes. Man knows instinctively that death means "paying" for all enjoyments. The person who is to die would *logically* enjoy life to the utmost, while it lasts. He does the reverse. He knows that by reducing the enjoyments, as the growth, he has less to pay for, at the end.

The only *solution for the problem of immortality,* which is actually that of the fear of death, is to distribute the value experiences so that less of the horrors of death is left to the end. In all higher, more farsighted cultures people adopt more resigned attitudes, as if choosing the feelings of closeness of death. Life becomes more restricted, therefore more elaborate, refined or enriched, and longer-lasting. Future science will enable men to manage their experiences, of equal values and disvalues, so that they can leave as little of the fear of death for the last moments as they wish.

If dying then becomes a more peaceful event, like falling asleep, the problem of immortality cannot bother much anybody. Then man will turn to attaining his only possible and meaningful immortality, of adding his tiny share to the unimaginably miraculous human destiny.

On the other hand, attempts to find emotional satisfactions about immortality, through psychology or philosophy, can only lead to neurotic fixations. The anxiety about death will increase as other worries become less significant. Then seeking to avoid that anxiety can only deepen it, because ultimately such avoidance is "exaggerated"—impossible in reality. In short, not assurances of immortality, but suffering the disillusionment beforehand should be the goal.

Belief in immortality is, certainly, man's deepest truth. It is also utterly crazy. Even a tiny organic change can distort person's experiences to unrecognition. How can any meaningful experience continue when the whole organism has disintegrated? And the organic experiences are the only reality that has any meaning for man.

Above all, the immortality men want, in the way they want it, is even logically impossible. They want it as a freedom from the fears of death. But all satisfactions or values of man's existence ultimately derive from the fears of death, as the needs of existence or survival. Therefore to want freedom from these fears, through the immortality assurance, and also to want the values, is like asking for *mountains without valleys*—which even God cannot give us.

We may say a few words about *religion*. All peoples have religions. For there is so much that they miss in their world, emotionally and cognitively, which they add as the supernatural part in it, like missing pieces in a jig-saw puzzle.

The primitive man has gods and spirits as providers for what he needs and as explanations for what he does not understand. More civilized men equally believe in God as source of values, like love, that they desperately need most; or as the ultimate intelligence where understanding is missing most. When modern physicists—unaware of the totally universal, unregistrable causal source —were faced with mystery, they postulated a mathematician God.

But such religions, *bound to men's values, are demeaning*. One can see this more clearly from primitive beliefs in providential gods only where calamities, failures of crops or dangers reign and not where things, like air, light or the ground, are always "providentially" given. Here, obviously, the beliefs in gods originate from the godlessness of the world.

The same is true of our religion as long as it is dominated by value beliefs. For causally the real sources of values are factual disvalues, wants or absence of what is needed. God as source of values is incongruous in every way. It has been always asked why did He create evils—while it is clear that values are meaningless without their opposites. The old philosophical double-talk is too transparent for the modern men. They turn to the God-is-Dead religion.

Even *God as intelligence* is a ridiculous human concept, though it has been favored in more intellectual religious interpretations. As we saw, intellect is a very clumsy capacity, of proceeding by the generalized "ones," whereas nature works with myriads of elements at once. The only advantage intellect has is that it can relive or remember the past and thus project future from it. If one such, inferior advantage makes the decisive difference, the world of human intellect must be limited indeed.

The only *nondemeaning belief* in God is one that recognizes the utter limitedness of man. The Unknown must be endlessly different from anything men can conceive. Every advance in knowledge reveals this. Thousands of universes may be existing in thousands of dimensions that may be passing through the space around you. In what strange ways the Unknowable relates to us we cannot know. We only know that not human purposes or providence, but opposition, chaos, difficulty or restriction are the causal sources of reality, evolution, progress or human capacities. And this causation is bringing the future of unimaginable miracles.

The *practical religion* does embody the recognition of the principle of restriction as well as of the unfathomable strangeness of God. The simple believers are closest to true religion. They see restrictions as the commandments of God and they bow in awe before a strange, severe, humanly incomprehensible will of God.

Religions become fatuous when learning is used to support them. Anything men can say or pretend to know about God is preposterous. As the ultimate reality He is the ultimate mystery, and man is too ridiculously limited to know anything about it. Men have not yet emerged even from their own shells, their humanistic, value delusions, as we have seen. Use of learning in religion only expands meaningless confusion about the unknowable.

To explain anything about God amounts to a comic inanity. Yet thousands of books are being written and uncountable words said every day on the "truths" about the humanistic God, by millions of highly learned men. The plain waste of talent and effort is appalling.

The Unimaginable Future of Man as Self-Creator

Once causally understood sciences of man are established, his progress will change completely. He will then be doing by conscious plan what has been done up to now by blind cultural selection. We may stress the revolutionary reversal of the causal logic itself, that will have to be the beginning of the future human sciences, however they are to come about. If the present real, technologic sciences have brought miracles equal to powers formerly attributed to gods, sciences of man will change the very dimensions of progress. Man will become a creator of men capable of still greater creation of capacities as the very sources of new progress. In short, the future will be as unimaginable as the necessary principles of its sciences are presently unthinkable.

Probably the first thing man will want to attain, in his self-creation, will be *increased longevity*. The present ideas and efforts to extend life favor stimulation and direct improvements, by use of stimulants and tonics of all kinds, from ginseng to novocaine, enzyme activating vitamins or dopamine increasing L-dopa.[9,11] We can refer here to Benjamin Frank in this country, Ana Aslan in Romania, or V. P. Filatov in Russia.[9] Such improvements are attained by increasing the rate of living at deeper levels, by the stimulation.

But it is almost self-evident to common sense that length of life is increased in direct proportion to slowing down of the rate of living, by restrictions, exactly opposite to the positively felt improvements. The widest, classic studies of longevity, by Raymond Pearl, Max Rubner or T. K. Van Voit, established the principle of the slower rate of longer living as axiomatic;[9] a later, Gallup survey confirmed it.[17] As can be expected, the experimentally "logical" modern theories have pointed out the restrictive functioning or the lower rate of living of aging organisms, as a direct cause of aging.[9] It is rather overlooked that particularly the aging organisms, while conserving their limited reserves, prolong their lives by the restrictive, slower rate of living.

Experiments on *retardation of maturity* in animals and on their *underfeeding,* by C. M. McCay, C. A. Hochwelt, B. N. Berg, J. H. Northrop, H. S. Sims, and others,[9,17] showed surprising increase in longevity, and a normal development, of the animals. Other studies and experiments have shown that life is extended by various restrictions slowing down the rate of living: by starvation diets, feeding of antioxidants, freezing, hibernation or enforced inactivity.[9,11,14]

Studies on *longer living peoples,* in South America, Asia or Russia,[10] show that they live under limitedness of means and absence of artificial stimulation or of "improvements" of life. Alexander Leaf, one of the leading researchers on such peoples, characterizes their lives by "penury and hard work."[10] This describes well a restrictive way of life without stimulating improvements.

Of course the "scientific" observers of all times have hailed direct stimulation, notably some increased sexual activity, as means of rejuvenation. One can think here of early *rejuvenators,* Brown-Sequard, Lejeune, or Voronoff. They all could demonstrate, in stimulation treatments, exciting improvements, which did not last. The early enthusiasm about sex hormones ended in disasters.[9] Experiments show that testosterone injected in old horses produces initial spurt of vigor but leads to disastrous changes.[17] Common sense has always shown that those who lead intense sexual lives age sooner. Women live longer; and their active sex life ends earlier, biologically and socially.

Once the role of restrictions and the paradox of "improvements" are understood, science can invent radically new means for *slowing down the rate of living* and thus extending the period of life. Restrictions can be imposed unlimitedly; and they are sources of releases as capacities. Longer lives of higher animals have been correlated with their larger brains, which act as restrictive systems.

Science only has to learn to do with more complex organic structures what can be done with simpler forms. Plants, like spinach or sisal, when trimmed down continuously or prevented from flowering, grow for years and years. Insects prevented from maturing, as when their wings are clipped, live many times longer than usual. Science may finally be able to prolong man's life, by more complex restrictions, for presently unthinkable periods, perhaps extending it manifold. Such life would, probably, be rather like a suspended vegetation in a laboratory environment. But higher mental activity would be enriched by it.

Here we may indicate that perhaps the most radical changes the scientific progress will bring will be in the human *sense of values.* When the prosaic causality of values is understood, the present, inviolable sacredness of our most certain, and fixational values will be broken. For instance, the beauty of woman, or man, is a value born in the biologic, reproduction needs that are as blindly compulsive and crude as are, say, the instincts to kill and devour. Most value sources of beauty are equally vulgar. Moreover, all our emotionally sacred values derive from their negative, infernal causal opposites, to begin with.

The inconceivable *strangeness of the future existence* of man may be considered here. Could we accept humanly different, "monstrous" forms for man, however unimaginably rich they may be—forms adapted to functioning with an excessively large brain, or to living on Mars or in the oceans? We do not have to accept the present science-fiction speculations. Yet the richness of variety of human forms could well be among the possible proudest or most "beautiful" achievements of man.

Man would be choosing here between values of blindly crude natural compulsions, and those of intellect of man finally understanding what is happening, inside or around him. He would be enhancing the achievements of mind, which distinguishes him from animals or makes him truly human. Could it all be viewed as man's final choice between the *animal drives* and the *mind* in him?

But first we may look at some problems of human progress that are becoming acute even now—the problems of human *eugenic planning*. Modern science has already the means, such as the artificial insemination, that could replace our animal ways of reproduction with intelligently planned conceptions and births of persons with higher capacities. The availability of such means, on the one hand, and the violent objections against their use, on the other, are vividly described in the *Future Shock* of Alvin Toffler, who refers to such authorities as J. Lederberg, J. B. S. Haldane, E. S. E. Hafez, R. D. Hotchkiss, T. J. Gordon, and A. Neyfakh.[3]

The objections show that all planned eugenics *seem presently abhorrent* to our sense of humaneness, ethics or natural human rights. Any progress can be used for good or bad, therefore can be easily condemned beforehand. When people feel strongly about something, they find every justification for their feelings; the arguments become endless. The strong value feelings here have grown through age-long fixations. People have attached their value experiences to the ways children have been always conceived and born. Anything different has to appear repugnant.

In general, man has strongest value fixations about his body, because the ways it exists are always there, and fixation grows through mere repetition of valuations. Operating on human body, even after death, remained sacrilegious—except for priests in rituals—up to the modern times.

There is plenty of justification for distrusting modern science when it wants to help improve us organically. If scientists admit that they cannot understand the causes of the functional diseases of which most modern men die, how can they be trusted with the involved eugenic problems? At least intuitively people may feel this way. But some eugenic methods, like the *artificial insemination*, are so clear causally that science can apply them without misunderstandings.

We admit, parents may reasonably want so see themselves physically repeated in their children. But cultural conditioning can change such attitudes. If the educational or spiritual values are emphasized and the parents want their moral qualities best expressed in their child, then they can be most successful with a child of higher mental capacities, wherever his genes come from. This more spiritual emphasis, corresponding to the general trend of our culture, could be easily promoted. In practice, adoptive parents soon learn to love their adopted child as strongly as if he was their own.

More "sacrilegious" would be *planned selection* by elimination of undesirable births. Here, again, change in cultural attitudes would be important. Only twenty years ago abortion was generally considered a murder. Now it is an operation on the woman's body, free for her to choose. The change has come together with increasing universal pressures of overpopulation. The next, very important step would be elimination if selectively required of a fetus or even pre-conscious infant to promote births of more capable individuals and to prevent defectives from becoming conscious.

This could be easily branded as atrocious "infanticide," unmentionable presently.[5] In reality, by permitting defective infants to become conscious beings, the present world is inflicting the cruelest degradation, on millions of persons who have to continue as shameful burdens for themselves and others.

Here we have to make it clear that the only decisive criterion should be the human, *conscious happiness and sufferings*. It would not have mattered anything to me if I had been killed, or even vivisected, before I acquired consciousness, which starts only months after birth. Permitting emergence of abnormal persons when this can be prevented without the slightest suffering, concern or even conscious realization is a cruel, practically most criminal act.

It should be stated without reservations, though, that once consciousness has developed, the suffering cannot be prevented by any means, drugs, anesthetics, or other manipulation of consciousness. Even a totally deranged person suffers and has to be cared for so that he can live his full life.

With this in mind, somebody has to start mentioning the unspeakable "infanticide," when it is the most humane thing men can do. Dr. James Watson, the discoverer of the DNA structure, has urged legalization of infanticide, to "save a lot of misery and suffering." But generally, "elimination of defective babies . . . is not spoken of until recently."[5] The great argument against elimination of any birth has been the sanctity of life. But life without consciousness is like nothingness. Animals have the same biologic life as we, but they do not even know that they or anything is there. Should their killing be compared to genocide?

It is *not life, but consciousness or feeling*, suffering and pleasure, that matters. The preconscious infant knows as little as does an animal or fish that he himself, or anything else exists. Surely the fetus is the beginning of the future person. But so is the ovum and sperm. Should we start crying about their destruction?

Everybody knows that compassion for the newborn infant or even for the child to be born is one of the strongest human feelings. Survival of species dictates it. But men should learn to control their strong, automatic instincts if they can prevent dehumanizing suffering, for millions of persons and tragic shame for their parents. If by cultural education the parents learn to abstain from investing love in the fetus there is no deep sorrow about its loss.

By a selection among infants to be born, science could *improve the human capacities,* surely by at least one third at first. Capacities, or defects, could be discovered from the fetus, before birth. Techniques for doing so are progressing rapidly.[5] But present scientific criteria, favoring increased releases as sources of capacities, would be misleading here as well. The present IQ measurements, in general, are so controversial because the main source of practical intelligence is the capacity to bear restrictions, which do not appear as favorable to modern scientists. But the future sciences will make possible reliable selection here. This together with new methods—beyond the present ideas about artificial insemination or implants of ova—should certainly enable men to do more for themselves than presently is done in animal breeding, where qualities are often doubled.

Even a general increase of the IQ to, say, 130 would bring in a couple of generations more human improvement than has been attained in millenia. For, if the IQ is selected right, with the restriction aptitude as the main criterion, most of the present problems would disappear. These problems depend on the abilities and behavior of the people, ultimately determined by their capacity to bear restrictions. If the IQ is doubled, as it certainly will be at some point in the future, the world will become a presently inconceivable utopia.

The possibilities here are unique. By artificial insemination and planned selection men can choose the best combinations of traits in the whole genetic stock, while in natural reproduction only one, blind, chance combination determines what the person will be.

But, as we saw, planned human eugenics is still abhorrent in our culture, and reasons against it are easily found. Thus it is argued that under such planning people will be turned into experimental robots subjected to the whims of their dictatorial managers. Actually, parents will simply want mentally superior children and will use the planned eugenics to get them. Decisions will, certainly, be crucial; and highly specialized experts will be required to make them. But do not doctors now decide matters of life and death for us, with aid of specialists?

Nor has planned eugenics to become racist. Every race has some specific superior qualities which will be selected to obtain as perfect gene combinations as possible. Ideas about conservation of racial "purity" are selfishly stupid. So is the refusal to study race differences, which obviously exist. The "ideal" man of the future will embody the best mixture of genes from all races. The separate "races" will disappear. The choice of the combinations will have to be scientifically precise, which will preclude racial prejudices.

Geneticists may warn that the richness of genetic variability should not be destroyed—that all traits of all races should be preserved. Such "richness" may be infinite when it consists of abnormalities or defects, while each perfect quality is essentially one and the same for all men.

People of all races know and want higher intelligence, just as they know what a perfectly beautiful, desirable human body is, from whatever combination of racial characteristics it comes. Within these limits variability can be useful; but we do not have to conserve traits of low intelligence or physical imperfection. How men know what constitutes perfect human traits is as miraculous as our capacity to distinguish healthy foods or beautiful things.

What is worst of all, presently *the human race is being overpopulated by persons with lower capacities*. Now the more intelligent families have only a couple of children, while the least intelligent have many. A couple of near morons may produce a half dozen children, uneducable, unemployable, potential criminals, cared for by welfare, who will produce more of the same.

This is *the vilest unnoticed crime* against everything that is noble in man and humanity. It amounts to a degradation of the human race, as well as to the increase of suffering, through crime, poverty and violence, that people of low capacities breed. Even traditional scientists, like Bentley Glass, point out the perpetuation of genetic defects with the improved modern medical means.[5]

The present neglect to intervene against this degradation of humanity is unbelievable. Nobody would be hurt by an intervention here. The less intelligent people who have the many children are not the ones who greatly love children or are ready to care for them. They simply have them because of their uncontrolled, thoughtless ways of life, and because the government supports the children and the mother. Having more children often becomes profitable business for welfare recipients.

But our deeply rooted attitudes are such that even a suggestion of any limitation measures here would be scandalous. Nothing but a change in attitudes is required for population control.[12] The thoughtless parents would be glad to have no children if they were supported for that and could easily avoid having them. A little effort could help them to have such support and freedom.

When science finally succeeds in selecting all men with higher capacities—ultimately, one can assume, with IQ's many times higher than ours—the *overpopulation will not be a problem*. People of higher intelligence tend to have fewer children. Rather need for more population will become the problem. Progress will be proportional to the number of highly capable persons and great societies strenuously competing for discoveries and huger amounts of pooled means. It has been calculated that our earth could support 200 billion people even with our present technology.[11] Past standards of what can be done have always been and will be enormously exceeded. Experiments with animals show that they remain totally unaggressive if they are born and raised in overcrowded conditions.[11]

Educational conditioning will increase with the progress. Man is always born an animal and has to be turned into a cultural being by uncessant conditioning. In the future education, probably, dozens of experts from all fields will care for each individual, as he is conditioned and lives in a kind of laboratory environment. The present *ideas that future men will have nothing to do*[5] are shortsighted. Above all, the conquest of space and search for other intelligent beings will take immense efforts.

Humanists are looking with dismay at the *increasing conditioning* of people even within our present progress. The future is viewed as a nightmare of dictatorial regimentation. In truth, restrictive conditioning can enrich capacities and motivations so that people can live with perfect love and reason. Mental or behavioral impoverishment is what makes people hateful and irrational.

Everybody wants only the positive, satisfactory, reasonable capacities or motives—and knows what they are, but lacks them because of the impoverishment. Restrictive conditioning can provide unlimited enrichment. Well conditioned people working for unselfish reasons or with love for all, in their "beehive" society, can have utopian benefits for everybody and the freedom to do their selfless work that they want. Of course, any conditioning is effectively attained only through deeply ingrown moral, restrictive tradition, as it has been in the atmosphere of "free" countries, and not through governmental enforcement or "scientific" techniques.

How the future men will live is unpredictable. A couple of hundred years ago our present technologic inventions would have been hardly imaginable. And the future will bring sciences of man which will, necessarily, *change everything in and around men in unprecedented ways.* We may as well visualize the future man as living in a biologic suspension, staying in a computerized room resembling a machine or laboratory, without even a need to move. In few decades men will study, work and socialize by tele-communications.

In the end man will be able to be "present," to see, even to "touch" things, at any place he wants, even on a planet or a star, without moving from his room. New radaring techniques permitting a focusing on objects at distance would be required. But in view of the rapid advances in such techniques, man will be able, in few centuries, *to have all the sensations he wants of things at any distance.* Men can do better than bats or dolphins.

Also, the interests of future men will, probably, be more abstract, like being interested in what may seem mere numbers and data but may reveal intricate new wonders in the mechanisms of the universe, working on a distant star. Thus the tele-presence, best suited for obtaining such numbers or data, might serve unlimited interests for future men. Mere abstract data can be tremendously exciting even to us. Think of how the world today would celebrate a signal from a galaxy indicating that intelligent beings could have transmitted it. It would capture news headlines for months.

Man as intelligent being is bound to conquer the universe around him. But he is physically too puny to do so by his bodily presence. To reach even a single, closest star man would have to travel for thousands of years. *Tele-presence is the only way.* Even so, new breakthroughs would be required, to overcome the light-year delays in the "radaring." We can hope that different, other "Fields" may be discovered, permitting higher transmission speeds. The universe is, almost necessarily, limitless in possibilities, as may be judged from its fundamental phenomena like the Field that have not yet been even suspected by scientists.

A more limited possibility would be *control of time* which is

nothing more than a relationship of changes. Men could stop everything inside and around them for a hundred years, then work for
a few days, and go back to "sleep," as in the *2001: A Space
Odyssey.*[9] Any waiting, for hundreds or thousands of years, could
thus be reduced to days.

Intellectual and nonqualitative values, like progressive interests
or rationally selfless love, will dominate the lives of future men.
We saw that such interests or love are created by imposing nonsatisfactions or restrictions felt as disvalues. Qualitative enjoyments, whether of beauty, sublime experiences or fulfilling love,
will be probably disparaged, because they derive from opposite
sources or lead to opposite feelings. The strangest change will result from complete sublimation of biological or sexual value feelings into intellectual interests.

Future men will be finally *free of the biologic values, like
beauty, sexual attraction, masculinity* or physical excellence? Individuals preoccupied with such interests will be, conceivably,
viewed as cases of mental retardation. They will be in fact relatively retarded, by having less of undivided intellectual interests
than others. This change will make the future value world weird
in various ways, if viewed from the present standards. But cultural
values are always relative. Many customs from different places
and times look weird to us.

In the end, man will function only intellectually, through his
brain, since all qualitative value enjoyments defeat themselves;
and the future men will be free of physical effort. We may go
along with the futurist vision of *man functioning as an extensive
brain.* The peculiarity of the brain is that it acts as a peripheral,
biologically less vital outgrowth, with minimum of releases of flow
of life; brain does not even cause pain when cut. The brain could
well be greatly expanded, by continuous genetic improvements. It
has increased disproportionally during the latest periods of evolution. It, evidently, functions at the lowest rates of living or aging
—if protected from the person's degenerative enjoyments.

Thus biologically the brain is like an unessential extension of
the organism and can function rather detachedly from it. Engineering the functions of the brain would not be grave biologically.
But the brain is clearly the organ of intellect, by which man will

conquer the universe and create himself. The brain could also be made immortal?

By cloning—so much discussed presently—exact copies could be created for the individual. These copies could be grown without permitting their higher brains or consciousness to develop. Then their other organs could be used as transplants to keep the individual alive; there would be no organic rejection. This is not more absurd than people with full life of the brain or consciousness dying because their other organs fail.

No supranatural or "higher" nature of the intellect or mind has to be assumed. The mind is a natural or mechanistic product, though because of its multiple complexity we have to use integrated concepts like pleasure to understand it. The *mechanistic* reality is the simplest one; and what is simple is, in essence, most universally determining, revealing or "divine." The simple, greatest past discoveries about the universe show this. The most universal, mechanistic principles are simplest exactly because they govern in the same order everything outside and inside all minds.

But the humanistic theories about man's final transformation and redemption postulate a *spiritual* world of mind or intellect as the final stage. One can think here of the noogenesis of Teilhard de Chardin[16]—as well as of the Kingdom of God of Kant or the Transfiguration of Toynbee—and various similar visions of a mind finally ruling the world.[6] The mind here is seen as a nonmechanistic, "higher," spiritual consciousness of beatific sublime quality, to be attained through the perfection and deepening of our *value experiences.*[16] We saw the inevitable self-defeat of these experiences in man as a stable organism; and he can exist only as such organism, however far he progresses.

Actually, every imaginable miracle lies within the limits of mechanistic processes. For instance, if consciousness—which has evolved mechanistically—could be combined with the multiplicity of interaction of natural, living processes, we could have virtually limitless miracles. Think what you could do if you could grasp and direct consciously, by plan, every molecule inside you at every instant, as nature does.

A being capable to *act consciously in the multiple ways of living processes* could transform himself into any imaginable new form or create new living beings, just as man now can move his limbs or create tools. He would understand, predict, re-create, cure or perfect in himself anything as easily as we now understand, predict or control the working of machines. He could even predict the future or resurrect the past, just as man now can predict future changes or reconstruct past forms in his dealing with separate things in his environment. All this would amount to miracles of creation, resurrection of the past or knowledge of the future, attributed to gods.

We admit, it is difficult to conceive how the conscious processes could be so combined with the multiple capacities of living nature (though our miraculously revealing pleasure reactions point to such possibilities). For instance, to resurrect past events of a world, its elements should first become integrated with the conscious organism. This is impossible. But the point is that mere mechanical principles already operating in nature can offer greater miracles than the humanistic theorists have dared to imagine.

Technology together with a mechanistic science of man will bring all the miracles man will need. The technologic progress should and will accelerate, in spite of the protests by humanistic purists.[6] Educational and physical requirements for each person will increase enormously, as we saw, and will have to be provided by increased production. The *antigrowth prophets,* like those of the prestigious Club of Rome, are not too farsighted. Exhaustion of resources cannot be a problem, if energy is plentiful. Every time men have exhausted a resource they have created a better substitute.

The sooner men face the shortage of oil and coal, the more intense will be the development of sources like the thermonuclear fusion, which can provide limitless energy. Even the breeder reactors could, presumably, provide plenty of energy for hundreds of years. The principles of fusion are known, since the fusion bomb has been exploded. Development difficulties may seem insurmountable. But unexpected technologic breakthroughs have been always found by men in desperate need.

Nor will the *pollution* suffocate us. Its problems require less revolutionary changes than did the urban canalization and plumbing. New methods could even yield materials and benefits from disposal of wastes or from thermal pollution. Our most vocal environmentalists are naive victims of fixations and esthetic prejudices. Pollutions that uncomfortably restrict enjoyments are far less harmful than the pleasures men seek through modern intensified improvements.

The present environmental perfectionism seems rather humorless, in perspective. Could not the technologic ugliness become fashionable, as did the gothic style—and the smears of modern painting? Or, the cute, most noticed endangered species may be less interesting scientifically than some unnoticed microorganisms, and could be conserved in zoos.

Even in the *technologic sciences* the future will bring surprises. Presently we may not be able even to think of the possibilities of principally new future discoveries. Our sciences are still mystified by the very essentials, the universal causal realities like the Field, from which our physical world derives. The Field concept is only an example for thinking of new possibilities in the evidently unlimited universe. Thus different forms of matter, energy or universal mechanisms could well be discovered in the future.

Radical surprises are to be expected in the *sciences of life* and genetics. The living process is a negative fire, as a chain-reaction "burning" against the Field. It is therefore an energy source potentially more powerful than are the other chain reactions, the ordinary fire or atomic reactions. Science can amplify, gigantically, any haphazard forces of nature. It *could create living processes of any form or intensity*. All kinds of elements could be "burned" by living processes. The only condition needed would be the presence of energy, from sun, natural heat or other radiation. One could envision luxurious new kinds of growth "burning" forth on deserts or the moon, to serve as sources of energy.

Science could design even a living process capable of absorbing the energy from the usual earth environment, which is far above the minus 459 degrees or zero energy. It all would amount to accumulating in usable quantities the energy that always acts, infinitesimally, around the atoms. This is not different from what happens in usual living growth, except that more intense kinds of life would be created; one can think, for illustration, of kinds of stronger fire, like the acetylene fire. The decisive point is the understanding of what life is.

Practical miracles would come through *the use of the capacity of living nature to work with myriads of elements* at every point and instant. (We speculated about the combination of this capacity with consciousness—a hardly conceivable possibility.) Nature, in this capacity, is incomparably superior to any machine men could ever build. The simple green leaf producing starch, performs a work of an extremely efficient "machine."[3] Use of such "machines," through microbiology, is supposedly one of the great modern advances, more promising than other industrial progress; the use of microbiology in Japan, as a start, is referred to.[3] By designing such "machines," in new ways, industry could produce far more efficiently than by use of nonliving machines or laboratories.[3]

Integration of living tissue in physical mechanisms or metal machines has been speculated about.[3] Here we should, however, consider the limitations of mind or its inability to follow the multiplicity of nature. Man builds machines, with isolated elements, exactly because mind can deal only with "one" thing at a time. Therefore a living process in a machine would be uncontrollable in any detail by man. How could it then be of any use in the machine?

The only way a living process can be controlled in detail by mind is the interaction between the two within the human organism, by the reactions of pleasure or displeasure—by the consciousness. Thus we are back to man himself, bearer of the consciousness, as the only possible addition to machines. Rather, changes in the myriad capacities of man as organism, or radically new adaptations by him to environment, or to machines, could bring the greatest revolution.

But, as we saw, men will first have to decide whether they want the rich variety of specialized human forms—*men adapted to live on planets or in space*—who would appear as monsters according to our present standards. It is naive to visualize the future men as *pretty replicas of the contemporary man,* in beautiful forms depicted by science fiction or TV shows. Depending on standards, one can view new human forms either as sublimely desirable or as unspeakably monstrous. We explained that our biologically or sexually determined sense of beauty will rather diminish.

Future men, seeking and probably finding other intelligent beings, on other galaxies, would hardly be repulsed by "monstrous" forms of themselves. If such change of mind evolves, the possibilities will be immense, under the increasing skills of genetic engineering.

Men adapted to live normally even in space conditions or to travel in space with minimal assistance from machines could, conceivably, be created in the end. Instead of dealing through and with the help of complex, enormously costly machines, men would be able to work and live in *miraculously efficient ways by direct adaptation.* Philip Slater, writing of the future "monsters," concludes that the existing technology will become obsolete, as nobody will "bother with anything as clumsy and rigid as a machine when living monsters with specialized adaptations can be created to do the same tasks."[6] Actually, the future men will be far too intelligent to do the work of machines. Their adaptations will be miracles of easier and totally different existence, even with the use of machines.

But it is true that machines are helplessly clumsy in comparison with living processes. Life endures where machines of steel fail, and the brain can do what no computer can. The simple, microscopic amoeba has, supposedly, more "circuits" in it than the best computer.

The rich variety of specialized human forms would be created by crossing of animal traits already evolved in their miraculously purposive myriad ways, rather than by direct engineering of genes. The present gene engineering, as well as most of microbiology, proceeds under the preposterous *assumption that living forms can be created or changed mechanically.* As we have stressed repeatedly, a living mechanism works through myriad purposive processes at every point and instant; and they have to concur with other infinite processes in the organism. Viable changes can be obtained only by dealing with organic wholes, like enzymes.

Scientists now speak of dangers of gene engineering. It is feared that a new extremely virulent microorganism, virus or bacterium could result from changing the genes. Laws are proposed to stop gene engineering. The belief of modern geneticists that the disruptive gene mutations can produce new adaptive forms finds here its parallel. We saw how untenable such belief is.

Even if a mere mechanic change of genes were to create a new form that continues living, its adaptability or virulence would require long, gradual evolutionary conditioning. Since by million-year adaptations the existing microbes have already attained the highest possible viability or virulence under the given conditions, the new form can be only far less virulent. In practice, theorists do not realize how difficult it is for a microbe to become pathogenic, as Bernard Davis of the Harvard Medical School has pointed out. Other practical experts, such as James Watson, have also objected to the "hysteria" against gene engineering. Combination of already evolved traits is the way new virulent strains of germs have been created.

Genetic engineering can develop new, viable forms by *combining whole, already existing adaptive animal traits, by crossing either chromosomes or reproductive cells.* The aim would be to change radically the traits of man, while conserving the capacities of his mind. By continuous crossings of human chromosomes with those of more and more disparate living forms, science could finally create men capable to live under any conditions, in space, on planets and stars or to do anything, with minimal use of machines; these would be used only where, for instance, metallic hardness or explosive force be required.

Of course, such new forms can, imaginably, be attained only slowly through numerous generations and with new genetic techniques. But science is stupendously resourceful where causal, scientific understanding is clear and only techniques, however complex, are to be perfected. And human insights will change immensely, even in the next few thousand years—in *ways necessarily so new as to appear abhorrent to us.*[5]

If the repugnance against the "monstrosity" of unusual human forms is overcome, and the techniques are endlessly perfected, the future men might well exist in all conceivable living forms, and do everything that limitless use and combination of matter and energy in the universe make possible.

Thinking of the now fashionable fiction about colonies and

travelers in space, we can visualize veritable space societies of the future. Limitless combination of specialized intelligent forms would enable such *societies to live, grow and travel in any conditions of space*. The energy always present in space could be used—conceivably through new, powerful kinds of living processes, requiring small amounts of matter to be "burned" by such processes and reused. Biological "machines," as well as technological tools, would be used by specialized men with capacities of any necessary combination.

Intelligent forms capable to change and adapt limitlessly would turn such society into a living organism of the universe finding other, strange intelligent beings and interacting with them under their conditions. Any scenario, ugly or beautiful, that you can conjure, would be within the possibilities of such future. And it would be rather pompous to think that our present human forms will remain, for all future ages, glorious ideals, even for a self-creating man with experiences of, say, intergalactic scope.

In brief, men as intelligent beings enabled to adopt specialized forms or to adjust to new conditions could accomplish every conceivable miracle. And the painful prejudice of viewing strange forms of man as monstrous will probably vanish as man becomes a citizen of the universe in his thinking. Similar prejudices in the past, against differences in races or religions have disappeared. The infidels in Medieval thinking were hardly human. The inhabitants of the New World discovered by Columbus were described as strange creatures.

The above progress is rather *more feasible than the enormous spaceships or wheels* with earth-like vistas that are presently speculated about as possible in near future. Consider how many billions of dollars are required to build and operate even one, fragile, three-man spaceship. When you use living nature, under its principles, it works for you with its astronomic multiplicity of purposiveness and adaptability, at the cost of pennies and with tiny controls.

Scientists, and fiction writers, used to our technologic progress, naively expect everything from it and overlook other, far more revolutionary possibilities. When sciences of man become established, scientists will see how much more can be attained by changing and expanding man's living capacities. Man's physical puniness and weakness as well as the inventiveness and adaptability of living forms become advantages in such efforts, while technologic power and skills are ridiculous against the immense hostile forces in the universe. Living process in its very weakness, as we saw, has reversed the forces of the universe and its entropy.

We may as well conclude on this general note. If we go into more detail we might add further "monstrosities." Nothing can be predicted exactly. The extreme, "monstrous" scenario may merely serve to indicate how strange the future will be, in our terms. The future progress will have to be inconceivably different because it will have to follow the universal causal principles of opposition and restriction, as well as of value relativity, that are unthinkable under our present humanistic truths.

The practically important more immediate goal would be, simply, a scientific advancement of the restrictions, presently rejected in human sciences. Man's organic limitedness is the decisive universal fact. But he can, and inevitably will, increase his capacities endlessly, because these capacities are satisfactions or releases deriving from needs as nonsatisfactions or restrictions which can be increased without limits.

In this endless increase of man's capacities lies his redemption or the only immortality he can attain. Through his capacities man will become a self-creator changing himself at ever-accelerating pace. Think of how immense such change and progress have to become through ages. We can conceive the miraculous destiny of man as little as an insect can conceive our life of consciousness, which also evolved mechanistically, but by blind selection, instead of science.

Our very inability to imagine man's future is the promise of our immortality, because the final destiny of man may well be so miraculous as to justify or redeem our every possible effort or incredible aspiration. Besides, the immortality that man now wants —as freedom from fears of death while he has values or joys of life—is as impossible as mountains without valleys.

REFERENCES

CHAPTER I (pp. 1-30)

1. U.S. Bureau of the Census, *Statistical Abstract of the United States,* U.S. Government Printing Office, Washington, D.C., 1978, pp. 50, 51, 62, 64, 65, 68, 86.

2. Selye, Hans, *The Stresses of Life,* McGraw-Hill Book Co., New York, 1976, pp. 171, 187, 370, 385, 389, 391, 414, 433, 484.

3. Friedman, Meyer, and Rosenman, Ray H., *Type A Behavior and Your Heart,* Alfred Knopf, New York, 1974, pp. 37, 48, 52, 62, 77, 83, 109, 117, 123, 161, 193, 214, 254.

4. U.S. President's Commission on Heart Disease, Cancer and Stroke, *Report to the President,* U.S. Government Printing Office, Washington, D. C., 1970, pp. 3, 4, 12, 22, 29, 33, 48.

5. Miller, Benjamin F., and Galton, Lawrence, *Freedom from Heart Attacks,* Simon & Schuster, New York, 1972, pp. 34, 59, 79, 122, 135, 137, 202, 256.

6. Ancowitz, Arthur, *Strokes and Their Prevention,* Van Nostrand Reinhold Co., New York, 1975, pp. 59, 87, 106, 123.

7. Dietrich, Edward B., and Fried, John J., *Code Arrest: A Heart Stops,* Saturday Review Press, New York, 1974, pp. 15, 23, 26.

8. Galton, Lawrence, *The Silent Disease: Hypertension,* Crown Publishers, New York, 1973, pp. 3, 5, 7, 53, 62, 77, 82, 112, 128, 144.

9. Levi, Lennart, *Stress: Sources, Management and Prevention,* Liveright Publ. Co., New York, 1967, pp. 36, 55, 63, 64, 80, 101, 142, 164.

10. McQuade, Walter, and Aikman, Ann, *Stress,* E. P. Dutton & Co., New York, 1974, pp. 3, 6, 12, 23, 31, 78.

11. Lamott, Kenneth, *Escape from Stress,* G. P. Putnam's Sons, New York, 1974, pp. 27, 29, 32, 37, 49, 163.

12. Finnerty, Frank A., and Linde, Shirley Motter, *High Blood Pressure,* David McKay Co., New York, 1975, pp. 2, 3, 31, 48, 114, 174, 178, 181, 194, 276.

13. Likoff, William, Segal, Bernard, and Galton, Lawrence, *Your Heart,* J. B. Lippincott Co., Philadelphia, Pa., 1972, pp. 79, 82, 89, 117, 141, 167, 170, 193.

14. Carruthers, Malcolm, *The Western Way of Death,* Pantheon Books, New York, 1974, pp. 21, 24, 89, 97, 125, 129, 132.

15. Blau, Sheldon Paul, and Schultz, Dodi, *Arthritis,* Doubleday & Co., Garden City., N. Y., 1974, pp. 11, 23, 79, 111, 126.

16. Lowenstein, Bertrand E., and Preger, Paul D., *Diabetes,* Harper & Row, New York, 1976, pp. 4, 17, 23, 67, 153, 179.

17. Hilgard, Ernest R., *et al.*, *Introduction to Psychology*, Harcourt Brace Jovanovich, Inc., New York, 1975, pp. 38, 150, 290, 547.
18. Tushnet, Leonard, *The Uses of Adversity*, Thomas Yoseloff, New York, 1966, pp. 52, 61, 63, 64, 71.
19. Graham, M. F., *Prescription for Life*, David McCay, New York, 1966, pp. 16, 26, 154.
20. Perlin, Seymour, *ed.*, *A Handbook for the Study of Suicide*, Oxford University Press, New York, 1975, pp. 74, 109, 157, 158, 206.
21. Samuelson, Paul A., *Economics*, McGraw-Hill Book Co., New York, 1976, pp. 212, 234, 253, 758, 761.

CHAPTER II (pp. 31-61)

1. Selye, Hans, *The Stresses of Life*, McGraw-Hill Book Co., New York, 1976, pp. 169, 171, 179, 187.
2. Stumpf, Samuel E., *Philosophy: History and Problems*, McGraw-Hill Book Co., 1977, pp. 18, 43, 76, 268, 280, 374.
3. Morgan, Clifford T., and King, Richard A., *Introduction to Psychology*, McGraw-Hill, New York, 1975, pp. 223, 227, 283, 382, 388, 392.
4. Pugh, George E., *The Biological Origin of Human Values*, Basic Books, New York, 1977, pp. 62, 205, 213, 248, 327.
5. Elbin, Paul N., *Paradox of Hapiness*, Hawthorn Books, Inc., New York, 1975, pp. 18, 39, 143, 176, 188.
6. Lazarus, Richard S., *The Riddle of Man*, Prentice Hall, Englewood Cliffs, N. J., 1974, pp. 111, 163, 230, 312, 335, 561.
7. Mussen, Paul, Rosenzweig, Mark R., *et al.*, *Psychology*, D. C. Heath & Co., Lexington, Mass., 1976, pp. 15, 78, 215, 216, 463, 464, 570-598.
8. Kendler, Howard H., *Basic Psychology*, W. A. Benjamin, Inc., Menlo Park, Cal., 1974, pp. 133, 280, 323, 326, 327, 663, 679.
9. Campbell, H. J., *The Pleasure Areas*, Delacorte Press, New York, 1973, pp. 64, 186, 291, 297, 299.
10. Chapman, Anthony J., and Foot, Hugh C., *eds.*, *Humor and Laughter: Theory, Research and Applications*, Wiley-Interscience, New York, 1976, pp. 126, 159, 244, 298, 337, 381.
11. Dubos, Rene, *Beast or Angel?*, Charles Scribner's Sons, New York, 1974, pp. 36, 74, 154, 168, 172.
12. Garan, D. G., *The Key to the Sciences of Man*, Philosophical Library, New York, 1975, pp. 11, 27, 28, 102, 263, 516.

CHAPTER III (pp. 62-95)

1. Selye, Hans, *The Stresses of Life*, McGraw-Hill Book Co., New York, 1976, pp. 171, 179, 252, 370, 373, 375, 384, 387, 442.
2. Friedman, Meyer, and Rosenman, Ray H., *Type A Behavior and Your Heart*, Alfred Knopf, New York, 1974, pp. 48, 52, 84, 86, 109, 111, 115, 123, 161, 189, 230, 254.
3. Miller, Benjamin F., and Galton, Lawrence, *Freedom From Heart Attacks*, Simon & Shuster New York, 1972, pp. 20, 59, 104, 123, 132, 142, 257.

4. Burn, J. Harold, *Drugs, Medicines and Man,* Charles Scribner's Sons, New York, 1966, pp. 17, 22, 115, 116, 184, 215.

5. Galton, Lawrence, *The Silent Disease: Hypertension,* Crown Publishers, New York, 1973, pp. 7, 39, 55, 107, 114, 123, 128, 144.

6. Cooley, Donald G., *The Science Book of Wonder Drugs,* Franklin Watts, New York, 1964, pp. 81, 97, 134, 140, 158, 184, 201, 201, 230.

7. Finnerty, Frank A., and Linde Shirley Motter, *High Blood Pressure,* David McKay Co., New York, 1975, pp. 31, 48, 113, 114, 171, 176, 180, 183, 191, 198.

8. McQuade, Walter, and Aikman, Ann, *Stress,* E. P. Dutton & Co., New York, 1974, pp. 10, 23, 59, 78, 136, 191.

9. Fishbein, Morris, *ed., Heart Care, an Authoritative Guide by Twenty Experts,* Hanover House, Garden City, New York, 1960, pp. 6, 51, 105, 152, 166, 173, 179, 198, 208.

10. *Conference on the Psychophysiological Aspects of Cancer,* Annals of the New York Academy of Sciences, Vol. 125, pp. 773-1055.

11. Richards, Victor, and Scott, Denise, *Cancer,* University of California Press, Berkeley, Cal., 1972, pp. 243, 260, 261, 262, 267.

12. Blau, Paul Sheldon, and Schultz, Dodi, *Arthritis,* Doubleday and Company, Garden City, N. Y., 1974, pp. 23, 66, 70, 71, 103, 109, 113, 115, 126.

13. Calabro, John J., and Wykert, John, *The Truth About Arthritis Care,* David McKay Co., New York, 1971, pp. 37, 51, 58, 61, 73, 81, 86, 158, 211.

14. Lowenstein, Bertrand E., and Preger, Paul D., *Diabetes: New Look at an Old Problem,* Harper & Row, New York, 1976, pp. 4, 9, 19, 23, 24, 38, 46, 67, 69, 96, 115, 144, 155, 179, 215.

15. Laufer, Ira J., and Kadison, Herbert, *Diabetes Explained,* Saturday Review Press, New York, 1976, pp. 34, 38, 71, 83, 84, 101, 128, 135, 152, 159.

16. Pfeiffer, Carl J., *ed., Peptic Ulcer,* J. B. Lippincott, Philadelphia, Pa., 1971, pp. 5, 59, 72, 96, 116, 136, 160, 303.

17. Bogoch, Abraham, *ed., Gastroenterology,* McGraw-Hill Book Co., 1973, pp. 136, 358, 361, 369.

18. Garan, D. G., *The Key to the Sciences of Man,* Philosophical Library, New York, 1975, pp. 211, 217, 219, 221, 224, 226, 229, 231, 233, 239, 247, 253.

CHAPTER IV (pp. 96-131)

1. Freedman, Alfred M., Kaplan, Harold I., and Sadock, Benjamin J., *Comprehensive Textbook of Psychiatry,* The Williams & Wilkins Co., Baltimore, Md., 1975, pp. 353, 453, 706, 811, 851, 892, 992, 1023, 1202, 1216, 1232, 1241, 1258, 1260, 1933, 2156, 2587.

2. Menninger, Karl A., *et al., The Vital Balance,* The Viking Press, New York, 1977, pp. 162, 264, 285, 357, 385, 399.

3. Korchin, Sheldon J., *Modern Clinical Psychology.* Basic Books, New York, 1967, pp. 59, 353, 355, 380, 428, 429, 611.

4. White, Robert W., and Watt, Norman F., *The Abnormal Personality,*

Ronald Press Co., New York, 1973, pp. 83, 146, 171, 215, 248.

5. Cole, Jonathan O., ed., *Psychopathology and Psychopharmacology*, The Johns Hopkins University Press, Baltimore, Md., 1973, pp. 85, 89, 102, 113, 162, 217, 246, 269.

6. Kalant, Osiana G., *The Amphetamines*, University of Toronto Press, Toronto, Canada, 1973, pp. 31, 55, 89, 134, 160, 173.

7. Hilgard, Ernest R., *et al.*, *Introduction to Psychology*, Harcourt Brace Jovanovich, New York, 1975, pp. 38, 150, 167, 232, 290, 529, 533, 547.

8. Morgan, Clifford T., and King, Richard A., *Introduction to Psychology*, McGraw-Hill Book Co., New York, 1975, pp. 127, 184, 189, 205, 213, 225.

9. Detre, Thomas P., and Jarecki, Henry, *Modern Psychiatric Treatment*, J. B. Lippincott, Philadelphia, Pa., 1971, pp. 108, 217, 505, 520, 529, 587, 636.

10. Arieti, Silvano, and Chrzanowski, Gerard, *New Dimensions in Psychiatry*, John Wiley & Sons, New York, 1975, pp. 86, 101, 233, 279, 284, 308, 322.

11. Flach, Frederick F., *The Secret Strength of Depression*, J. B. Lippincott Co., Philadelphia, Pa., 1974, pp. 52, 126, 159, 185, 247.

12. Mussen, Paul, and Rosenzweig, Mark R., *Psychology: An Introduction*, D. C. Heath & Co., 1976, pp. 86, 91, 216, 464, 571.

13. Kendler, Howard H., *Basic Psychology*, W. A. Benjamin, Inc., 1974, pp. 146, 172, 289, 323, 327, 380, 663.

14. Burn, J. Harold, *Drugs, Medicines and Man*, Charles Scribner's Sons, New York, 1968, pp. 41, 114, 129, 132, 148, 215, 224.

15. Johnson, G., *The Pill Conspiracy*, Sherbourne Press, Los Angeles, Cal., 1967, pp. 22, 45, 47, 52, 56, 86, 90, 95, 163, 164.

16. Maher, Brendan A., *Principles of Psychopathology*, McGraw-Hill Book Co., New York, 1966, pp. 192, 235, 436, 472.

17. Kline, Nathan S., *From Sad to Glad*, S. P. Putnam's Sons, New York, 1974, pp. 116, 119, 122, 127, 129, 133, 139, 141,159, 205.

18. Modell, Walter, and Lansing, Alfred, and the Editors of Life, *Drugs*, Time Inc., New York, 1970, pp. 7, 58, 150, 151, 163.

19. Freud, Sigmund, *The Problems of Anxiety*, Modern Library, New York, 1936, (1929), pp. 15, 28, 41, 51, 52, 55, 67, 72, 76, 83, 106, 109, 115.

20. Robert, Marthe, *The Psychoanalytic Revolution*, Harcourt Brace Jovanovich, New York, 1966, pp. 48, 68, 110, 111, 248, 249, 386.

21. Garan, D. G., *The Key to the Sciences of Man*, Philosophical Library, New York, 1975, pp. 113, 115, 117, 129, 132, 159, 163, 169, 177, 179, 186, 191, 198, 201.

CHAPTER V (pp. 132-164)

1. Jencks, Christopher, *Inequality: A Reassessment of the Effect of Family and Schooling in America*, Basic Books, New York, 1972, pp. 120, 185, 206.

2. Silberman, Charles, *Crisis in the Classroom*, Random House, New York, 1970, pp. 67, 70, 74, 203, 262, 319, 322, 522.

3. Wilson, John A. R., *et al.*, *Psychological Foundations of Learning and Teaching*, McGraw-Hill Book Co., 1974, pp. 40, 73, 99, 128, 153, 177, 180, 191, 210.

4. Powell, Marvin, and Mangum, Robert E., *Introduction to Educational Psychology*, Bobbs-Merrill Co., New York, 1971, pp. 80, 195, 196, 240.

5. Klausmeier, Herbert J., and Goodwin, William, *Learning and Human Abilities*, Harper & Row, New York, 1975, pp. 20, 70, 91, 375, 425, 457.

6. Sorenson, Herbert, *Psychology in Education*, McGraw-Hill Book Co., New York, 1971, pp. 310, 311, 347, 375, 430, 511.

7. Gross, Ronald, and Gross, Beatrice, *Radical School Reform*, Simon & Schuster, New York, 1970, pp. 38, 187, 206, 211, 214, 244.

8. *Newsweek*, April 23, 1973, pp. 113 ff.

9. Spock, Benjamin, *Raising Children in a Difficult Time*, W. W. Norton, New York, 1974, pp. 144, 183, 207. 261.

10. Piaget, Jean, *Science of Education and the Psychology of the Child*, The Viking Press, New York, 1971, pp. 34, 70, 142, 185, 210.

11. Jones, Howard M., *The Pursuit of Happiness*, Harvard University Press, Cambridge, Mass., 1968, pp. 128, 153, 159, 160, 163, 164.

12. Erikson, Erik H., *Childhood and Society*, W. W. Norton, New York, 1966, pp. 132, 240, 256.

13. Maslow, Abraham, *Toward a Psychology of Being*, Van Nostrand, New York, 1970, pp. 48, 103, 169, 171, 173, 197.

14. McKinney, Fred, *et al.*, *Effective Behavior and Human Development*, Macmillan Publ. Co., New York, 1976, pp. 69, 115, 152, 309, 316, 326, 361, 382.

15. *Time, Weekly Newsmagazine*, October 13, 1975, pp. 71ff.

16. *Newsweek*, September 6, 1976, pp. 56ff.

17. *International Encyclopedia of Social Sciences*, The Macmillan Co., New York, 1967. Vol. II, pp. 226-237, 239, 240, 241; Vol. IV, pp. 410, 415, 423, 446, 457, 460; Vol. XV, pp. 375-396.

18. Bell, Daniel, *The Coming of Post-Industrial Society*, Basic Books, 1973, pp. 121, 165, 337, 460.

19. Samuelson, Paul, *Economics*, McGraw-Hill Book Co., New York, 1976, pp. 218, 246, 267, 757, 779.

20. Galbraith, John K., *New Industrial State*, Houghton Mifflin Co., Boston, Mass., 1971, pp. 2, 135, 146, 271, 309.

21. Garan, D. G., *The Key to the Sciences of Man*, Philosophical Library, New York, 1975, pp. 265, 276, 314, 315, 326, 330, 332, 335, 343, 347.

CHAPTER VI (pp. 165-189)

1. DeWolf, L. Harold, *Crime and Justice in America*, Harper & Row, New York, 1975, pp. 4, 6, 106, 173, 223.

2. Phelps, Thomas R., *Juvenile Delinquency*, Goodyear Publ. Co., Pacific Palisades, Cal., 1976, pp. 75, 77, 79, 80.

3. Firestone, Harold, *Victims of Change*, Greenwood Press, Westport, Conn., 1976, pp. XI, XIII, XV, 13, 74, 80, 151, 188.

4. Cortes, Juan B., with Gatti, Florence M., *Delinquency and Crime*, Seminar Press, New York, 1972, pp. 137, 183, 189, 256, 348, 357.

5. Sanders, William B., *Juvenile Delinquency*, Praeger Publ., New York, 1976, pp. 28, 34, 46, 52, 105, 134, 175, 215.

6. *Time*, *Weekly Newsmagazine*, June 30, 1975, Vol. 110, No. 27, pp. 10-24.

7. Neumeyer, Martin H., *Juvenile Delinquency in Modern Society*, Van Nostrand, New York, 1969, pp. 56, 87, 91, 97, 146, 173, 192, 287.

8. Eriksson, Torsten, *The Reformers*, Elsevier, New York, 1976, pp. 216, 221, 247, 248, 249, 250.

9. Duffee, David, and Fitch, Robert, *An Introduction to Corrections*, Goodyear Publ. Co., Pacific Palisades, Cal., 1976, pp. 273, 335, 337, 341, 342, 345, 375.

10. The Joint Committee of ABA and AMA on Narcotic Addiction, *Drug Addiction*, Indiana University Press, Bloomington, Ind., 1968, pp. 37, 41, 47, 56, 87, 106, 125, 136.

11. Wilner, David M., *ed.*, *Narcotics*, University of California Press, Berkeley, Cal., 1965, pp. 17, 32, 40, 45, 56, 63, 88, 134, 189, 191.

12. U.S. Commission on Marihuana and Drug Abuse, *Drug Use in America*, U.S. Government Printing Office, Washington, D. C., 1976, vols. 1-4.

13. Platt, Jerome J., and Labate, Christina, *Heroin Addiction*, Wiley-Interscience, New York, 1976, pp. 71, 78, 104, 110, 113, 116, 124, 292, 299, 305, 314, 317, 322.

14. Johnson, Eric, and Carroll, Eleanor, *eds.*, *Drug Use: Epidemiological and Sociological Approaches*, John Wiley & Sons, New York, 1974, pp. 6, 7, 9, 10-14, 149, 238, 279, 306, 323, 351, 365.

15. Marin, Peter, and Cohen, Allan Y., *Understanding Drug Use*, Harper & Row, New York, 1971, pp. 19, 22, 25, 34, 137, 140, 141.

16. Masters, William H., and Johnson, Virginia E., *The Pleasure Bond*, Little, Brown & Co., Boston, Mass., 1975, pp. 59, 96, 139, 174, 192, 254, 266, 267.

17. Hettlinger, Richard, *Sex Isn't That Simple*, The Seabury Press, New York, 1974, pp. 44, 85, 87, 88, 113, 115, 167, 186.

18. Hunt, Morton, *Sexual Behavior in the 1970s*, Playboy Press, Chicago, Ill., 1974, pp. 61, 99, 131, 122, 186, 250, 362.

19. Barzun, Jacques, *Science: The Glorious Entertainment*, Harper & Row, New York, 1965, pp. 278, 279.

CHAPTER VII (pp. 190-221)

1. Huxley, Sir Julian, *et al.*, *The Humanistic Frame*, Harper & Row, New York, 1972, pp. 25, 29, 188, 196, 243, 445, 607.

2. Sorokin, Pitirim A., *The Way and Power of Love*, The Beacon Press, Boston, Mass., 1963, pp. 180, 229, 313, 314, 343, 456, 478.

3. Otto, Herbert A., *ed.*, *Love Today*, Association Press, New York, 1972, pp. 27, 47, 151, 172, 183, 254, 268, 272, 273.

4. Barzun, Jacques, *Science: The Glorious Entertainment*, Harper & Row, New York, 1964, pp. 227, 235, 254, 279, 290, 298, 305.

5. Jones, Howard M., *The Pursuit of Happiness,* Harvard University Press, Cambridge, Mass., 1966, pp. 128, 153, 159, 160, 163, 164.

6. May, Rollo, *Love and Will,* W. W. Norton, New York, 1973, pp. 104, 153, 201, 233, 286, 307.

7. Bronowski, Jacob, *The Ascent of Man,* Little, Brown, & Co., Boston, Mass., 1976, pp. 14, 19, 226, 265, 319, 343, 357.

8. Fromm, Erich, *The Sane Society,* Holt, Rinehard & Winston, New York, 1976, pp. 206, 208, 310, 311, 356.

9. Muller, Herbert J., *The Children of Frankenstein,* Indiana University Press, Bloomington, Ind., 1970, pp. 5, 7, 11, 13, 373, 378, 405, 415.

10. Flink, James J., *The Car Culture,* The MIT Press, Cambridge, Mass., 1975, pp. 113, 139, 140, 190, 191, 233.

11. Elsen, Albert E., *Purposes of Art,* Holt, Rinehart & Winston, New York, 1977, pp. 36, 102, 219, 243, 276, 321, 388, 406, 467.

12. Gombrich, E. H., *Art and Illusion,* Princeton University Press, 1970, pp. 6, 29, 359, 381, 388, 389.

13. Biasin, Gian-Paolo, *Literary Diseases,* University of Texas Press, Austin, Texas, 1974, pp. 11, 12, 19, 26, 123, 124, 155.

14. Russell, Bertrand, *Problems of Philosophy,* Oxford University Press, New York, 1959, pp. 21, 117, 200, 243, 251, 308, 326.

15. Stumpf, Samuel E., *Socrates to Sartre,* McGraw-Hill Book Co., New York, 1975, pp. 27, 49, 228, 271, 305, 365, 374.

16. Garan, D. G., *The Key to the Sciences of Man,* Philosophical Library, New York, 1975, pp. 56, 62, 75, 92, 438, 448, 452, 463.

CHAPTER VIII (pp. 222-256)

1. Einstein, Albert, and Infeld, Leopold, *The Evolution of Physics,* Simon & Schuster, New York, 1961, pp. 124, 141, 158, 196, 256, 303.

2. Whittaker, Sir Edmund, *From Euclid to Eddington,* Dover Publications, New York, 1960, pp. 53, 82, 118, 155, 178, 201, 247, 263.

3. Planck, Max, *The New Science,* Meridian Books, New York, 1959, pp. 97, 113, 170, 174, 205, 264, 268.

4. Bridgman, P. W., *The Way Things Are,* Harvard Univeristy Press, Cambridge, Mass., 1959, pp. 157, 173, 188, 191, 206, 207.

5. Schroedinger, Erwin, *Science, Theory and Man,* Dover Publications, New York, 1957, pp. 59, 131, 177, 195, 200.

6. American Foundation for Continuing Education, *The Mystery of Matter,* Oxford University Press, New York, 1965, pp. 102, 109, 535, 539.

7. Mittelstaedt, Peter, *Philosophical Problems of Modern Physics,* D. Reidel Publishing Co., Hingham, Mass., 1975, pp. 213, 250, 287, 294.

8. Heisenberg, Werner, *Across the Frontiers,* Harper & Row, New York, 1974, pp. 16, 71, 184, 219, 221.

9. Handler, Philip, *Biology and the Future Man,* Oxford University Press, New York, 1970, pp. 20, 21, 165, 172, 175.

10. Oparin Alexander I., *Life, Its Nature, Origin and Development,* Academic Press, New York, 1962, pp. 7, 14, 55, 65, 111, 113, 159.

11. Phillips, Edwin A., *Basic Ideas in Biology,* The Macmillan Co., New York, 1971, pp. 609, 617, 618, 633.

12. Dobzhansky, Theodosius, *Genetics of the Evolutionary Process,* Columbia University Press, New York, 1972, pp. 1, 59, 64, 98, 136.

13. Papazian, Haig P., *Modern Genetics,* W. W. Norton, 1967, pp. 165, 220, 265.

14. Garan, D. G., *The Key to the Sciences of Man,* Philosophical Library, New York, 1975, pp. 380, 382, 383, 387, 392, 394, 402, 411, 420.

CHAPTER IX (pp. 257-293)

1. Kahn, Herman, and Wiener, Anthony J., *The Year 2000,* The Macmillan Co., New York, 1967, pp. 110, 196, 207, 349, 351.

2. Huxley, Sir Julian *et al., The Humanist Frame,* Harper & Row, New York, 1972, pp. 39, 355, 428.

3. Toffler, Alvin, *Future Shock,* Random House, New York, 1971, pp. 169, 173, 176, 178, 180, 205, 209, 274, 283, 305, 324, 362, 386.

4. Dubos, Rene, *A God Within,* Charles Scribner's Sons, New York, 1972, pp. 148, 193, 194, 206.

5. Still, Henry, *Man-Made Men,* Hawthorn Books, Inc., New York, 1973, pp. 149, 151, 167, 169, 210, 218, 225.

6. Slater, Philip, *Earthwalk,* Doubleday, New York, 1974, pp. 20, 33, 40, 204, 211.

7. Muller, Herbert J., *Uses of the Future,* Indiana University Press, 1974, pp. 56, 87, 88, 97, 98, 124.

8. Kuhns, William, *The Post-Industrial Prophets,* Weybright & Talley, New York, 1971, pp. 65, 138, 193, 217, 259.

9. Rosenfeld, Albert, *Prolongevity,* Alfred Knopf, New York, 1976, pp. 107, 113, 115, 117, 127, 128, 130.

10. Leaf, Alexander, *Youth and Old Age,* McGraw-Hill Book Co., New York, 1975, pp. 129, 145, 183, 209, 211.

11. Warshofsky, Fred, *The Control of Life: the 21st Century,* The Viking Press, 1970, pp. 20, 21, 85, 88, 180, 181.

12. Kostelanetz, Richard, *ed., Social Speculations; Visions of our Time,* William Morrow, New York, 1971, pp. 64, 79, 107, 108, 216, 223, 224.

13. Tiselius, Arne, and Nilsson, Sam, *eds., The Place of Value in a World of Facts,* Wiley-Interscience, New York, 1971, pp. 19, 52, 199, 207, 294, 305, 382, 416.

14. Gordon, Theodore J., *The Future,* St. Martin's Press, New York, 1965, pp. 10, 17, 34, 89, 124, 179.

15. Falk, Irving A., *ed., Prophecy for the Year 2000,* Julian Messner, New York, 1970, pp. 76, 77, 84, 139, 152.

16. Teilhard de Chardin, Pierre, *Toward the Future,* Harcourt Brace Jovanovich, New York, 1975, pp. 60, 96, 183, 217.

17. Garan, D. G., *The Key to the Sciences of Man,* Philosophical Library, New York, 1975, pp. 69, 78, 85, 481, 487, 489, 493, 501, 509.

INDEX

A

Addiction: and the vicious-circle compulsion, 47, 174-80; general but "scientifically" incomprehensible, 21, 116, 174-75; inevitable under the opposite causation, 47, 165, 176-77; to drugs, alcohol, smoking, coffee and other means, 21-23, 165, 174. *See also* Drug addiction.

Adler, Mortimer J., 139, 267.

Against ourselves, 31-49: our opposite reactions as "ingenious" as our overenjoyments, 23, 46, 61, 98-100, 110; the why and how of it, 30-31, 43-49, 63, 146, 265; worsening brought by improvements, 2, 42-44, 94, 109-14. *See also* Opposite or relative causation.

Alchemistic, "scientific" logic: and direct improvements vs. opposite causality, 54, 135-36, 269-70; the belief in ideational factors as sources, 40, 139, 146 (if it were true, we would all be supermen, 40, 54-55); in behavioral theories, 144-45, 149, 154; in education, 132, 139, 143; in humanistic thought, 190, 196, 265-67; in psychiatry, 96-97, 101-07, 109-15; in psychology, 97, 122-24; in social science, 154-55; inevitable under the improvement-from-improvement logic, 32, 122, 124; of adding more satisfactions as capacities, 61, 132, 266-67. *See also* Like-from-like logic.

Alchemy, virtual modern, 53-60: as belief in nonopposite value causality, 53-54, 97, 114-15; a dangerous fallacy, 135-36, 143-44, 190-91; governing all sciences about man, 94-96, 121-22, 132, 266; inevitable under modern "scientism," 58, 95-96, 143; inherent in direct improvement logic, 53, 62-63, 135; leading to endless complexity, 58-59, 130-31, 220; of accepting easy, ideational causes, 53, 139, 267; of direct increase in positive feelings, 61, 96, 256-66; of formulas and techniques as factors, 61, 122-23, 154-55; of improvements by drugs, artificial means, 89-90, 115-17, 269-70; of never-felt unconscious experiences as causes, 57, 108, 128; of learning and reasoning as determinants, 55, 139, 154.

Anxiety: caused by overenjoyment of security, 102-03; emerging from "nowhere"—from continuous, unnoticed background, 102. *See also* Stress.

Art and esthetics, 203-08: absurdities through fixation, "originality" and confusion, in, 206-07; as a superstitious cult, 203-08; confusion due to myriad complexity and opposite causality of beauty, 205, 207; does not have to remain an absurd cult, 207-08; fame through absurd sensationalism due to fixation, 205-07; the "impossible" opposite causal

as causes of, 167-72; simple but "illogical" cause of, 165, 172-73; unprecedented increase of, 11, 166-67; worsening through improvement re, 167, 171-73.

Cultural fixations, 197-203: as "neurotic" customs enslaving us, 199, 201, 203; decisive obstacles to progress, 200, 203; lack of understanding of, and enslavement to, 198, 200, 202; modern culture governed by, 197, 199, 201, 203; their most insidious effect, waste of surpluses, 198-99, 203; ways of life becoming sacred truths through, 200-02, 210-11. *See also* Fixations.

D

Diabetes: as self-inflicted, increasing disorder, 9, 81-83; "beneficial" improvements as causes of, 81-82; its admitted causal mystery, 81; its overimprovement etiology, 82-83; paradoxical overstimulation syndrome of, 82; recent reversals of certitudes re, 81-82.

Diseases functional: absent in Nazi concentration camps, 17; admitted mysteries causally, 4, 63, 87; and doctors afflicted by them most, 20, 72; caused by overimprovements, excessively pursued freedom from stress, 2-10, 29, 62, 64; causes of 80% of deaths, 2-3; not afflicting primitive peoples or animals, 30, 64, 94; self-inflicted, 2-9, 62, 99-100; stress as their recognized cause, 1, 5, 7, 30, 62, 66; stress increasing excessively through its avoidance, and, 30, 62, 92; their paradoxical role as nature's remedies, 5, 65, 110, 115, 121; their simple overimprovement etiology, 30, 31, 62-66, 97-100. *See* Arthritis; Cancer; Diabetes; Heart disease; Hypertension; Ulcer, peptic. *See also* Medicine, modern; Stress; Vicious circle.

Disorders, self-inflicted, modern, 10-12: and evidence of disorder from overenjoyed improvement, 30-31, 92, 94, 100; increasing with improvements, 12-20, 102, 120, 166, 174; typical modern social disorders, 11-12. *See* Complexes; Crime; Diseases, functional; Drug addiction; Family disintegration; Mental disorders.

Drug addiction, 174-181: and typical arguments about marijuana, 179-80; immediate beneficial effects of drugs, and, 21, 177-78; incredibile "scientific" confusion vs. real science, on, 175-78, 180; inevitable under pursuit of increased satisfactions, 165, 174-75; the key, pleasure motivation missed in theories on, 176-78; real science the only possible help, 180-81; typical overenjoyment disorder, 174-75, 180-81; worsening through improvement, in, 21, 174, 179-81. *See also* Addiction; Against ourselves; Satisfaction or pleasure release.

Drugs: and self-defeat of drug therapies, 115-17; can only cause opposite aftereffects, 21, 89-90, 270; perfect mental improvement and disorder, from, 96-98, 269; sublimest feelings followed by equal horrors, from, 47, 194, 267; their disastrous aftereffects, 89, 116, 194; their miraculous initial "curing" effects, 57-58, 64-65, 115-17.

Dubos, René J., 42, 218, 265.

E

Economics: the dismal science, 28, 162; its underlying, pyschologic bases misunderstood, 28-29, 162-63; the paradox of progress through restriction missed, 162, 164; recession behavior opposite to normal drives vs., 28, 163; recessions, through economic and psychologic overenjoyments, 28-29, 163-64.

Education: "alchemistic" logic of in-

Improvements, organic: and the paradox of stress, 11-13, 20, 29-30, 66, 99-100; artificial, and their disastrous aftereffects, 57-58, 88-89, 270; causes of disorders but felt as relief, 31, 43, 83, 93; disorders from excessive, 2, 14, 61, 89, 92-93; experimentally always appearing beneficial, 31, 88, 93; in modern work and living conditions, 14-16, 18-20, 120-21; leading to insidious worsening, 6, 43, 62-63, 94-95; now turning into overenjoyments, 2, 13, 63-64, 258; unique modern, concurrent with disorders, 13-20, 121, 258; the vicious circle and, 2, 44, 63, 98-100. *See also* Diseases, functional; Disorders; Overenjoyment.

Intellect: and belief in the power of reason, 40, 54, 139; can become as disastrous as it is vast, 151-52, 268; powerless as motivational source, 40, 139, 151; prodigious tool, only, 151-52. *See also* Thought and reasoning.

J

James, William, 149, 194, 217, 271.
Jencks, Christopher, 134, 141.

K

Keynes, John Maynard, 28, 162.

L

Laing, R. D., 111, 145.
Laugh, the unique capacity of man, 41-42.
Life, theory of, 244-49: the Field-matter interaction and causal insights for, 244, 246-48; life as "negative fire," 244-45, 247-48; main phenomena and miracles explainable by the Field action, 245-47, 249; present speculations untenable re, 247-48. *See also* Physics.
Like-from-like logic: absurd for sciences about man, 58, 60, 154; contrary to value causality 220, 268;

imitated everywhere, from exact sciences, 46, 58-59, 266; in humanistic thought, 31, 53, 190; would be alchemic in human sciences, 31, 58, 61, 143-44. *See also* Alchemistic "scientific" logic; Opposite or relative causation; "Scientism."
Literature, 208-11: causal understanding missed most in, 208-10; creating causally distorted worlds, 207-10; fixational cult of classics re, 210-11; perpetuating passionate value delusions and "logical" truths, 209-10; writers practically least wholesome, having least of causal intuition, 209-10.
Longevity, 275-76: increased only in the average, 3; modern, stimulation methods for, 275-76; restriction the effective, potentially limitless method, 275-76.
Love: as satisfaction requiring equal need, conditioned nonsatisfaction, 192-93; excessive hate from exaggerated love, 153, 157-58; its "impossible," opposite causal sources, 192, 193; a pleasure requiring value opposites 136, 192 (if it came directly, all men would enjoy it boundlessly, 40, 47-48, 193). *See also* Humanistic value delusions.

M

Marcuse, Herbert, 182, 219, 265.
Maslow, Abraham H., 54, 145, 219.
May, Rollo, 102, 145, 193.
Mead, Margaret, 16, 138, 161.
Medicine, modern, 62-94: and doctors dying at highest rates from functional diseases, 20, 72; can do more harm than good for the main, functional diseases, 64, 72, 87, 93-94; its admitted lack of causal understanding, 67, 78, 81, 95; its awesome "progress" with wrong causal logic, 63, 92-93; perpetuates the direct-improvement blunder of our

tivity of knowledge, 40, 211-12; its causal value delusions about Mind, 214-15; its self-defeat, 40, 211, 215-16; perpetuating the value delusions, 213-14 (*see* Humanistic value delusions).

Physics, 222-44: admitted causal confusion even in physics, 222, 242-43; causal explanations by a universal Field vs., 223-26; the Field as unknowable as water is to fish, re, 222, 224-25, 244, 256; the theoretical mysteries explained by the universal Field, 227-30, 232-36; the unseen cause of gravity, electromagnetism, cosmic phenomena, 236-42. *See also* Relativity; Value reactions.

Pleasure, 36-39: always appearing beneficial, 31, 93, 191, 221; as the drive to overadjustment and disease, 36, 43, 270; its centers in animals' brains, 36; the mechanism that makes man "tick," 37, 152; miraculously precise source of causal "insights," 38-39, 124, 286; misregarded in psychology and science, 37, 56, 152; renders nature unfathomably miraculous, 38, 286; representation of the life force itself, 37, 152, 154; restriction the causal source of, 34, 121, 132, 257, 293; universality of pleasure, 37, 154, 156, 292.

Progress: *see* Cultural fixations; Future progress; Modern cultural "progress"; Technology and materialism.

Psychiatry, modern: and the trend of increasing mental disorders, 10, 120; direct improvements as its goals, 96, 115, 120; doing more harm than good, 120-21; its "alchemistic" direct-improvement logic, 97-98, 115 (if that logic worked, we would have utopia, viii, 32, 53, 58, 115, 169-70); mental disorders from strongest improvements, by

drugs, vs., 96-98, 116; psychiatrists committing suicides at highest rates, and, x, 20; psychotherapy as extensive, useless treatment, in, 119-20; reversal of its very logic overdue, 97, 121; trying to suppress directly the functional disease, nature's remedy, 110, 115; vs. shock therapy, as "absurd," best treatment, 118-19, 121. *See also* Drugs; Mental disorders; Neuroses; Overenjoyment; Psychoses.

Psychology, 122-31: the "alchemistic" logic of more improvement from improvement, in, 46, 58, 96, 122; endless theories and confusion, in, 59, 130-31; failure through imitated scientism, 124-27; its "alchemistic" belief in ideational causality, 54-56, 122-23; its imitation of experimentalism, 53, 123-27; pleasure, that makes man "tick," ignored, 37-38, 123; a virtual modern alchemy, 58, 96, 122-23. *See also* Alchemistic, "scientific" logic; Behavioral theories; Freudianism; "Scientism," from physical sciences.

Psychoses, 109-15: admitted mysteries causally, 102, 111-14; and the overenjoyment capacity of psychotics, 98, 110, 112; as nature's pressures toward normalcy, 110-11, 121; their paradoxical, opposite causation, 98, 101, 109-14; their overenjoyment etiology, 100-02.

Psychosomatics: generality of psychosomatic etiology, 65-66; using diametrically wrong causal logic, 66.

R

Relativity: equal inner disvalue for every value, 34, 52, 96-98, 196, 265; evident from what psychologists accept as true, 46, 52; extinction of sensation and value by continuation, 48-49, 52, 122, 124; its "unscientific" commonplace universality, 33, 61; most universal values

57; the opposite value reactions of eras misinterpreted, 161; the paradox of satisfactions and hardships missed, 158-59; reversals in political systems, democracy, communism . . . 160-61; vs. unwanted and unintended, opposite, negative reactions, 155-58.

Sociobiology, vs. the exclusive rule by conscious pleasures, 150-51.

Stress: actually organism's natural remedy, 5, 66, 91, 110, 115, 121; avoided to excess by modern man, 1, 13, 24, 62, 94, 121, 217-18; cause of disorders if avoided excessively, 66, 94-99, 121; its paradoxical increase through avoidance, 2, 30, 121, 174, 218; present theories on, untenable, 24, 25, 220-21; recognized cause of diseases and disorders, 68, 101-02, 218, 269.

Suicide: its paradoxical cause, 25-26.

T

Technology and materialism: confusedly blamed for modern ills, 48, 219, 286. *See also* Humanistic value delusions.

Thought and reasoning: believed decisive in behavior, 54, 122-23, 154-55; powerless as behavioral causes, 40, 132, 144, 154-55. *See also* Conflict; Intellect.

Toynbee, Arnold J., 158, 160, 265, 285.

U

Ulcer, peptic: its admitted causal mystery, 83; overimprovement and conflict as causes of, 83-85; paradoxical role of stress in, 84; self-inflicted, increasing disorder, 9, 83.

Unconscious, the: as "logical" explanation of the opposite reactions (*see* Opposite causation), 46, 61, 128; the contradiction of unconscious feeling, re, 56-57, 108, 128; its "ingeniousness' as great as that of overenjoyed improvements, 46, 53, 61; prescientific personification, 128. *See also* Freudianism; Neuroses.

V

Vicious circle, the: impoverishment thinking, 39, 211-12; decrease by addition and increase by subtraction, in, 49, 124, 197, 265; deriving from basal organic values, 191-97, 216; determining all behavior, 154, 217; extinction by continuation of, 48-50, 52, 122, 124; governed by opposite causality, 61, 192-96, 292; their opposites equal each other, 102-07, 109-14, 191-96; universal values noticed or "known" least, 35, 50, 135-36; worsening through improvement of, 6, 14, 44, 63, 92. *See also* Contrast; Humanistic value delusions; Like-from-like logic; Opposite causation; Organic limitedness; Relativity.

Vicious circle, the: impoverishment through overenjoyed improvements, and, 5, 31, 98-100; inevitable under improvement drive, 31, 44, 93; its insidious cumulative effect, 2, 44, 63-64; source of malignant impoverishment, 2, 44, 63.

W

Watson, James, 247, 279, 290.

Wheeler, John A., 226, 243-44.